Contents

The Atheist Handbook to the Old Testament

Volume One

The Atheist Handbook to the Old Testament
Volume One

Joshua Bowen

Digital Hammurabi Press
Mechanicsville, MD.

Library of Congress Control Number: 2021906052
ISBN: 978-1-7365920-2-1

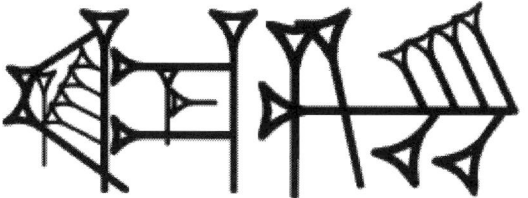

Acknowledgements

A special thanks goes out to Joel Baden, Francesca Stavrakopoulou, and Aron Ra, who took the time to read through the manuscript prior to publication. Their suggestions were invaluable and made the book all the more academically rigorous and publicly accessible.

I would also like to thank the gentlemen at The Atheist Round Table for all of their enthusiasm and support, not only for this book, but also for *Did the Old Testament Endorse Slavery?* I cannot think of a time that I have interacted with them live in which they did not hold up one of my books and instruct the audience to go purchase a copy. Austin, Jeff, Mike, and Steve, I thank you.

This also goes for Michael from *The Canadian Atheist Podcast*, who has consistently supported and encouraged publications like this one. In addition, Jay Pacic and Jefferson Spatchcock have been incredibly supportive of my work, along with our good friends MathPig and Momma Atheist. We appreciate all that you do.

I would like to extend gratitude to my good friend Bobby Ilapogu for reading through sections of the manuscript while it was still in draft form. His insights and suggestions were often adopted into the book.

A shout out to Skylar for the time he spent listening to me bounce around a variety of ideas. Thank you for being my sounding board on all those occasions.

As always, I would like to thank my brilliant and supportive wife Megan Lewis for all the work that she has put into this book. All of the illustrations and overall polish that you see in these pages are directly attributable to her. You are my everything.

Finally, to all of our supporters – particularly in the online atheist and skeptic community – I want to extend sincere thanks. I hope that this series will help make our interactions with Christian apologists more productive and meaningful.

Introduction

"Atheists don't understand the overall point of the Bible".

"Atheists have to read these passages REALLY out of context to come to that conclusion!"

"There *are* no unfulfilled prophecies, atheist! You just don't understand how prophecy works!"

"If atheists understood the entire picture of the Old Testament – and how it is fulfilled and completed in the New Testament – these passages about slavery, rape, and genocide wouldn't be so problematic for them".

Atheists are accused of a lot of things, not the least of which is playing fast-and-loose with the Bible. Cries of "Context! Context! Context!" are waiting around every corner in nearly every debate or discussion between atheist and apologist. Social media provides a wide variety of platforms from which Christian apologists of all shapes and sizes can hurl accusations of sloppy exegesis and malicious "cherry-picking" toward the skeptic.

To be fair, these charges can sometimes be valid; there is no shortage of hot-headed atheist trolls who seem to live only to humiliate their competition. And there is no question that there are many well-meaning atheists who have not yet been equipped with the tools necessary to fully understand some of the nuances of the Old Testament. In cases like these, an apologist with even a general understanding of the narrative of the Bible and a basic grasp of Christian theology can call out an atheist for not knowing the specific background of a passage like 1 Samuel 15 and walk away from the debate with their head held high.

Two things need to be said about these all-too-common occurrences. First, you don't need to know all of the details of a particular story to have a valid critique of many of God's commands in the Old Testament. No knowledge of the book of Enoch and the heavenly watchers is necessary to have a problem with God drowning the entire world with a flood. You can lack a detailed comprehension of slave adoption practices at Nuzi, yet still condemn the owning of another human being as property. A firm grasp on the extent of child sacrifice in ancient Palestine is not required to identify the call for mass genocide or forced relocation in the book of Joshua as a bad thing.

While you might not *need* this contextual understanding, it can certainly *help*. In fact, that is the point of this publication. *The Atheist Handbook to the Old Testament* is specifically designed to fill the gap, as it were, between the appropriate criticisms that are made by atheists and skeptics and the contextual details that would bring the Old Testament into greater focus. If you are armed with the literary, historical, archaeological, and even linguistic data involved in a particular passage or topic, your argument is far less likely to be overshadowed by an apologist's demand for context.

It's worth taking a brief moment here to note that "Old Testament" is a Christian label for a collection of Jewish texts and is a label used here primarily for the readers' ease of understanding, many of whom (I anticipate) come from a Christian background – whether or not they are atheists. Indeed, some of the criticisms made by atheists about Christianity were originally criticisms levelled at Judaism and the "Jewish" god by Christians.

Now, back to our conversation about context! Let's take 1 Samuel 15. I cannot tell you how many times I have heard the following interaction (or something similar):

Atheist: "Your God is good? He is the ground and basis for morality? Then how do you explain 1 Samuel 15:3? "'Now go and strike Amalek and utterly destroy all that they have; do not have compassion on them, but *put to death every man, woman, child, infant, bull, sheep, camel, and donkey*"'??"

Christian Apologist: "Do you even know who the Amalekites were? What they did to Israel? Why God commanded that they be punished? Do you know anything about the context of this passage?"

Atheist: "What difference does the context make? God commanded the Israelites to wipe out everyone!"

Christian Apologist: "So you don't know the context, you don't know why God commanded this... can I assume you don't know about war rhetoric in the ancient Near East either?"

Atheist: "This is crazy. Why can't you just deal with what I am saying?"

Christian Apologist: "I am! If you don't know the context, you can't properly understand what is going on in this passage!"

With this short "call for context", the apologist has successfully moved past the incredibly problematic command of genocide that has been the topic of constant debate among scholars and theologians for millennia. Yet, as you can probably tell, the audience watching this debate would almost certainly feel as though the apologist got the better of the atheist (whether everyone would admit it or not).

What could the atheist have known that might have helped in this interaction? Well, *let's take a look at the context*. 1 Samuel 15 is part of the larger story of King Saul, the first king over Israel. Saul has made a number of blunders and is cast in a poor light in the book of 1 Samuel. Here in chapter 15, Saul is told by Samuel that God has ordered him to go conquer the Amalekites. Now, without going into a great deal of detail, the Amalekites were a group of people that had been opposed to Israel since as early as the Exodus from Egypt.

In Exodus 17:8-16, we can see that the Amalekites attacked Israel following their exodus from Egypt. In this famous story, the Israelites succeed in defeating the Amalekites in battle as long as Moses is able to hold his staff in the air above his head. After the battle had been won the text reads:

> "And Yahweh said to Moses, 'Write this as a memorial in a scroll, and impress it upon Joshua, for I will surely wipe out the memory of Amalek from under the heavens'. So Moses built an altar and he called it 'Yahweh is My Banner'. And he said, 'Because a hand was against the

throne of Yah, *Yahweh will be at war with Amalek from generation to generation*" (Exodus 17:14-16, emphasis mine).

Now it makes sense when we read in 1 Samuel 15:2, "Thus says Yahweh of Hosts, 'I will punish Amalek for what they did to Israel, for how they obstructed them when they came up out of Egypt". Saul is being ordered by God *to exact revenge* upon the Amalekites for what had happened generations before, and God's command to Saul was completely in keeping with Exodus 17.

But what about the question of ancient Near Eastern war rhetoric? I'm going to save that one for later (come on, I can't give everything away in the introduction!). But you see my point: it wouldn't take a great deal of research and reading to come away with a solid, overall understanding of the context of this passage. This knowledge would have allowed the atheist to respond, "Actually, I *do* know the context... now, how do you explain this call for genocide?"

The problem, of course, is trying to find a resource that brings together information about the narrative of the Old Testament, wider ancient Near Eastern history and culture, archaeological methods and data, and specific examples of commonly debated topics between atheists and apologists.

Oh, wait... you've already found it.

This publication is specifically written to give you the information and tools that you need to properly understand the Old Testament, particularly in the context of debates or discussions, be it with strangers online, friends, or even your own family. The goal is not to enable you to be arrogantly combative or antagonistic, but rather to be able to speak as a well-informed non-specialist with respect to some of these highly debated topics.

Each volume in this set will seek to provide the reader with information that takes into account at least four aspects of the Old Testament; the narrative of the Old Testament, the broader historical background, the archaeological data, and debated passages.

The books in this series will have the following layout: first, I will explain the actual narrative of the Old Testament: what is the story that the canonical or final form of the Hebrew Bible is trying to tell? From the creation of the world to the events following the return from the Babylonian exile, the Old Testament has a story all its own. In this regard, the point is not to challenge the historicity of the Exodus from Egypt or the conquest of Canaan; these are issues that will be addressed in other chapters. Instead, we want to understand the content and flow of the story *on its own terms*, much like we would study the storyline of the *Epic of Gilgamesh* without worrying about whether he was actually able to kill a giant bull from heaven.

Second, I will cover the broader background of the ancient Near East, both with respect to its history and culture. What can we say about the history of the ancient Near East? What was their religion like? Was their culture so different from what we know about ancient Israel? A broad understanding of the wider ancient Near East can place the events described in the Old Testament into an overarching framework, making it easier to assess and contextualize its claims. This book will focus on the history of Mesopotamia, while volume II will cover other aspects of ancient Near Eastern culture, as well as Egyptian history.

Third, I will discuss the importance of archaeological evidence, including an overview of how archaeologists excavate, and examples of how archaeological data can help to illuminate questions about the biblical text.

Finally – and perhaps most importantly to the reader – we will encounter the chapters specifically discussing some of the more debated topics in the Old Testament. I will cover issues like the authorship of the Pentateuch, Ezekiel's prophecy against Tyre, homosexuality, violence and genocide, and slavery, just to name a few. The goal is to properly evaluate the relevant texts, archaeological evidence, and secondary literature (i.e., what scholars have written about the topic), comparing them to what apologists often argue with respect to these issues. At the time of writing, there are two volumes planned for this publication. The first – the one you are in possession of – will be laid out in a way that follows the four goals mentioned above. This brings up an important point: I will be citing a LOT of scholars. If you have read my book *Did the Old Testament Endorse Slavery?*[1] you have seen that I am bound and determined to let you know what scholars in the field say about these issues. Because of this, you will find that I quote scholars liberally in the body of the text. The rationale for this is actually quite straightforward: I am not an expert in all of the areas that I will be discussing in this series. While I am well trained in both the Hebrew Bible/Old Testament and the ancient Near East, there are people that dedicate their academic careers to the topics that we will be discussing. Thus, we want to see not only what the original texts and archaeological data say, but how the scholars in the field interpret that material, and what the consensus is among them.

What do I mean by "consensus"? Scholarly consensus refers to what mainstream scholars in a particular field agree to be the case concerning a particular topic.[2] This isn't to say that consensus is always correct, or that academics always agree on everything; indeed, rigorous scholarly debate is a crucial part of the academic process. However, by adhering to consensus scholarship, I am ensuring that the reader is not inadvertently steered towards fringe, or disproven theories.

Chapter one lays out a detailed summary of the story of the Old Testament from creation, through the time of the patriarchs, to the Exodus from Egypt and the wanderings in the wilderness, ending at the death of Moses. The second half of the narrative will be covered in volume II.

Chapter two will provide the reader with a general overview of ancient Near Eastern history, from the beginning of the 3rd millennium B.C.E. until the conquest of Alexander the Great.

Chapter three will cover the topic of archaeology, beginning with how archaeology actually works, as well as the history of "biblical archaeology", describing its development from the early 19th century to the present day. We will then examine two well-known people groups from the Old Testament that are illuminated by archaeological evidence: the Canaanites and the Philistines.

Finally, chapters four through seven present detailed analyses of four important and oft-debated topics in the Old Testament. Chapter four looks at the question, "Did Moses write the Pentateuch?". Through the investigation of contradictions and inconsistencies in the narrative of the Pentateuch, I will consider whether it was written by one person, or if the process was more complex than that.

Chapter five covers the dating of the book of Daniel, laying out in detail the evidence for a late date of composition, along with the most common apologetic arguments and what scholars have to say about them.

Chapter six moves on to the topic of slavery in the Old Testament, including an analysis of data from the New Testament and from the Antebellum South.

Finally, chapter seven deals with the failed prophecy against Tyre found in Ezekiel 26, including information on the history of the period, linguistic evidence on the text itself, and some of the more common theological interpretations that are presented by apologists to reconcile the glaring problems that exist with this prophecy.

A few final points are worth noting before we dive in. First, unless otherwise indicated, all translations from the Bible are my own. Second, in order to keep the technical aspects of the book to a minimum, I tend to use simple transliterations when representing foreign words. For example, instead of writing the Hebrew word for "slave" as עבד, I will write it *eved*. While this lacks some precision, I think the benefits of this type of simplicity outweigh the costs, particularly for the reader. Finally, I have opted to use endnotes in place of my more common footnotes, primarily because I am leaving the majority of the quotations in the body of the text. This will keep the main pages of the book from being cluttered with short citations.

It is my sincere hope that this series will be immensely helpful to the atheist/skeptic community, Christian apologists, and anyone who is interested in the study of the Old Testament.

---

[1] Bowen 2020a.
[2] Bowen 2020a: 5-6.

CHAPTER ONE
The Story of the Old Testament:
From Creation to Moses

Introduction

Lily Sloan: "You broke your little ships. See you around, Ahab".

Jean-Luc Picard: "'And he piled upon the whale's white hump the sum of all the rage and hate felt by his whole race. If his chest had been a cannon, he would have shot his heart upon it'".

Lily Sloane: "What?"

Jean-Luc Picard: "Moby Dick".

Lily Sloane: "Actually, I never read it".[1]

This brief exchange upon the Starship Enterprise speaks volumes to us, not about the Borg or resisting the urge to seek revenge, but about being familiar with the content of things that you discuss. In this scene, Lily knew enough about *Moby Dick* to make reference to its basic plot but was unable to recognize or contextualize the actual content of the story. Unfortunately, this is an all-too-frequent occurrence in discussions about the story of the Old Testament.

The analogy actually works in two ways. On the one hand – as we just saw – you can be caught off-guard by the context of a story if you haven't actually read or studied it. However, as was the case with Lily, you can be absolutely right about the overall point that you are making, even if you are unfamiliar with the whole story. Similarly, if you find yourself in a debate on the topic of violence and genocide in the Old Testament, as we saw in the introduction, you might bring up God's command to slaughter the Amalekites in 1 Samuel 15. However, if someone asks you a particular question about the context of the passage, or who the Amalekites were and why they were being punished, unfamiliarity with the story will make your valid point fade into the background.

The purpose of this chapter is to provide the first part of an overview of the narrative of the Old Testament. From the creation of the world to the return of the exiles from Babylonia, the Old Testament has its own storyline. Familiarity with the overall story will allow you to place particular passages and events into their appropriate narrative settings, giving you the confidence to address cries of "Context! Context!" in debates and discussions. In this chapter, we will cover the Old Testament story from creation to the death of Moses; in volume II, we will pick up the narrative with Joshua's conquest of Canaan and conclude with the events following the return of the exiles from Babylon.

This chapter is not intended to address the veracity or historicity of the claims of the Old Testament. Whether there was a "Tower of Babel", or if Daniel's three friends were actually thrown into a fiery furnace is irrelevant here. Our only objective is to "tell the story" of the Old Testament. As there are accurate historical details in the Hebrew Bible – particularly events that are chronologically later – there will be some overlap between the story and actual historical events. Again, however, the focus is on *knowing what the Old Testament story is*, and how the authors painted the picture of human history in the text.

The Primeval History

"When God began to create the heavens and the earth" (Genesis 1:1). While the creation story found in Genesis 1:1-2:4a differs significantly from what we see in Genesis 2:4b-25, the basic idea is the same: Yahweh, the God of the Israelites, was the creator of this world. In Genesis 1, the world's initial state was watery chaos, and by the power of his word, God speaks things into existence, giving them their proper place in the cosmos. For six days, God creates all that is. On the first day, God creates the light and separates it from the darkness. On day two, he creates a dome in the sky, which holds water above it. The third day sees the dry land, seas, and vegetation created. On the fourth day, he creates the sun, moon, and stars. On the fifth day, God creates the animals in the sea and the birds. Finally, on day six, he creates the animals that live on the land, along with humans, who are quite distinct from the animal kingdom. On the seventh day, God rests.

The second creation story in Genesis 2:4b-25 is much more animated and begins with the earth as a dry place that God then provides with water. God creates one man – Adam – and places him in the Garden of Eden to care for it. Noticing that Adam should not be alone and failing to find a suitable partner for him in the animal kingdom, God creates Eve from a rib that he took from Adam.

Chapter three opens on a new character, the serpent, who sets about to cause Adam and Eve to disobey the direct command of God. Although God allowed the two humans to eat from any of the trees in the garden, he forbids them to eat from the tree of the knowledge of good and evil. In spite of this, the serpent successfully tempts Eve with the fruit of the tree, and after she and Adam eat, God curses the serpent, the woman, and the man for their actions. They are ultimately thrown out of the Garden of Eden to make their way in the world.

Following their banishment, Adam and Eve have two sons – Cain and Abel – who grow crops and tend flocks, respectively. Abel brings an offering that God accepts, while Cain's offering is rejected. Cain then becomes angry and murders his brother. Because of this, Cain is cursed by God and driven from his presence. The remainder of Genesis 4 and 5 are primarily dedicated to showing the genealogy that ran from Adam down to Noah, the man who would be the righteous survivor of the worldwide flood.

Genesis 6 opens with an odd bit of information concerning angels mating with human women, and the complete wickedness that accompanies these events. "And Yahweh saw that the evil of mankind was great in the earth, and every inclination of the thoughts of their hearts was only evil all the time" (Genesis 6:5). Because of this wickedness, God decides to send a worldwide flood to destroy all living creatures, save for Noah and his family, the only righteous people left on the earth.

While there are two different flood stories intertwined in the narrative, causing some confusion in the details, the overall story is generally comprehensible. God tells Noah to build an ark and to take on board every species of animal in order to repopulate the earth following the flood. Noah obeys, and when the flood comes, it returns the earth to its primordial state of watery chaos (just like in Genesis 1). Once the waters subside, Noah sacrifices to God, who swears that he will never destroy the earth again with a flood. God commands Noah and his family to repopulate the earth in a manner quite similar to what we saw in Genesis 1.

A somewhat strange story follows, in which Noah plants a vineyard and gets drunk on the wine. His son Ham has an encounter of some kind with his father, who lies naked in his tent. Whatever the nature of the encounter, it leads Noah to curse, not Ham, but Ham's *son* (Noah's grandson) Canaan. Noah then blesses his own two sons, Shem and Japheth. Noah lives another 350 years and dies at 950 years of age.

Chapter 10 presents another series of genealogies, including the lines of Japheth, Ham, and Shem. In chapter 11, we see that the "whole world had one language and a common speech" (Genesis 11:1). Humanity decides to build a city, including a tower that would reach to heaven. God is displeased with their decision, and in order to keep them from working together to complete the tower, he confuses their languages, causing them to call off the work and go their separate ways. The place where this occurred was thus called Babel, "because there Yahweh confused the languages of the earth, and from there Yahweh dispersed them over the surface of all the earth" (Genesis 11:9b). Chapter 11 then closes with a continuation of the line of Shem, which makes its way down to Abram (later called Abraham). Abram lived in Ur – in southern Mesopotamia – with his father, two brothers, their wives, and his nephew. They all left Ur and traveled north to the city of Harran, where Abram's father died.

The Patriarchs: Abraham, Isaac, and Jacob

The bulk of the book of Genesis is taken up with the story of the patriarchs: Abraham, Isaac, and Jacob. By God's command, Abram leaves his home to come to Canaan, wanders about, and gains a great deal of wealth. He is promised by God that he will have a child, and his numerous descendants will inherit the land of Canaan. This is fulfilled in Abram's son, Isaac, and grandson, Jacob. Jacob then has twelve children, who become the twelve tribes of Israel. Chapter 11 closes on Abram and his relocation out of Ur to the city of Harran.

Abraham

Chapter 12 opens with God's command to Abram to "'Go out from your land and from your relatives and from the house of your father to the land that I will show you" (Genesis 12:1). Abram responds immediately, taking with him his wife, Sarai, and his nephew, Lot, traveling to the land of Canaan. He stops at the city of Shechem, where God confirms the blessing that will come to him; Abram responds by building an altar to Yahweh. He travels farther south near Bethel and builds another altar. Finally, he goes far south into the Negev.

A famine strikes the land of Canaan, so Abram goes even farther south into Egypt. As he travels, he realizes that, because Sarai – his wife – is so beautiful, the Egyptians will kill him and take her. Because of this, he tells her to lie and say that she is only his sister. In that way, not only will he not be killed, but they will treat him well for her sake. Of course, because they lie about their relationship, the Pharaoh feels free to take Sarai into his harem, providing Abram with a great deal of wealth in return. However, to ensure that Sarai remains pure, God causes the Pharaoh and his family to become ill. When the Pharaoh realizes what has happened, he scolds Abram and sends him away, but allows him to keep the wealth he had given him.

Abram returns to the Negev desert much wealthier than before and gives his nephew the option to settle wherever he sees fit. Lot chooses the area of Sodom and Gomorrah (before it had been destroyed), and Abram continues to live in Canaan. After Lot's departure, God appears to Abram and again confirms his promise to bless him. Abram moves north to Hebron and settles there, building another altar to Yahweh.

Genesis 14 involves the story of Lot being captured by a coalition of four kings from the east, and Abram valiantly taking just over 300 men to rescue him. When they return, the enigmatic Melchizedek king of Salem comes out to meet them, to whom Abram gives "a tenth of everything" (Genesis 14:20b). Abram then refuses to accept any gifts from the king of Sodom in return for his brave actions, so that only God would be able to get the credit for making him wealthy.

In Genesis 15, we get the first account of the covenant that God made with Abram, by which he would know for certain that he would receive the land of Canaan as an inheritance. As part of a covenant ritual, Abram is instructed to cut various animals in half and place the halves opposite one another, creating a type of aisle between them. Abram expects that he and God will somehow pass between the pieces in order to swear the covenant. In other words, the ritual essentially indicates that, if one were to break the covenant, they would die like those animals had. However, when the moment comes, God causes Abram to fall asleep, and God alone passes through the animal carcasses, indicating that the covenant was laid on God alone, making it unconditional in nature. We learn that Abram's descendants would become enslaved in a foreign country and remain there for four hundred years.

The promise had been given and the covenant had been made; Abram was going to be the father of many nations, and his descendants would inherit the land of Canaan. Abram, however, was still childless. In Genesis 16, Sarai comes up with her own plan to remedy the situation: Abram is to sleep with Hagar, her slave, and have a child through her. The plan works, at least as far as Abram and Sarai were concerned: Hagar becomes pregnant. It instantly backfires when Sarai becomes infuriated and complains to Abram: "'My wrong be upon you; *I* set my female slave in your lap, and she sees that she is pregnant, and I am now belittled by her! May Yahweh judge between me and you!'" (Genesis 16:5). Abram's solution: "And Abram said to Sarai, 'Your female slave is in your power; do to her what is pleasing in your eyes'" (Genesis 16:6). Hagar is then mistreated by Sarai, and she runs away. But the angel of Yahweh comes to Hagar and tells her to return to Sarai and submit to her, with the promise that Hagar would have many descendants through her son, whom she is to name Ishmael. Hagar returns home and gives birth to Ishmael.

More than a decade later, God returns to Abram and reminds him of the covenant that was made with him and changes his name from Abram to Abraham, "because I have made you a father of a multitude of nations" (Genesis 17:5b). There is an additional stipulation set in place by God: all of the males in the household must be circumcised. God then changes Sarai's name to Sarah and promises that she will bear a son. Abraham responds to this in disbelief: "And he said in his heart, 'Will a son be born to a hundred-year-old man? And will Sarah give birth at ninety?'" (Genesis 17:17b). God promises that he will accomplish it, and in response, Abraham circumcises all the males of his household.

Chapter 18 tells the story of three divine visitors who come to Abraham and promise that Sarah will have a son the following year. As the men prepare to leave, Yahweh (one of the three visitors) tells Abraham that Sodom and Gomorrah – where his nephew Lot is living – has become so wicked that God is about to destroy it. Abraham pleads with God, who eventually agrees that if he finds ten righteous people in the city, he will not destroy it. No such group of ten is found.

Two angels arrive in Sodom in the evening, and Lot urges them to come in and reside with him for the night. However, the men of the city surround the house and demand the two individuals be brought out so that they might have sex with them. Lot steps out, locking the door behind him, and attempts to persuade the men to reconsider their actions, offering instead his two daughters in the guests' place. When they refuse and begin to try to force their way in, the two angels open the door, pull Lot inside, and strike all the men there with blindness.

The two angels then warn Lot to take his family and leave the city, as God is about to destroy it. After some prodding, they leave the city (only his wife and two daughters with him) and head toward the city of Zoar. Although they were commanded not to look back, as God rains burning sulfur upon the city, we see, "But his wife looked back, and she turned into a pillar of salt" (Genesis 19:26).

In Zoar, Lot and his two daughters take up residence in a cave. The two daughters, fearful that they will not find a husband with whom to have children, plot to get their father drunk and have their way with him. Their plan is successful, and the older daughter gives birth to Moab, while the younger gives birth to Ben-Ammi, forefather of the Ammonites.

A familiar story reappears in chapter 20, as Abraham is again on the move, going south into the Negev, taking up residence in Gerar. While there, Abraham tells Abimelek, the king of Gerar, that Sarah is his sister; thereupon, Abimelek takes Sarah into his harem. God comes to Abimelek in a dream and tells him that he is going to die because Sarah is married. Abimelek awakes, confronts Abraham, gives him a wealth of sheep, cattle, and slaves, and allows him to choose to live wherever he likes. He then gives Sarah 1,000 shekels of silver (that's a lot of silver). Abraham then prays for Abimelek, and God removes his curse from the king and his household.

Isaac

As God had promised, Sarah gives birth to Isaac. Again, however, there are problems with Hagar and her son, Ishmael, who begins to mock Isaac. Abraham sends Hagar and Ishmael away into the desert, and when they exhaust their water supply and are about to die, God comes down and rescues them. The chapter continues with a short etiological story about how Beersheba got its name ("well of seven" or "well of oath").

We now come to one of the most famous stories in the patriarchal narrative: the sacrifice of Isaac. God comes to Abraham in Genesis 22 and commands him to sacrifice Isaac to him as a burnt offering. Given the narrative build up from Genesis 12 concerning the importance of Abraham having a son, this is an incredibly dramatic point in the narrative. Abraham immediately complies, taking Isaac on the journey to the region of Moriah. Isaac and Abraham go up to the mountaintop alone, and just as Abraham takes the knife and is about to kill his son, the angel of Yahweh stops him, saying "'Do not stretch out your hand against the boy, and do not do anything to him, for now I know that you fear God, as you have not withheld your only son from me'" (Genesis 22:12). God provides a ram to be offered in Isaac's place, and Yahweh reconfirms his promise to Abraham.

Sarah dies in Hebron at 127 years of age. In order to obtain a place to bury his wife, Abraham approaches the Hittites, among whom he is residing as an alien in Canaan, purchasing from them the cave of Machpelah and the surrounding field – where he will inter Sarah's body – for 400 shekels of silver.

Abraham then commissions his servant to return to his relatives in Harran and find a wife for his son Isaac, in order that Isaac might not marry a Canaanite woman. When the servant arrives, he stops at a well and prays that the woman he is to choose for Isaac would come out to the well and offer him and his camels a drink. Before he can finish his prayer, Rebekah comes out (the granddaughter of Nahor, Abraham's brother) and draws water for him and the camels, even offering them a place to stay for the night.

When they arrive at Rebekah's home, the servant tells her brother, Laban, about his mission and his prayer to God for a sign, which Rebekah fulfilled. "Laban and Bethuel answered saying, 'The word has gone out from Yahweh; we are not able to speak to you bad or good. Here is Rebekah. Take her and go, and she will be a wife for your lord, just as Yahweh has said'" (Genesis 24:50-51). In the morning, when the servant was preparing to return with Rebekah to Canaan, her brother and mother ask for her to remain for at least 10 days before setting off.

The servant presses them, and the decision is ultimately left up to Rebekah whether she will leave immediately or insist on the traditional ceremonies involved in the betrothal process. Rebekah agrees to leave immediately. When Rebekah and the servant come close to their destination, Isaac sees them at a distance from a field where he was meditating. Their eyes meet in dramatic fashion, and Isaac takes her home to become his wife and comfort him after the death of his mother.

In chapter 25, Abraham dies at 175 years of age, but not before fathering several more children with a new wife, Keturah. After giving gifts to the children of his concubines, he sends them to live in the east, and leaves everything else to Isaac. He and Ishmael bury their father in the cave of Machpelah, where Sarah had been buried.

Rebekah then faces the same problem that Sarah had faced: she could not conceive. Isaac prays to God on her behalf, and she gives birth to twins, Jacob and Esau. Esau, the firstborn, is an outdoorsman and hunter, while Jacob is more of a homebody. Esau comes in from the field one day, absolutely famished, and begs Jacob for some of his stew. Jacob sells him a bowl in exchange for Esau's birthright (quite an expensive meal!).

Now, you might not believe it, but Isaac falls into the same trap that his father had twice before. There is a famine in Canaan, and Isaac goes to Abimelek, the king of Gerar, and – just as his father did – lies about his wife, Rebekah, saying that she is his sister. This time, Abimelek happens to see Isaac and Rebekah caught in an intimate physical embrace and determines that she is actually his wife. Abimelek is enraged, but after scolding Isaac, he decrees that Isaac should be protected, and they are allowed to stay among the Philistines, where they ultimately become quite wealthy (see a pattern here?).

Eventually, Isaac's great wealth becomes a problem for the Philistines, who request that he leave. After a brief stay in the valley of Gerar – and some arguments about wells – he moves to Beersheba. God appears to him and promises to bless him; in response, Isaac builds an altar. Abimelek then comes to Isaac and they swear a peace treaty.

Jacob

If you have heard of Jacob and Esau, you have probably heard the story about Jacob stealing his older brother's blessing away by tricking their father, Isaac. In Genesis 27, Isaac is getting old and is close to death. He instructs Esau to go kill a wild animal and prepare a meal for him from it; Isaac would then bless Esau. Rebekah overhears the conversation and – because she prefers Jacob to Esau – comes up with a plan to trick Isaac into blessing Jacob instead of Esau. She cooks a meal for Isaac and covers Jacob with goat skins in order to make him hairy like his brother.

The ruse works, and Isaac blesses Jacob as the firstborn son. When Esau returns and learns what has happened, he is enraged and plots to kill Jacob after he mourns the death of his father. When Rebekah finds out about this, she sends Jacob away to her brother Laban in Harran to keep him safe, and perhaps to find a wife. Somewhat oddly, in chapter 28, Isaac calls Jacob to himself and blesses him. He then instructs him to take a wife when he goes to Harran.

On his way to Harran, Jacob stops for the night and has a strange dream about a stairway to heaven. In the dream, God affirms – as the God of Abraham and Isaac – that he will extend the promises that he made to his father and grandfather to him. Jacob arrives at Harran and falls in love with Laban's daughter, Rachel. A deal is struck between Laban and Jacob: Jacob would serve seven years in order to marry Rachel. However, at the end of the seven years, Laban tricks Jacob, giving him Leah (the older sister) instead of Rachel. Laban eventually gives Jacob Rachel as a wife as well, and Jacob works for Laban a further seven years.

Because Jacob loves Rachel more than Leah, God causes Leah to conceive, but not Rachel. This begins a competition of sorts between the two sisters to produce more children for Jacob. Leah bears children, and because Rachel cannot conceive, she (in the same manner as Sarah) gives Jacob her maid, Bilhah, who then gives birth to two sons. Leah does the same, giving Jacob her maidservant Zilpah, who also bears sons. Leah gives birth to more children, and God finally allows Rachel herself to bear a son: Joseph.

After Joseph's birth, Jacob seeks to leave Laban and return to Canaan. As payment for his work, Jacob proposes that he take Laban's flocks out to pasture, and all of the spotted or speckled animals that return with him are to be his. Jacob, of course, does not leave this process to chance, and works a form of sympathetic magic (magic involving symbolic associations between objects), strategically growing his flock in size and strength. "So the man became very, very wealthy, and he had great flocks, and female and male slaves, and camels, and donkeys" (Genesis 30:43).

This does not sit well with Laban. God commands Jacob to leave for home. After loading up his family and possessions, Jacob leaves, but as they depart, Rachel steals some household idols from Laban. Laban learns of their departure and chases after them. Before Laban reaches them, God comes to him in a dream and warns him not to harm Jacob. When Laban overtakes Jacob, he accuses him of fleeing and stealing his household gods. As Jacob knows nothing about Rachel's actions, he denies having stolen them. When Laban checks the tents, Rachel pretends to be menstruating, so that she can stay seated on the camel's saddle, where she had hidden the idols.

Having not found the idols, Jacob and Laban argue, ultimately swearing an oath to one another using a heap of stones. Laban declares, "'This heap is a witness, as is the pillar, that *I* will not cross over to you past this heap, and *you* will not cross over to me past this heap and this pillar for evil'" (Genesis 31:52). The next morning Jacob and Laban depart from one another.

On the journey back, Jacob sends messengers ahead to his brother Esau, who return and inform Jacob that Esau is coming out to meet him. Fearful for his safety, he divides his company into two groups, ensuring that at least one group would remain safe. As he approaches Esau, he sends gifts ahead of him, instructing the messengers to say that he will be along shortly.

That night, after Jacob sends the rest of his party across the river, "a man wrestled with him until the break of day" (Genesis 32:24b). This divine being changes his name from Jacob to Israel, "'because you contended with God and with men and you overcame'" (Genesis 32:28b).

This rather enigmatic passage ends with Jacob limping, having had his hip injured, which explains why "the children of Israel do not eat the socket of the hip joint" (Genesis 32:32a).

Finally, the moment arrives when Jacob is confronted by Esau. Much to his surprise, Esau is elated to see him. He attempts to return all of the gifts that Jacob had sent ahead to him, but Jacob insists that he keep them, and Esau eventually relents. Jacob tells Esau that he must move slowly with his young flock and that Esau should go ahead of him back to Seir. Jacob ultimately makes it back to Canaan, to the city of Shechem, but camps outside of it. He purchases land and builds an altar to God.

We then read the story of Jacob's daughter Dinah, who is raped by Shechem, the son of Hamor the Hivite. Shechem then tells his father Hamor to get Dinah for him as a wife. Dinah's brothers are incensed, but Hamor pleads with them to intermarry with his people and to settle among them. The brothers seek revenge and trick the people of the city into being circumcised. While they recover from their circumcisions, Simeon and Levi (two of Jacob's sons) kill all the men of the city. Jacob scolds Simeon and Levi for bringing potential retribution upon them from the Canaanites and Perizzites living in the land.

God then commands Jacob to go to Bethel and build an altar. Jacob removes all of the foreign gods from his household that were brought from Harran, then sets out for Bethel and builds the altar. After leaving Bethel, Rachel dies giving birth to her son, whom she names Ben-Oni ("son of my trouble") as she dies. Jacob, however, calls him Benjamin ("son of the right hand"). Rachel is buried between Bethel and Ephrath.

They then move to just beyond Migdal Eder, and Reuben sleeps with Bilhah, Jacob's concubine. Finally, they arrive back at Hebron. Isaac then dies, and Jacob and Esau bury him.

Joseph

The narrative then turns to Joseph, Jacob's favorite son. His brothers' jealousy, coupled with Joseph's dreams about ruling over his family, cause his brothers to plot his murder. Joseph goes to see how his brothers are doing as they are tending the flocks, and upon his arrival, they throw him into a pit. Although there are different versions of the story in Genesis 37, each one ends with Joseph being sold into slavery in Egypt.

Genesis 38 interrupts the story of Joseph in Egypt to describe the life of one of his brothers, Judah. Judah marries a Canaanite woman who bears him three sons: Er, Onan, and Shelah. Er marries a woman named Tamar, but because of some wicked behavior, God kills him. Judah instructs Onan to sleep with his brother's wife to ensure his dead brother's name gets passed on. However, whenever Onan has sex with her, he ejaculates on the ground. Because of this wicked act, God also kills him.

Judah promises Tamar his third son, Shelah, but asks her to wait some time so that Shelah can grow up. Secretly, however, he fears that God will kill Shelah as he did his first two sons and so he delays giving Shelah to Tamar. Tamar gets tired of waiting and pretends to be a prostitute so that Judah will sleep with her. He does, and Tamar becomes pregnant and gives birth to twins.

After this interlude, the story returns to Joseph, who is sold to Potiphar, one of the Pharaoh's officials. God blesses Joseph while he is there and he gains Potiphar's favor. However, Potiphar's wife attempts to sleep with him, and when Joseph refuses, she accuses him of trying to rape her. As a result, Potiphar throws Joseph in prison. While in prison, he meets a baker and a cupbearer, who each have dreams that Joseph correctly interprets. He reveals that, according to the dreams, the cupbearer will be restored to his former position, but the baker will be executed. This, of course, is what happens.

Two years later, the Pharaoh himself has a dream, and the cupbearer remembers that there is a man in prison that can interpret dreams. The Pharaoh calls for Joseph, who interprets the dream, telling him that there will be seven years of plenty followed by seven years of famine. Thus, the Pharaoh should store up grain during the first seven years in order to prepare for the years of famine. The Pharaoh is so impressed that he elevates Joseph to a high administrative position to oversee the collection and storage of the food. Joseph is 30 years old and is given a wife by the Pharaoh, who bears him two sons: Manasseh and Ephraim. After the seven years of plenty, the famine strikes the land, and people from all over the world come to Egypt to get food to survive.

Jacob, still in Canaan, sends his sons to go get grain from Egypt. When they arrive, Joseph recognizes them, but they fail to recognize him. Keeping his identity a secret, he accuses them of being spies. They deny it and say that their family – including their youngest brother – is back in Canaan. Joseph demands that they bring their youngest brother (Benjamin) to Egypt; he will keep one brother in prison while the others go and get Benjamin in order to verify their story.

After the brothers return to Canaan, Jacob refuses to let Benjamin go, fearing he will die like Joseph did. Ultimately, however, he relents, and sends the brothers back with Benjamin, along with precious gifts. When they arrive, after having a meal with Joseph, they are provided with grain; however, a silver cup is hidden in Benjamin's grain sack at Joseph's request. As the brothers make their way back to Canaan, Joseph sends his steward to stop and search their bags, knowing that the cup will be found in Benjamin's bag. They are brought back to Joseph, accused of stealing the cup, and this time Joseph demands to see their father, saying that he will keep Benjamin hostage until he arrives.

The brothers plead with him to not do this, and finally Joseph can no longer hold out. He reveals himself to them, and they all embrace. The Pharaoh instructs Joseph to have his family come down to Egypt to live. The brothers return home and they all, including Jacob, make their way down to Egypt. Along the way, at Beersheba, Jacob offers sacrifices to God. As the family approaches Goshen in Egypt, Joseph races out to meet them and embraces his father. The family then settles in Egypt.

The famine continues to worsen, and eventually Egypt itself runs out of food. The Egyptians come to Joseph and sell all that they have to him in order for him to sell it and buy food with the proceeds. Eventually, they have to sell themselves as slaves, along with their land, to Joseph. However, Joseph is able to sustain the people.

Jacob lives in Egypt for 17 years, until the age of 147. Before he dies, he makes his sons promise to bury him with his fathers in Canaan. When Jacob falls ill, Joseph brings his two sons to him to be blessed by their grandfather. Genesis 48 and 49 are mostly taken up with Jacob blessing Joseph's two sons, along with Joseph and his brothers. Finally, Jacob dies, and Joseph and his brothers take him back to Canaan and bury him in the cave of Machpelah.

Fearing that Joseph will now seek retribution against them, his brothers plead for mercy. Joseph, however, reassures them that he holds no grudge. They all live in Egypt, where Joseph dies at 110 years of age. He is embalmed and buried in Egypt as the book of Genesis ends.

The Exodus from Egypt

Following the death of Joseph and his family, the Israelite population increases in Egypt. However, the memory of who Joseph and his family were is lost on the new Pharaoh, and he enslaves the Israelites, fearing that they might side with an enemy if Egypt is attacked. Under the oppression of slavery, the Israelites multiply even more. Thus, Pharaoh implements a new policy: the midwives are to kill all the newborn Hebrew males. When the midwives fail to carry out their responsibility, the Pharaoh gives a blanket order to the Egyptians to kill all Hebrew newborn males.

A couple from the tribe of Levi then have a son; his mother hides him for three months, eventually placing him in a reed basket and setting him adrift on the Nile. He floats down the river to where the Pharaoh's daughter is bathing, and she takes the child and adopts him, naming him Moses. Moses's sister, meanwhile, is secretly watching all of this transpire and suggests – at precisely the opportune moment – that she bring a Hebrew woman in to serve as a wet nurse. The Pharaoh's daughter agrees, and his sister goes and gets her mother, who comes and nurses him (and is even paid for her efforts!).

When Moses grows up, he sees an Egyptian beating an Israelite. Moses kills the Egyptian and hides his body. He then flees from Egypt out of fear and goes to live in Midian, where he marries Zipporah. While he is living outside of Egypt, the Pharaoh dies, and God determines that it is now time to bring his people out of Egypt.

God appears to Moses in the form of a burning bush and instructs him to go down to Egypt and lead the people out. Moses protests, but God insists, ultimately allowing Moses to bring along his brother, Aaron. God promises that the people will listen, and that – after some miraculous persuasion – the Pharaoh will also relent and let the people go.

Fearing that the people will not believe him, God gives Moses supernatural aids, including a staff that will turn into a snake, the ability to turn his own hand leprous, and the ability to turn the water of the Nile into blood. Moses returns to his father-in-law and states his plans. On the way back to Egypt, we see an interesting episode where God plans to kill Moses. However, his wife Zipporah circumcises their son and Yahweh relents. Moses and Aaron arrive in Egypt and speak to the Israelite elders, performing the supernatural signs for the people, who then believe their message.

Moses and Aaron go to Pharaoh and deliver God's message. Pharaoh refuses to release the people, and instead orders that straw no longer be provided for making bricks, making the Israelites' jobs even harder. The people complain to Moses and Aaron about what they have brought on them. Moses then laments to God, which sets in motion the acts of God against the Pharaoh. Aaron performs the sign of changing his staff into a snake; Pharaoh responds by summoning his own sorcerers, who perform the same thing. However, Aaron's staff swallows the staffs of the sorcerers. Nevertheless, Pharaoh continues to refuse to let the people go. Moses and Aaron then turn the Nile river to blood; yet again, the Egyptian sorcerers are able to perform this miracle, and again Pharaoh does not budge.

God then sends plagues of frogs, gnats, and flies. He causes the Egyptian livestock to get sick and die, and causes boils to break out upon all the people and animals. He sends hail, which strikes everywhere but Goshen, where the Israelites live. He brings locusts, a plague of darkness, and finally the death of all the firstborn children of Egypt. Only those who put the blood of the Passover lamb on their doorposts and lintel live.

The final plague causes Pharaoh to relent, and he orders the Israelites to leave Egypt. The Israelites ask the Egyptians for goods to take with them on their way, and God causes the Egyptians to respond favorably. "Now the residence of the children of Israel when they resided in Egypt was 430 years. And it came to pass at the end of the 430 years that – on that very day – all the hosts of Yahweh went out from the land of Egypt" (Exodus 12:40-41).

In order to ensure that the Israelites would not be attacked and thereby return to Egypt in fear, God leads the people the long way out of Egypt, through the desert. He guides them during the day with a pillar of cloud and a pillar of fire at night.

Once the Israelites leave, the Pharaoh changes his mind and pursues them with his army. Moses parts the Red Sea with his staff and the people pass through on dry ground. The Egyptians pursue them regardless and are engulfed by the waters.

The Israelites then travel through the desert for three days but are unable to find any water to drink. They finally stumble across a source of water at a place called Marah, but the water is bitter and undrinkable. The people complain and Moses throws a piece of wood into the water, causing the water to suddenly become pure. This cycle of the people complaining, Moses crying out to God, and God solving their problem becomes a pattern in much of the story from this point forward.

The Israelites then leave Elim and camp in the Desert of Sin, where they again begin to complain about the conditions. "O that we had died by the hand of Yahweh in the land of Egypt, when we sat by the pots of meat and ate bread to the full! For you have brought us to this desert to kill all this assembly with hunger!'" (Exodus 16:3). God informs them that, in order to feed them, he is going to provide them with a substance known as "manna". The manna will appear on the ground each morning, except for on the seventh day of the week. They are to go out and collect the manna and use it up each day. However, on the sixth day, they are to collect twice as much and rest on the seventh day.

Leaving the Desert of Sin, they arrive at Rephidim, but there is no water, and the people begin to complain again. God commands Moses to take his staff and strike a rock, which will then produce water. While camped at Rephidim, the Amalekites attack them. Joshua fights with them, while Moses ascends to the top of a mountain and holds up his staff. As long as Moses is able to hold up his hands, the Israelites are successful in the battle; but when he lowers his hands, they begin to lose. Aaron and Hur help Moses keep his hands in the air, even to the point of propping him up with a rock. This attack by the Amalekites sets a precedent for future generations: "And Yahweh said to Moses, 'Write this as a memorial in a scroll, and impress it upon Joshua, for I will surely wipe out the memory of Amalek from under the heavens'" (Exodus 17:14).

Moses's father-in-law, Jethro, comes to visit, and Moses recounts all of the things that Yahweh had done for the Israelites. Just hearing about these miraculous events causes Jethro to proclaim,

> "'Blessed be Yahweh, who delivered you from the hand of Egypt and from the hand of Pharaoh, who rescued the people from under the hand of Egypt! *Now I know that Yahweh is greater than all the gods,* because of this thing (that he did to) those who behaved insolently toward them!'" (Exodus 18:10-11, emphasis mine).

This story contrasts the faith of Jethro (a non-Israelite who believes because he has *heard* about the things that God has done) and the lack of faith of the nation of Israel (who has actually *seen* these things, yet continues in unbelief). The following day, Jethro advises Moses – who is attempting to judge all matters among the people himself – to appoint other men to help him judge the smaller cases. Moses agrees and sets up "officials of thousands, hundreds, fifties, and tens" (Exodus 18:25b). Jethro then returns home.

Three months after leaving Egypt, the Israelites come to the Desert of Sinai and camp in front of Mt. Sinai. Chapters 19-31 essentially recount the giving of the law to Israel and primarily concern legal obligations and ritual procedures, contributing little to the narrative. Moses receives these laws and customs from God and is instructed to deliver them to the Israelites.

In chapter 32, Moses is up on Mt. Sinai, and Aaron is with the people, who are beginning to get impatient with how long this process is taking.

> "And the people saw that Moses delayed in coming down from the mountain, and the people assembled to Aaron and said to him, 'Go up and make us gods who will go before us, since this man Moses, who brought us up from the land of Egypt, we do not know what has become of him'" (Exodus 32:1).

Aaron instructs the people to provide him with the golden earrings that they are wearing, and he melts them down and fashions a golden calf from them. He then builds an altar in front of it, and the people offer sacrifices and celebrate a festival.

Meanwhile, on the mountaintop, God tells Moses to get down the mountain, because the people are acting wickedly. "'I have seen this people, and they are a stiff-necked people. And now leave me alone and I will burn with anger against them and consume them, and I will make you into a great nation'" (Exodus 32:9-10). God's plan is to start over with Moses, destroying the rest of the nation of Israel. Moses, however, pleads with God not to do this, and God relents.

"And when he drew near to the camp and saw the calf and dancing, Moses burned with anger and threw the tablets out of his hands and smashed them at the bottom of the mountain" (Exodus 32:19). Moses then takes the calf and turns it into a powder, making the Israelites drink it mixed in water. He confronts Aaron, who blames the actions on the people:

> "And Aaron said, 'Do not burn with anger my lord! *You* know this people, that they are wicked! And they said to me, "Make us gods who will go before us, since this man Moses, who brought us up from the land of Egypt, we do not know what has become of him". And I said to them, "Whoever has gold, take it off and give it to me". And I threw it into the fire, *and this calf came out*'" (Exodus 32:22-24, emphasis mine).

In other words, they wanted it, and all I did was throw some gold into a fire, and *somehow* a calf just came up out of the fire!

Moses then rallies all the Levites to himself and orders them to take a sword, go throughout the camp, "'and each man kill his brother and each man his friend, and each man his neighbor'" (Exodus 32:27b). After they had killed about 3,000 people, Moses says, "'You have been devoted this day to Yahweh, for each man was against his son and his brother, so he has given you a blessing this day'" (Exodus 32:29). Finally, God sends a plague among the people because of their sinful actions. God then informs the Israelites that he will no longer go with them, because if he did, he would have to kill them for their sin. Moses pleads with God either to go with them or not to send them away from that place. God agrees, and Moses ascends back up the mountain and receives a new set of tablets with the commandments. He remains on the mountain 40 days and 40 nights. When he comes back down, his face is radiant, and he has to put a veil over it.

The remainder of Exodus essentially concerns the setting up of the tabernacle (the earthly dwelling-place of Yahweh) and the ritual processes involved with it. At the end of chapter 40, we see God's glory descending on the completed tabernacle.

> "And the cloud covered the tent of meeting, and the glory of Yahweh filled the tabernacle. And Moses was not able to come to the tent of meeting, because the cloud rested upon it, and the glory of Yahweh had filled the tabernacle" (Exodus 40:34-35).

The book of Leviticus, is primarily concerned with laws and procedures about the priesthood and keeping the Israelite people holy; even the short narrative portions concern purity. For example, in Leviticus 8-10, we see that Aaron and his sons are ordained as priests, and in chapter 10, Nadab and Abihu, Aaron's sons, offer "strange fire before Yahweh" (Leviticus 10:1) and are killed by God. Why? "And Moses said to Aaron, 'This is what Yahweh spoke of when he said, "I will be sanctified among those who draw near to me, and I will be revered before all the people"'" (Leviticus 10:3). Those who approach God must be holy and obey the commands and ritual regulations. The same is true in chapter 24, when the son of an Israelite woman and an Egyptian father "cursed the name" (Leviticus 24:11).

Wandering the Wilderness

The book of Numbers has narrative portions that describe the continual failure of the Israelites to trust God as they make their way through the wilderness. The book begins with God commanding Moses to take a census of the nation (primarily for purposes of war) and describes how the people are to be organized. In chapter 10, the Israelites leave Sinai, making their next stop in the Desert of Paran. We then see story after story about Israel's faithlessness towards God.

In Numbers 11:1-3 we read,

> "Then the people were like those who complain about calamity in the ears of Yahweh, and Yahweh heard, and he burned in anger, and the fire of Yahweh burned them and it consumed them to the edge of the camp. And the people cried out to Moses, and Moses prayed to Yahweh, and the fire subsided. And the name of that place was called Taberah, because the fire of Yahweh burned among them" (Numbers 11:1-3).

We see here that the people complain leading God to send fire to consume them.

Immediately following this incident, in the same chapter, the people complain that they don't have any meat to eat and they have to make do with manna. In response, God gives them what they want... sort of.

> "And a wind went out from Yahweh and it brought quail from the sea and left them beside the camp about a day's journey on each side, and about three feet upon the ground.

And the people got up all that day and all that night and
all the next day and gathered the quail" (Numbers 11:31-
32a).

Sounds pretty good, right? Well, not so much. In verse 33 we read, "The
meat was still between their teeth, before it was chewed, and the anger
of Yahweh burned against the people and Yahweh struck the people
with a very great plague". Here again, we see the people complain and
God responding by killing many of them with a plague.

In the next chapter, Miriam and Aaron speak against Moses. "And the
anger of Yahweh burned against them and he went out. And the cloud
turned aside from the tent, and suddenly Miriam was leprous, like snow,
and Aaron looked at Miriam and she was leprous!" (Numbers 12:9-10).
Again, God's judgment is immediate, divine in origin, and causes a
disease as punishment.

One would think that, eventually, the people would realize what
happens when you rebel against God. They never do, which is a
significant point in the book.

In chapter 13, God commands Moses to send spies from each tribe into
Canaan to get the lay of the land.

"And see what the land is like, and the people who are
dwelling upon it: are they strong? Weak? Few or many?
And what is the land like where they are living? Is it good
or bad? And what are the cities like that they are living in.
Are they in camps or within fortifications? And what is the

land like? Is it productive or lean? Are there trees in it or not?'" (Numbers 13:18-20a).

When they return, they report on the high quality of the land, but on the might of its inhabitants; it would be impossible to take it. Only Caleb and Joshua state that they should go up and take the land.

In chapter 14, the people rebel after they hear this report about the inhabitants of the land that they are to conquer. And what is God's response?

> "And Yahweh said to Moses, 'How long will this people disrespect me? And how long will they not trust me, with all the signs that I have done in their midst? I will strike them with a plague and dispossess them, and I will make you into a greater and mightier nation than them'" (Numbers 14:11-12).

Don't worry; Moses again talks him down. However, Israel isn't going to get off scot free:

> "And the men whom Moses sent to spy out the land and returned and caused all the congregation to murmur against him by bringing a bad report about the land, those men, who brought out the bad report about the land, died by the plague before Yahweh" (Numbers 14:36-37).

Here we see the pattern again: the Israelites anger Yahweh – then receive a divine punishment, which is often a plague or disease directly from God. In this case, God tells the Israelites that all those who were part of the group that was delivered from Egypt would not enter the promised land.

In Numbers 16, a man named Korah rebels against Moses (and thus against God). Yahweh's response is unsurprising:

> "And Korah assembled all the congregation to them to the doorway of the tent of meeting, and the glory of Yahweh appeared to all the congregation. And Yahweh spoke to Moses and Aaron saying, 'Separate from the midst of this congregation so that I can consume them instantly'" (Numbers 16:19-21).

Sound familiar?

> "And they fell on their faces and said, 'O God, the god of the spirits of all flesh, this one man sins, and you will be angry with the entire congregation?' And Yahweh spoke to Moses, saying, 'Speak to the congregation, saying "Get up from around the tent of Korah, Dathan, and Aviram"'" (Numbers 16:22-24).

Then Moses gives the people a way to know if God was at work: if those rebellious individuals continued living and died at a ripe old age, then God did not send Moses (this does not bode well for them); however, if the ground opens up and swallows them, that would indicate that they were guilty.

> "And when he had finished speaking all these words, the ground split that was under them, and the earth opened its mouth and swallowed them, and their houses, and all the

people who belonged to Korah and all his property"
(Numbers 16:31-32).

One would think that this type of miraculous judgment would be enough
to get the people's attention. However, in Numbers 16:41 we see the
Israelites again complaining, this time that Moses and Aaron were
responsible for the deaths. Really? And God's response? "'Get away from
the midst of this congregation, so that I might consume them instantly'"
(Numbers 16:45a).

This time, however, we do not see Moses and Aaron pleading with God
to spare the people, perhaps because they realize that God's punishment
has already begun. And what is it? You probably guessed: a plague.

> "And Moses said to Aaron, 'Take the censer and put fire on
> it from the altar, and set incense on it, and go quickly to
> the congregation and atone for them, for the anger has gone
> out from Yahweh: the plague has begun!'" (Numbers
> 16:46).

So what happens? Aaron offers incense for the people and the plague
stops, but not before killing nearly 15,000 people (Numbers 16:47-50).

In Numbers 20, we see a second episode where Moses produces water
from a rock. The Israelites travel to the Desert of Zin and camp at
Kadesh, but there is no water. Unsurprisingly, the people complain. God
instructs Moses to speak to the rock in order for it to produce water, but
in his anger, Moses strikes the rock (twice). Yahweh's response:

> "And Yahweh said to Moses and to Aaron, 'Because you
> have not trusted me in order to sanctify me before the eyes

of the children of Israel, therefore you will not come with this assembly to the land that I have given them'" (Numbers 20:12).

Moses then sends messengers to the king of Edom (the descendants of Esau) seeking passage through their land. Moses promises that they will not take any of their produce or cause them any inconvenience; they will stick to the main highway. In spite of all this, the king of Edom denies them access (Numbers 20:17-18). Instead of passing through Edom, therefore, they travel from Kadesh to Mt. Hor, near Edom. There Aaron dies and his office is passed to his son Eleazar. They again set out and the king of Arad attacks Israel; Israel swears to God that, if he will allow them to defeat the king of Arad, the Israelites will utterly destroy their cities. God then delivers them into the hands of the Israelites, and they utterly destroy them (Numbers 21:3).

Leaving Mt. Hor and going around Edom, the people again complain, so God sends venomous snakes to kill the Israelites, who then cry out for help. Moses is told to erect a bronze snake on a pole; anyone who looks at the serpent will be cured. The people then travel from place to place, ultimately reaching Moab. On the way, as they did with Edom, they request to pass through the land of Sihon king of the Amorites. They receive a similar response and ultimately conquer Heshbon, Sihon's city. The same thing happens to Og, king of Bashan.

Chapters 22-24 recount the story of the Moabites and Midianites who, upon seeing the great number of Israelites, hire a diviner named Balaam to come and curse the Israelites on their behalf. After some convincing, Balaam comes to curse the Israelites, but is met by the angel of Yahweh;

however, only Balaam's donkey sees the angel. The donkey refuses to continue on (and smashes Balaam's foot in the process). Balaam then beats the donkey, who turns to him and asks why he is beating him (Numbers 22:28b). After a short conversation between these two, Balaam is allowed to see the angel, who tells him that he may go with the messengers of Moab and Midian, but he must only say what the angel tells him to say.

When he arrives, Balaam has rituals performed in preparation for cursing Israel on behalf of Balak, the Moabite king who hired him. However, Yahweh gives Balaam a message, which turns out to be a *blessing* on the nation of Israel rather than a curse. Balak is furious and tries again, this time in a different place. Again, Balaam blesses Israel rather than cursing them. Several more attempts at cursing Israel are made, only to have them blessed. In the end, not only is Israel blessed, but her enemies are cursed. Both Balaam and Balak ultimately return home.

This brings us to Numbers 25, a critical chapter with respect to the rest of the book. The Israelite men are having sex with Midianite women and worshipping their gods, resulting in a plague. The tipping point comes when an Israelite man and a Midianite woman walk in front of Moses and the people, and then enter into the man's tent to have sex. In Numbers 25:7-9, Phineas takes up his spear, chases after the couple into their tent, and thrusts the spear through them both, pinning them to one another. This stops the plague, but only after killing 24,000 Israelites.

This is just what we would expect: the people rebel (worshipping other gods), God sends a divine plague against the Israelites, and when a priest makes "atonement" for the sins of the people, the plague immediately stops, but not before killing thousands of people.

After another census is taken and Joshua is established as Moses's successor, we come to Numbers 31, where God commands the Israelites to destroy the Midianites. The people go and capture the Midianite women and children, along with animals and many of their possessions. But Moses isn't happy; they had allowed all the women to live. Since these were the women that caused the Israelites to sin in Numbers 25, Moses commands, "'And now kill every male among the little ones and kill every woman who has slept with a man. But all the little girls who have not slept with a man, spare them for yourselves'" (Numbers 31:17-18). In the end, all the males and every non-virgin woman are killed, but the virgin women are taken as plunder.

In chapter 33 there is a summary given of the journey that Israel took through the wilderness, from the time they left Egypt until they arrived on the plains of Moab. This is essentially where the book of Deuteronomy begins; it is Moses's farewell address – prior to his death – where he recounts all of the history of the people prior to coming to the border of Canaan. He reiterates the law and the covenant with them, which they accept. After blessing the tribes, Moses finally dies in chapter 34, climbing up Mt. Nebo and looking out over the land of Canaan. Moses is buried in Moab, and Joshua takes over for him.

This ends part one of the two-part summary of the story of the Old Testament. We have covered the narrative from the creation of the world to the end of the wilderness wanderings. In volume II of *The Atheist Handbook to the Old Testament*, we will pick up with Joshua's conquest of the land and cover through the period of the judges, the united and divided monarchy, the exile, and the return from exile.

---

[1] Scene from *Star Trek: First Contact* (Paramount Pictures, 1996). The full quote from *Moby Dick*: "He piled upon the whale's white hump the sum of all the general rage and hate felt by his whole race from Adam down; and then, as if his chest had been a mortar, he burst his hot heart's shell upon it" (Melville 1851: 267).

CHAPTER TWO
The History of the Ancient Near East

Introduction

It has become quite fashionable in online debates and discussions for someone to bolster the validity of their position by noting, "Well, in the context of the ancient Near East..." Of course, as an Assyriologist (someone who studies the languages and cultures of the ancient Near East – particularly Mesopotamia), I always get a bit of a jolt when someone brings the ancient context of the Old Testament into the discussion. While this context is crucial to understanding the Old Testament more fully, it can often be difficult to know whether the sources you've found are reliable and factual. In addition, people often read a book or an online article that happens to mention some aspect of the ancient Near East as it relates to the Bible, and suddenly they feel like an expert on the topic (and even comment like one!). This is very likely not the case; the study of the ancient Near East is full of several sub-disciplines, including the fields of Assyriology, Egyptology, Archaeology, Art History, Old Testament and Northwest Semitics, and parts of Classical studies. Each discipline has its own nuances and complexities, and academics in these fields spend entire careers devoted to the study of this region. Nonetheless, it is absolutely critical for anyone who is studying the Old Testament in its original context to understand the cultures that made up the varied tapestry of the ancient Near East. Believe me, this is no simple task.

When we talk about the "ancient Near East", that designation can include quite a few regions during quite a few time periods. The history of the ancient Near East is generally considered to extend from around the end of the fourth millennium B.C.E. down to the conquest of Alexander the Great in the late 4th c. B.C.E.[1] The term also encompasses a wide geographic area, from the Persian Gulf to the Red Sea and from Iran to Turkey. Egyptian culture and history is also vital to a complete understanding of the region, and in volume II we will explore Egyptian history, providing the reader with a far more complete historical background to the history of the ancient Near East.

How does one get a handle on the broad chronological and geographical scope that is indicated by the designation "ancient Near Eastern context"? And why should we care about it in the first place? Isn't it enough to understand what the writers of the Old Testament were doing when they penned their ancient documents?

Depending on your purpose in reading an ancient text like the Hebrew Bible, it may not be necessary to place the texts in their ancient setting. Some interpretive methods do not require such an understanding. However, for many people seeking to better understand the Old Testament, a proper comprehension of the context of the wider ancient Near East is absolutely critical to the discussion.

This chapter will provide a broad, basic exposure to the overall history of the major periods and events in the ancient Near East. The goal is to give the reader enough background to effectively situate themselves historically when they encounter things like "the Amarna texts", "Sargon of Akkad", or "the Neo-Babylonian period". These terms will bring to mind a general context and historical setting, which will make it easier for the reader to understand things like, "When Nebuchadnezzar took over the newly-formed Neo-Babylonian Empire…"

Obviously, there is no way that this single chapter can provide a complete grasp of all aspects of every major area and time period that make up the ancient Near East. However, the chapter will cite enough resources and provide adequate bibliographic information that the interested enthusiast will be able to dig into any of the major periods. A useful and accessible starting point for such an investigation is Marc Van De Mieroop's *A History of the Ancient Near East ca. 3000-323 BC.*[2]

Given our particular interest in the historical data that we can glean from the ancient Near East, we will begin our investigation with the period after writing was invented (around the end of the fourth millennium B.C.E.), ending with the rule of Alexander the Great in 331 B.C.E. This is a conventional ending point for many scholars; Van De Mieroop explains:

> "I have chosen to take Alexander as the last figure of the political history of the ancient Near East, because while the changes he instituted were probably not momentous for most of the people at that time, our access to the historical data is transformed starting in his reign".[3]

To give the reader an idea of how this chapter will be structured, let's take a quick look at the major periods that we will investigate. Remember, this is not an exhaustive assessment of the history of the ancient Near East; we are only going to hit the highlights, focusing on periods and events that are essential for an introduction to the topic. Much of our analysis will focus on Mesopotamia, the land between the Tigris and Euphrates rivers, as most of the political history centers on that region. We will begin with the 3rd millennium B.C.E., including the city-states of the Early Dynastic period, the empire founded by Sargon of Akkad, and the far-reaching bureaucratic governance of the kings of the Ur III period (ca. 2100-2000 B.C.E.).

We then examine the first half of the 2nd millennium B.C.E., including the trade colonies of the Old Assyrian period and the constant political maneuvering that ultimately came to a head with Hammurabi of Babylon. Following a major collapse in the middle of the 2nd millennium, we pick up our survey again with a time of international diplomacy: the Amarna period. This comes to an end with another great collapse, brought about in part by the Sea Peoples around 1200 B.C.E.

It will be at this point in our survey that Palestine or the southern Levant enters into the picture, as several nations begin to form in that region. We follow the Neo-Assyrian Empire as it gains momentum, bringing the history of Palestine into the picture when appropriate. The nation of Israel will fall in 722 B.C.E. to the Neo-Assyrian Empire; however, the Neo-Assyrian Empire itself ends little more than a century later in 612 B.C.E. at the hands of the Neo-Babylonian Empire. Judah falls in 586 B.C.E., and the Neo-Babylonian kings continue until they are conquered by Cyrus and the Persian Empire in 539 B.C.E. The Persians remain in power until Alexander the Great, whose conquest brings their power – and our historical survey – to an end.

The Third Millennium B.C.E.

The fourth millennium saw the origin and growth of cities, along with the invention of writing. Immediately thereafter, the early 3rd millennium B.C.E. was "characterized by the existence of city-states constantly interacting and competing with one another".[4] It is during this Early Dynastic period that the later *Sumerian King List* places famous rulers like Gilgamesh of Uruk. Later written works about the period were included in the Mesopotamian curriculum, which preserved them for later use by academics and historians.[5] While we cannot simply rely on these later works to tell us about the specific history of the period, it is clear that it was a time that was in many ways revered by those who came after: an early period of formation in the ancient Near East.

Between the years 2600 and 2450 – what scholars refer to as the Early Dynastic IIIa period – we see in the textual record that several cities were often grouped together, as if they formed some sort of coalition. These six cities were Uruk, Adab, Umma, Lagash, Nippur, and Shuruppak, and they have been dubbed the "Hexapolis".[6] This coalition was possibly headed by the king of the city of Kish, who played a significant role in the famous border conflict between two city states during this period: Umma and Lagash.

The Umma-Lagash Border Conflict

The border dispute between the cities of Umma and Lagash is one of the best-documented events in the Early Dynastic period and an excellent example of the constant interaction and competition between early city-states. Umma and Lagash were two cities between which lay fields known as the *guedena*, "edge of the steppe". Preserved in the writings of the kings of Lagash between 2500 to 2350 B.C.E. is a detailed record of a border conflict with their neighbor to the north, Umma.[7] The written accounts come from royal inscriptions from the city of Lagash; thus, they are only from the point of view of the Lagash rulers.[8] The battles are portrayed in these texts as a fight between the gods of the two cities: Ningirsu fighting for Lagash and Shara fighting for Umma. The conflict is even depicted visually in the famous "Stele of the Vultures", which shows Eanatum of Lagash victorious in battle over the ruler of Umma around 2460 B.C.E.[9]

There appear to have been five battles between these two city-states that were described in the different inscriptions from Lagash and seem to have been centered on the use of various fields and canals, particularly those to the north of Lagash.[10]

In the first conflict, Ur-Nanshe of Lagash defeated Pabilgaltuk, the leader of Umma, though we are not told specifically why in the text.[11] At that time, the king of Umma did something displeasing to the fields of the god of Lagash, Ningirsu (i.e., the fields of the *guedena*).[12]

Ur-Nanshe and his son Akurgal had problems with the rulers of Umma over the fields that lay in between the two cities, and the conflicts were cast as battles between their respective gods. It appears that the king of the city of Kish, Mesalim, stepped in as a mediator of sorts, establishing a boundary between Umma and Lagash; again, this is depicted as a divine action:[13]

> "Enlil, king of all the lands, father of all the gods, by his
> authoritative command, demarcated the border between

Ningirsu and Shara [the two gods of Lagash and Umma]. Mesalim, king of Kish, at the command of Ishtaran, measured it off and erected a monument there".[14]

Ush, the king of Umma, is said to have smashed this monument – the one set up by Mesalim – and entered the territory of Lagash. The text goes on to say that Ningirsu was responsible for defeating him in battle but does not seem to indicate the human agent through which this was accomplished. "Ningirsu, warrior of Enlil, at his (Enlil's) just command, did battle with Umma. At Enlil's command, he cast the great battle-net upon it, and set up burial mounds for it on the plain".[15] This corresponds well to the image carved into the "Stele of the Vultures", which shows the god holding a large net in which to ensnare his enemies.[16]

Trouble continued, however, with Urluma, the king of Umma, who – according to the text – failed to repay a loan given to him by Eanatum and rebelled against him.

> "Since he was unable to repay? that barley, Urluma, ruler of Umma, diverted water into the boundary-channel of Ningirsu and the boundary-channel of Nanshe. He set fire to their monuments and smashed them and destroyed the established chapels of the gods that were built on the (boundary-levee called) Namnunda-kigara. He recruited foreigners, and transgressed the boundary-ditch of Ningirsu".[17]

Diverting water that was destined for Lagash, burning monuments, destroying chapels, and recruiting foreign soldiers for battle against Lagash resulted in yet another significant conflict.

The text records that Enanatum (not Eanatum, but E*n*anatum) – the king of Lagash – then fought with Urluma of Umma, but Enanatum's son Enmetena was the one who ultimately defeated Urluma. When the dust settled, a man named Il, a temple administrator, had taken control of Umma and redirected the water channels (just like Urluma):[18]

> "At that time, Il, who was the temple-estate administrator at Zabala, had marched in retreat from Girsu to Umma. Il took the rulership of Umma for himself. He diverted water into the boundary-channel of Ningirsu and the boundary-channel of Nanshe, at the boundary-levee of Ningirsu".[19]

As we would expect, this was ultimately stopped and "righted" by the king of Lagash, Enmetena.

The final chapter of this story comes with the tables being turned against Lagash under the rule of Lugalzagesi of Umma. Lugalzagesi was able to march against Lagash (amongst other places), which was then under the rule of a man named Urukagina. He carried off valuable objects to Umma and destroyed the barley of the fields of Ningirsu. An inscription describes a lament of Urukagina, the man who – according to the text – had done no sin deserving of this:

> "The leader of Umma set fire to the Ekibira. He set fire to the Antasura and bundled off its precious metals and lapis-lazuli . . . In the fields of Ningirsu, whichever were cultivated, he destroyed the barley. The leader of Umma, hav[ing] sacked L[ag]ash, has committed a sin against Ningirsu. The hand which he has raised against him will be cut off! It is not a sin of Uru'inimgina, king of Girsu! May

Nisaba, the god of Lugalzagesi, ruler of Umma, make him (Lugalzagesi) bear the sin!"[20]

As Cooper aptly points out, we must remember that these inscriptions cannot simply be taken at face value; reconstructing the described events to reflect historical reality is a complicated matter. He writes concerning his reconstruction,

> *"The preceding narrative of the Lagash-Umma conflict is not a history.* In harmonizing the *obviously one-sided accounts of Lagash itself*, I have tried to reconstruct the historical tradition of the conflict at Lagash, as it circulated among the scribes who drew on it to compose the inscriptions of their employers . . . Rarely, evidence from outside Lagash, such as the inscriptions of Lugalkiginedudu or Lugalzagesi, could be utilized to broaden the perspective" (emphasis mine).[21]

The point of this section, however, was simply to provide an example of the conflicts that existed between the various city-states during this period. Only a short time later, a ruler would unite this region in an unprecedented fashion.

The Old Akkadian Empire

After Lugalzagesi defeated the city of Lagash, he moved his capital to the city of Uruk. Beaulieu writes,

> "Lugal-zagesi's conquest of Lagash heralds the end of the Early Dynastic period. He transferred his capital from

Umma to Uruk and embarked on a series of military campaigns aimed at uniting Babylonia under his rule".[22]

This would, however, bring him into conflict with a man who had established himself as the ruler of the famous city of Akkad and the founder of the Old Akkadian Empire: Sargon.

Sargon's origins are an interesting point of discussion. Edzard notes:

> "Sargon's past is dark, and it was already legendary early on. The Akkadian birth legend is an 'exposure story'. According to it, Sargon was taken in by a gardener as a foster son. Later, the goddess Ishtar would take a liking to the young Sargon, and paved the way for a great future for him".[23]

Several (later) literary texts – both in Sumerian and Akkadian – speak of different aspects of his life prior to kingship. For example, the Akkadian text from the first millennium B.C.E. referenced by Edzard above – *The Birth Legend of Sargon of Akkad* – is a pseudo-autobiography that speaks to Sargon's birth and early life.

> "I am Sargon the great king, king of Agade. My mother was a high priestess, I did not know my father . . . My mother, the high priestess, conceived me, she bore me in secret. She placed me in a reed basket, she sealed my hatch with pitch. She left me to the river, whence I could not come up. The river carried me off, it brought me to Aqqi, drawer of water. Aqqi, drawer of water, brought me up as he dipped his

bucket. Aqqi, drawer of water, raised me as his adopted son".[24]

Those readers familiar with the biblical story of Moses in the book of Exodus will recognize some similarities between the two stories!

Another interesting literary text is the Sumerian story of *Sargon and Ur-Zababa*, which tells of Sargon functioning as an official of Ur-Zababa, the king of Kish, prior to his rise to power in Akkad. The text also speaks of Lugalzagesi, to whom Sargon would not submit. This text appears to agree with what we see in the famous *Sumerian King List*, which tells us the following about Sargon: "In Agade, Sargon, whose father was a gardener, the cupbearer of Ur-Zababa, became king, the king of Agade".[25] Of course, we cannot be sure that any of this information is historically reliable; all ancient texts were written with a purpose, often politically motivated, and in this case the theme of an unavoidable destiny determined by the gods likely helped to provide legitimacy to Sargon's illegitimate rule.[26]

Whatever we can say about the founding of the Old Akkadian Empire under Sargon of Akkad, the creation of an empire was a significant development in the late 3rd millennium (and in the region altogether). Not only was Sargon's empire the first empire centered in Mesopotamia, but the Old Akkadian period gave rise to important cultural and political developments in the region.[27] Extending his political reach through force, Sargon was likely able to unite much of the north and south in Mesopotamia. Uniting what were historically disparate and conflicting city-states was no easy feat, and there is evidence that Sargon encountered substantial resistance from the Sumerian cities in the south. Sargon destroyed the fortifications of southern cities and installed Akkadians as rulers who would be loyal to the empire, laying the foundation for "the most enduring feature of the Akkadian Empire: dominion based on military power".[28]

Sargon's two sons followed him to the throne: Rimush and Manishtushu. Then came the incredibly influential grandson of Sargon, Naram-Sin. While Naram-Sin implemented many noteworthy changes, history chiefly remembers a major event that occurred during his reign: the "Great Rebellion".[29] At some point during his reign, at least two (possibly three) coalitions – from both the north and the south – came against Naram-Sin and his city, Akkad (Agade).

> "The rebel cities included Kish, Kutha, Dilbat, Lagaba(?),
> Sippar, Kazallu, Giritab, Apiak and Eresh in North
> Babylonia, all following Iphur-kishi; and Uruk, Ur,
> Lagash, Umma, Adab, Shuruppak, Isin, and Nippur in the
> South, all following Amargirid. *Hardly a single major
> Babylonian town remained loyal to Naramsin*" (emphasis
> mine).[30]

This Great Rebellion and the battles resulting from it are documented in numerous royal inscriptions from the time of Naram-Sin and after. One of the most famous inscriptions, which speaks of nine battles being fought in one year, contains the details of Naram-Sin's deification as a reward for his victory.

> "When the four quarters together revolted against him,
> through the love which the goddess Aštar showed him, he
> was victorious in nine battles in one year, and the kings

whom they (the rebels[?]) had raised (against him), he captured. In view of the fact that they protected the foundation of his city from danger, (the citizens of) his city requested . . . *that (Naram-Sin) be (made) the god of their city*" (emphasis mine).[31]

Westenholz notes,

"Both contemporaries and later generations were deeply impressed by these events. In Akkade, the City Fathers asked permission from the gods of Eanna (i.e., Uruk), Nippur, Tuttul, Kesh, Eridu, Ur, Sippar, and Kutha to build a temple for Naramsin in Akkade 'as the god of their city', 'because he in the time of crisis had strengthened the foundations of the city'. Naramsin was henceforth 'Akkade's god', at least to his officials".[32]

Whether the officials of the empire felt compelled to nominate him to kingship for personal reasons, or due to some "suggestions" from the king himself, his victory in the Great Revolt clearly left a significant impact. However, later memories of him and his reign are not so one-sided. For example, in a later literary composition known as *The Cursing of Agade*, Naram-Sin is depicted as acting in a rather impious manner. Cooper summarizes the critical portion of the story:

"Inanna suddenly turns against her protégés, seemingly because Enlil has refused permission for a proper temple to be built for her . . . She abandons Agade, the gods withdraw their favor, the city is in the throes of agony. Naramsin foresees the finality of the city's misfortune in a dream so dreadful that he is unable to talk about it, and he sinks into a seven-year depression".[33]

In response to Enlil's decision, Naram-Sin destroys his temple, the E-Kur.[34]

Other later texts seem to cast Naram-Sin in a "less-than-ideal" light as well, as he is remembered – for example – as a king who does not follow the will of the gods. Westenholz argues,

> "No doubt these mixed reviews go back to very different opinions about the king in his own time. While some admired his valor in warfare, and while almost all were awed by his victory in the Great Revolt, others saw his conduct, especially toward the gods, as dangerous hubris and arrogance".[35]

Following the reign of Naram-Sin, the Old Akkadian Empire ultimately fell into decline. However, the region saw a significant and far-reaching revival in the last century of the 3rd millennium, a time known as the Ur III period.

The Ur III Period (ca. 2100-2000 B.C.E.)

If you have been to a museum that has a cuneiform collection on display, no matter how small, you have more than likely seen an administrative document from the late 3rd millennium B.C.E. "The Ur III period, as it is generally known, produced abundant archival documentation estimated conservatively at *more than 100,000 tablets* and which keeps increasing with new discoveries" (emphasis mine).[36] This extensive documentation was the result of an administrative system that was quite developed and centralized, and – as we will see below – incorporated both the "core" of the Ur III state as well as the "periphery", particularly the lands to the east.

The Ur III period began with Utu-Hegal, the king of the city of Uruk, expelling a group of invaders known as the Gutians from Babylonia. Ur-Namma, the brother of Utu-Hegal, was the next to rule the region, and moved the capital to the city of Ur. Van De Mieroop writes, "Around 2100 Ur-Namma started the Third Dynasty of Ur (or Ur III dynasty), a succession of five generations of rulers from the same family".[37]

One of the great achievements for which Ur-Namma is still known is his collection of laws: *The Laws of Ur-Namma* (LU). In what would become standard practice, the law collection contained a prologue that spoke of the just and caring rule of the king.

> "I established freedom for the Akkadians and foreigners(?) in the lands of Sumer and Akkad, for those conducting foreign maritime trade (free from) the sea-captains [who had previously been in control of it], for the herdsmen (free from) those who appropriate(?) oxen, sheep, and donkeys" (LU A iii 114-124).[38]

The text continues to demonstrate the king's justice and mercy:

> "I did not deliver the orphan to the rich. I did not deliver the widow to the mighty. I did not deliver the man with but one shekel to the man with one mina (i.e., 60 shekels). I did not deliver the man with but one sheep to the man with one ox" (LU A iv 162-168).[39]

The prologue concludes: "I eliminated enmity, violence, and cries for justice. I established justice in the land" (LU A iv 170).[40]

Many of the individual laws would reappear in similar form in the later legal collections. A common thread that runs through these collections is the picture of the king establishing and maintaining that culture's idea of social justice. Laws like "If a man commits murder, this man will be executed" (LU 1), "If a slave marries a slave girl of his choice, (and) this slave is set free; (she) will not leave the household" (LU 4), and "If a . . . beats a gentleman's daughter and causes her to miscarry, he will pay thirty shekels of silver. If she dies, this man will be [executed]. If a . . . beats a gentleman's slave girl and causes her to miscarry, he will pay ten (*var.* five) shekels. If the slave girl dies, he will give slave for slave" (LU 33-36) may bring to mind similar laws found in the Old Testament (for example, Exodus 21:2-6, 12, and 22).

Perhaps the most famous king of the Ur III period is Shulgi, who reigned from 2094-2047 B.C.E. An important aspect of his reign that we will focus on here is how he structured his administration of the land into the "core" and "periphery". Sumer and Akkad were split into over 20 provinces, each with their own ruler, known as the *ensi*, "a title which no longer denoted independent rulership of a city-state but more the position of a governor . . . Military affairs in each province were entrusted to a royal deputy, the *shagina*".[41]

The system that made the whole thing work was called the *bala* (Sumerian "turn" or "rotate") system, in which the king assigned specific duties to the various core provinces and peripheral regions. In the core of the land, there was a system of redistribution that allowed the individual regions – who may have specialized in producing various commodities – to bring their goods to a central redistribution center and receive commodities from other regions in return. "It was a massive fund to which all provinces had to contribute and from which they could withdraw goods, enabling the state to use resources from all over its territory".[42]

The periphery was subjected to a different form of taxation. There were numerous *shagina* officials stationed throughout the periphery, who were responsible for collecting what was known as the *gunmada,* or "tax of the provinces". In essence, these local officials, as part of the Ur III administration, would collect (generally) livestock, either from their own land – given by royal grant – or from their subordinates, and would provide it to the *bala* system. The amount of their required contributions was dependent upon their military rank. Unfortunately for the periphery, they did not receive distributions from the *bala* system.

The end of the Ur III period saw an economic and political decline during the reign of its final king, Ibbi-Sin. One of his generals, Ishbi-Erra, was sent on a mission to procure grain for the king. However, Ishbi-Erra appears to have betrayed the king and ultimately established his own rule at the city of Isin. Also involved in the downfall of the city of Ur were external foreign forces, likely including the Amorites and the Elamites. Whatever events coalesced to bring about the fall of the Ur III dynasty, it ushered in another period in which independent states were constantly interacting with one another, either in conflict or as part of a coalition.

The Early Second Millennium B.C.E.

Following the highly centralized rule of the Ur III period at the end of the 3rd millennium, the various regions of Mesopotamia and Syria fragmented, and different cities were able to establish their own local rule. Some were even able to gain control of surrounding regions. This control, however, was ever-shifting, and much of the region ultimately fell under the sway of Hammurabi of Babylon in the mid-18th c. B.C.E. In spite of the somewhat chaotic political climate, there were industrious people who learned to thrive in that environment, both economically and politically. We will begin our discussion of this fragmented political situation by examining an entrepreneurial phenomenon that existed in the early 2nd millennium B.C.E.: The Old Assyrian trade network.

The Old Assyrian Period

During the first two centuries of the 2nd millennium B.C.E., we see an extensive network of commercial activity between Assur (a city in southern Assyria) and Anatolia (modern-day Turkey), in a city called Kanesh. "The system is known to us from the discovery of more than 20,000 tablets left by Assyrian merchants in a colony at the edge of the central Anatolian city Kanesh, some 1000 kilometers from Assur".[43]

Traders from the city of Assur in the east acquired tin and textiles from Assyria and the surrounding regions and transported those materials northwest into Anatolia (modern-day Turkey). There, they sold the tin and textiles for silver at a much higher rate – given the scarcity of these materials in Anatolia – and took that silver back to Assur to purchase more tin and textiles.

For example, let's say a merchant named Frank, who lived in Assur, took ten shekels of silver and purchased tin and textiles. He loaded that merchandise on a donkey and set out for Anatolia, where he was able to sell what he had purchased for 10 shekels for, let's say, 20 shekels.[44] He would then take that 20 shekels of silver, return to Assur, and purchase, perhaps, 15 shekels worth of tin and textiles (assuming he needed to use the remaining 5 shekels to live). He would then return to Anatolia, sell the 15 shekels worth of material for 30 shekels, and so on.

Van De Mieroop summarizes the process in this way:

> "Assur acted almost solely as a transit point in this trade. It imported tin from unknown sources in Iran or beyond and textiles from Babylonia . . . Donkey caravans were organized in Assur, each animal loaded with 150 pounds of tin and thirty textiles . . . When the caravan arrived in Kanesh, most of the donkeys were sold and the merchandise was exchanged for silver and gold, which was then taken back to Assur".[45]

You can imagine that, over time, traders developed more efficient means of moving and selling their products. For example, when Frank arrived in Anatolia, he had to accomplish a number of tasks. First, he had to find a place to stay. Then he had to find a buyer (or buyers). He also had to worry about thieves on his route back home. When he returned to Assur, he had to again procure more products, take care of his family, etc. Traders began to build the size of their businesses by assigning certain people to certain roles.

This ultimately led to an actual trading colony being established in the city of Kanesh in Anatolia, where people who lived in the city would receive the goods and have the responsibility for selling the products. Veenhof describes it in this way:

> "The range of action of the traders increased and must have resulted in more colonies and trading stations, also in more marginal areas, and to exploit these possibilities more capital, more traders and more personnel must have been needed. Increase of capital presumably led to the formation of 'joint-stock companies', which worked with a large capital . . . invested by shareholders".[46]

What makes this period intriguing for many people – in addition to what we learn about these economic activities – is the insight that we gain into the private lives of individuals. These traders were not part of the palatial system or working on behalf of some government agency. These were entrepreneurial families working in a private business. While the men acted as traders, this was very much a family business. Women normally remained in Assur, managing affairs in the city and communicating with their husbands and other male relatives in Anatolia. They were responsible also for either weaving the textiles used in trade themselves, or overseeing their creation by other women.[47]

Because these trade documents and letters were written by private individuals, it often allows us to see some of the more intimate details of their lives. Van De Mieroop cites a letter from a wife to her husband, who has been complaining to her about the poor quality of the textiles that she has been producing:

"'Why do you keep on writing to me: "The textiles that you send me are always of bad quality!" Who is the man who lives in your house and criticizes the textiles that are brought to him? I, on the other hand, keep on striving to produce and send you textiles so that on every trip your business gains ten shekels of silver"'.[48]

Given the nature of the business, it was customary for husbands to leave their families in Assur for extended periods of time. Van De Mieroop cites another letter that a woman wrote to her husband concerning the dire straits in which the family found itself following the husband's departure:

"'You wrote to me as follows: "Keep the bracelets and rings that you have; they will be needed to buy you food" . . . When you left, you didn't leave me one shekel of silver. You cleaned out the house and took everything with you. Since you left, a [terrible] famine has hit the city (of Assur). You did not leave me one liter of barley. I need to keep on buying barley for our food . . . Now I live in an empty house and the seasons are changing. Make sure that you send me the value of my textiles in silver, so that I can at least buy ten measures of barley"'.[49]

Thus, while the situation was by no means perfect for all members of the family, the Assyrian traders were able to adapt to their surroundings and establish a trade network that covered more than 600 miles, meeting the demand of their Anatolian buyers.

The Isin-Larsa Period

The political makeup of the first half of the 2nd millennium (2000-1600 B.C.E.) was similar to that of earlier periods – individual city-states, ruled by military leaders, embedded in an ever-shifting patchwork of rivalries and alliances.[50]

If you recall from the previous section, the final Ur III ruler, Ibbi-Sin, was said to have been betrayed by one of his generals, Ishbi-Erra, who established his rule in the city of Isin. He was able to free the city of Ur from the invading hostile forces that had taken it and began to extend his rule to different cities in Mesopotamia. The rulers of Isin attempted to maintain cultural continuity between the fallen Ur III state and their new seat of power; for example, the Sumerian language continued to be used extensively, including for literary and administrative purposes.[51] Although Sumerian was most likely a dead language by this time, the Isin ruler Lipit-Ishtar produced a new collection of laws in Sumerian, not unlike those created in the reign of Ur-Namma of the Ur III dynasty.

Many comparisons can be made between these two collections of laws. For example, in the prologue of the *Laws of Lipit-Ishtar* (LL), we see a similar focus on establishing justice and minimizing oppression:

> "At that time, the gods An and Enlil called Lipit-Ishtar to the princeship of the land – Lipit-Ishtar, the wise shepherd, whose name has been pronounced by the god Nunamnir – in order to establish justice in the land, to eliminate cries for justice, to eradicate enmity and armed violence, to bring well-being to the lands of Sumer and Akkad" (LL i 20-37).[52]

We also see similar legal rationale and law formulations:

> "If [a . . .] strikes the daughter of a man and causes her to lose her fetus, he shall weigh and deliver 30 shekels of silver. If she dies, that male shall be killed. If a . . . strikes the slave woman of a man and causes her to lose her fetus, he shall weigh and deliver 5 shekels of silver" (LL d-f).[53]

Another law shows concern for a wife whose husband no longer values her as he once did:

> "If a man's first-ranking wife loses her attractiveness or becomes a paralytic, she will not be evicted from the house; however, her husband may marry a healthy wife, and the second wife shall support the first-ranking wife" (LL 28).[54]

Eventually, the city of Isin lost control over much of its territory to the city of Larsa, which expanded its territory, primarily beginning with the capture of the city of Ur by Gungunum, the king of Larsa.[55]

The Rise of Hammurabi

The famous Hammurabi of Babylon came to power and eventually dominated Mesopotamia in the 18th c. B.C.E. After the fall of the Ur III dynasty, an outsider group known as the Amorites began to move into Mesopotamia. For example, around the city of Mari, which lies on the Euphrates River, there were four tribes of Amorites: the Sim'al, Yamina, Numha, and Yamutbal. The events that led to Hammurabi's domination are a bit complex, but are more comprehensible if examined individually. This section will focus on major powers involved in the region and the specific cities and powers that were involved leading up to Hammurabi's conquest: Mari, Babylon, Eshnunna, Larsa, and Elam. The fact that we can reconstruct events in such amazing detail is due to an archive of nearly 4,000 royal letters that were discovered in the palace of Zimri-Lim at the city of Mari.

Toward the end of the 19th century, the city of Mari was ruled by a man by the name of Yahdun-Lim. Both Yahdun-Lim and his son and successor, Sumu-Yaman, were assassinated. The throne of Mari was taken over shortly thereafter by Shamshi-Adad. This powerful and competent ruler eventually controlled much of northern Mesopotamia, and placed two of his sons over prominent cities, while he ruled from his capital, Shubat-Enlil. Ishme-Dagan, the eldest, ruled at Ekallatum, while his younger son, Yasmah-Addu, took over at the city of Mari.[56]

Following Shamshi-Adad's death, however, Yasmah-Addu was not able to hold on to control of Mari, and an Amorite from the Sim'al tribe named Zimri-Lim was able to come to power. The early part of his reign saw many rebellions and other conflicts that required his attention, after which (during a time of peace) he was able to focus his attention on the business of ruling, including royal building works and a census of the people.[57]

In the south, several kings ruled from smaller city-states, including Hammurabi of Babylon and Rim-Sin of Larsa, while the state of Elam to the east was an ever-present threat. The first major event in Hammurabi's rise to power was the defeat of the king of Elam, the major power to the east of the Zagros mountains. Elam's policy up to this point had been to have regular contact with and exert influence on Mesopotamia, but not to remain in the area to rule. A drastic change to this policy came in 1767, when Elam invaded and occupied various Mesopotamian states, "a policy of overextension that would ultimately lead to its defeat by Hammurabi only two years later".[58] Elam's crucial mistake came when they attempted to play Hammurabi off of the ruler of Larsa, Rim-Sin. In a message to Hammurabi, the ruler of Elam told the Babylonian king to provide him with troops in order to engage with Rim-Sin of Larsa. At the same time, however, he sent a similar message to Rim-Sin about Hammurabi. "When the two Mesopotamian rulers compared notes, they saw Elam's duplicity and agreed to join forces".[59]

Hammurabi sent messages to the king of Mari, Zimri-Lim, asking for additional troops to help defeat Elam. Although Zimri-Lim struggled to recruit troops, he was eventually able to do so. Hammurabi then requested similar support from Rim-Sin of Larsa; however, Rim-Sin refused to help for a variety of possible reasons – his Elamite roots, his old age, Larsa's economic decline, and/or a distrust of Hammurabi's motives.[60] This refusal would come back to bite Rim-Sin. Faced with military pressure, Elam eventually retreated back to their homeland.

Following Elam's defeat, Hammurabi turned his attention to the man who failed to support him against Elam: Rim-Sin of Larsa. In 1763, Hammurabi declared war and went on the offensive. With Mari's troops still under his command, he first took the city of Mashkan-Shapir, which was under the control of Rim-Sin's brother. Hammurabi then took Nippur and Isin, and finally reached Larsa, where he laid siege to the city. Despite Rim-Sin's advanced age, the defeat of Larsa was not an easy victory for Hammurabi, and the attacking king "built assault ramps and brought in siege engines, and continued to secure additional forces from his allies".[61] When Larsa did finally fall, Hammurabi had its walls torn down, and Rim-Sin was sent to Babylon.

This left only two powers in Mesopotamia: the cities of Eshnunna and Mari. After Hammurabi defeated Rim-Sin of Larsa, Zimri-Lim had become impatient and requested that his troops be finally returned to him. Hammurabi stalled, but ultimately allowed them to return to Mari. The ruler of Eshnunna, Silli-Sin, declared that he was independent from Babylon, and he and Zimri-Lim established a relationship which angered Hammurabi. Having just defeated Larsa, Hammurabi filled in the gaps from the loss of Mari's troops with soldiers from Larsa. He then turned and attacked Silli-Sin of Eshnunna, defeating the city in 1762.

Hammurabi then turned toward Mari, beginning an attack from the north and the south, gathering troops in Hanat, two day's march from Mari, and sending an additional 20,000 troops to the north of the city.[62] Mari was defeated, though Hammurabi had to return in 1759 to suppress an uprising, this time tearing down its walls. Hammurabi of Babylon was now the dominant power in the region. This is the start of the time period that Assyriologists refer to as the "Old Babylonian period".[63]

From Hammurabi to the Fall of Babylon

Hammurabi is probably best known from the law collection that he commissioned. While the previous sets of laws that we discussed were written in Sumerian, the *Laws of Hammurabi* (LH) were written in Akkadian. These laws were inscribed on quite an impressive monument, a basalt slab over 7ft tall, adorned at the top with a carved scene showing "Hammu-rabi standing before the sun-god Shamash, the god of justice, who is seated on a throne". [64] While it is not completely preserved, the stele contains a staggering 282 laws dealing with cases that include:

> "[J]udicial procedure; theft and robbery; slave sales and matters affecting slaves; agricultural and irrigation work and offenses; pledges, debts, deposits and loans; real estate sales and rentals; marriage, matrimonial property, and sexual offenses; inheritance, adoption and foster care; assault and bodily injuries; rates of hire for equipment, laborers, and craftsmen; failure to complete contracted tasks; renters' and shepherds' liabilities; and goring oxen". [65]

As we saw with the previous law collections, the prologue focuses on the king and the good that he had been commissioned to do for his people.

> "At that time, the gods Anu and Enlil, *for the enhancement of the well-being of the people*, named me by my name: Hammurabi, the pious prince, who venerates the gods, *to make justice prevail in the land, to abolish the wicked and the evil, to prevent the strong from oppressing the weak*, to rise like the sun-god Shamash over all humankind, to illuminate the land" (LH i 27-49, emphasis mine). [66]

Similarly,

> "When the god Marduk commanded me *to provide just ways for the people of the land (in order to attain)*

appropriate behavior, I established truth and justice as the declaration of the land, I enhanced the well-being of the people" (LH v 14-24, emphasis mine).[67]

As in the other law collections from the ancient Near East, many of the laws bear a passing to striking resemblance to those found in the Old Testament.

"If a man should kidnap the young child of another man, he shall be killed" (LH 14).[68]

"If a man has a claim of grain or silver against another man, distrains a member of his household, and the distrainee dies a natural death while in the house of her or his distrainer, that case has no basis for a claim. If the distrainee should die from the effects of a beating or other physical abuse while in the house of her or his distrainer, the owner of the distrainee shall charge and convict his merchant, and if (the distrainee) is the man's son, they shall kill his (the distrainer's) son; if the man's slave, he shall weigh and deliver 20 shekels of silver; moreover, he shall forfeit whatever he originally gave as the loan" (LH 115-116).[69]

"If an obligation is outstanding against a man and he sells or gives into debt service his wife, his son, or his daughter, they shall perform service in the house of their buyer or of the one who holds them in debt service for three years; their release shall be secured in the fourth year" (LH 117).[70]

While much more could be written on the reign of Hammurabi – and the remainder of his dynasty – it will suffice to briefly describe the remaining years of the Old Babylonian period. Hammurabi's reign represents the pinnacle of political unification of Mesopotamia during this period. Starting with his successor, Samsuiluna, Babylon's influence gradually receded. Samsuiluna was able to deal with a rebellion in the south by Rim-Sin II of Larsa, although his control over the south continued to wane. Following the reigns of the final kings of the Old Babylonian period – Abi-eshuh, Ammiditana, Ammisaduqa, and Samsuditana – the Hittites from Anatolia appear to have sacked Babylon, bringing about a "dark age".

> "The Hittite king Muršili (ca. 1600 B.C.E.) is said to have conquered Babylon in the 32nd and final year of the Babylonian king Samsu-ditāna, and by this to have ended the three-hundred-year-old so-called First Dynasty of Babylon".[71]

The Amarna Period and International Diplomacy

Following the fall of Babylon to the Hittites, the ancient Near East began to shift in the way in which individual nations interacted with one another.

> "During the centuries from 1500 to 1200 the Near East became fully integrated in an international system that involved the entire region from western Iran to the Aegean sea, from Anatolia to Nubia. A number of large territorial states interacted with one another as equals and rivals. Located between them, especially in the Syro-Palestinian

area, was a set of smaller states that owed allegiance to their more powerful neighbors, and which were often used as proxies in their competition".[72]

Much of what we know about this period of international diplomacy comes from a group of Akkadian cuneiform tablets that were found in Egypt during the late 19th century. These tablets are known as the "Amarna tablets" after the location of their excavation, the site of Tell el-Amarna, ancient Akhetaten, city of the infamous "monotheistic" pharaoh Akhenaten and his queen, Nefertiti.[73] The tablets date to the 14th c. B.C.E. and illuminate several decades in which various nations were interacting with one another in an unprecedented manner. At the site of Amarna were discovered 350 tablets which contain letters that can be split into two groups. The first group includes letters sent to and from the members of the "Great Powers Club" (Egypt, Babylonia, Assyria, Mittani, Hatti, Alashiya, and Arzawa), while the second group includes those letters sent between Egypt and her vassals in Syria-Palestine. If you consider the location of these vassal rulers, their kingdoms lie on the narrow strip of land that connects Egypt to the rest of the Near East. Control over this "land bridge" became a great source of contention between the major powers on either side of it, particularly the Egyptians to the south and the Hittites to the north.[74]

The Amarna letters that contain correspondence between the major kings reveal a new level of international diplomacy. For example, the standard greeting formula between equals shows kings addressing one another as "brother":

"Say [t]o Kadašman-Enlil, the king of Kardun[i]še (Babylonia), my brother: Thus Nibmuarea, Great King, the king of Egypt, your brother. For me all goes well. For you may all go well. For your household, for your wives, for your sons, for your magnates, your horses, your chariots, for your countries, may all go very well. For me all goes well. For my household, for my wives, for my sons, for my magnates, my horses, the numerous troops, all goes well, and in my countries all goes very well".[75]

Notice that the Egyptian king refers to the king of Babylonia and himself as "brothers", indicating an equal standing and a type of implied familial bond.

The vassal letters, however, contain no such terminology, as the vassal rulers were obviously not considered to be the equal of the pharaoh.[76] The local rulers – who were placed under the jurisdiction of locally-stationed Egyptian military officials – were required to provide Egypt with tribute, corvée labor, and other goods, services, and personnel.[77]

Given their subordinate role, the letters to and from these local rulers appeared very different.

"Say to Namḫurya, the son of the Sun, my lord: Message of Akizzi, your servant. I fall at the feet of my lord 7 times. My lord, I am your servant in this place. I seek the path to my lord. I do not desert my lord. From the time my ancestors were your servants, this country has been your country, Qaṭna has been your city, (and) I belong to my lord".[78]

Similarly, Rib-Hadda, king of Byblos, writes to the Egyptian king,

> "Rib-Hadda says to [his] lord, king of all countries, Great King, King of Battle: May [the lady] of Gubla grant power to the king, my lord. I fall at the feet of my lord, my Sun, 7 times and 7 times".[79]

The letters from the vassal rulers often concern pleas for support, including troops, provisions, and overall care. The letters to and from the great kings, however, show them engaging in international diplomacy, treating each other as part of a large family... including the pettiness that some familial relationships lend themselves to! In a letter from the Babylonian king to the king of Egypt, we see the not-so-subtle expression of dissatisfaction by the Babylonian king concerning the gifts that he had been given and the apparent slight he had received:

> "When you celebrated a great festival, you did not send your messenger to me, saying, 'Come t[o eat an]d drink.' No[r did you send me] my greeting-gift in connection with the festival. It was just 30 minas of gold that you [sent me]. My [gift] [does not amoun]t to what [I have given you] every yea[r]. I have built a [ne]w [house]. I[n my house] I have built a [l]arge [...]. Your [mes]sengers have see[n *the house and the* ... , *and are pleased. No*]w I am going to hav[e] a house-opening. Come [*yourself*] to [eat an]d drink with me. [*I shall not act* a]s you yourself did".[80]

The Amarna period reveals a new phase of international diplomacy that was developed among the great powers of the ancient Near East during the second half of the 2nd millennium B.C.E. At the same time, this group of letters illuminates the makeup of the land of Canaan during this period, giving us insight into the local vassal rulers that were subjects (primarily) of the Egyptian Pharaoh. This time of international relationships was not to last, however, and would ultimately give way to the rise of territorial states during the first millennium. The first of these – the Neo-Assyrian Empire – began to take shape in the late 2nd millennium, starting during the Amarna period and culminating during a time known as the Middle Assyrian period.

The Rise of Assyria (Middle Assyrian Period)

Although the history of the region is quite complex and involves a variety of nations, because the Assyrian Empire established itself as the dominant force during the first half of the first millennium, we will focus on the Assyrians and their development beginning in the Middle Assyrian period (ca. 1400-1000 B.C.E.). We first see the Assyrian state asserting its political importance during the Amarna period, under a king called Assuruballit I, who ruled from 1363-1328 B.C.E. In an attempt to establish himself as an equal among the "Great Powers Club", he wrote to the Egyptian king. This drew the attention – and not in a good way – of the king of Babylon, who considered Assuruballit to be his subordinate – one of his own vassals, in fact, who had no place in the Great Powers Club.[81] Nevertheless, Assuruballit I was able to gain strength and establish Assyria as a major power in the region.

Three other kings ruled during the 13th century that also had an early influence on Assyria: Adad-nirari I, Shalmaneser I, and Tukulti-Ninurta I. Their military campaigns focused mainly on the west, where they slowly incorporated the previous Mitanni state into Assyrian territory.[82]

These regular military campaigns would pave the way for the Neo-Assyrian Empire just a few centuries later.

By way of illustration, Tukulti-Ninurta I can be held up as an example of a prototypical Assyrian king. He established power and influence in the region for Assyria, largely through regular military expeditions. He is depicted as a great warrior for the gods in a literary text known as *The Tukulti-Ninurta Epic*, which describes how the Assyrian king sacked Babylon to the south and took captive its king.

> "The lines of battle were drawn up, combat was joined on the battlefield. There was a great commotion, the troops were quivering among them. Assur went first, the conflagration of defeat burst out upon the enemy, Enlil was whirling(?) in the midst of the foe, fanning the blaze, Anu set a pitiless mace to the opponent, Sin, the luminary, laid upon them the tension of battle. Adad, the hero, made wind and flood pour down over their fighting, Shamash, lord of judgment, blinded the eyesight of the army of Sumer and Akkad, Valiant Ninurta, vanguard of the gods, smashed their weapons, Ishtar flailed her jump rope, driving their warriors berserk! *Behind the gods, his allies, the king at the head of the army sets to battle*" (emphasis mine).[83]

The power of Assyria did not last long, however, as a great collapse befell the entire ancient Near East around 1200 B.C.E.[84] This regional decline affected nearly all of the eastern Mediterranean world, with the result that "[v]ery little is known about the centuries from 1100 to 900".[85] By the time of the first millennium B.C.E., we see that the ancient Near East had significantly changed and developed "into an age of empires".[86]

The Neo-Assyrian Empire

In the last section we saw that during the tail-end of the Amarna period, culminating in the Middle Assyrian period, Assyria developed into a powerful political force in its own right, exchanging letters and diplomatic gifts with other important states, most notably the Egyptians. This period marked a shift in the political organization of the Mesopotamian region, from a collection of disparate city-states into two territorial states – Assyria and Babylonia. It also saw the beginning of regular military campaigns by the Assyrian kings, which – together with this political shift – paved the way for the creation of the Neo-Assyrian Empire and set a pattern to be emulated by the Neo-Assyrian kings.

Assyria was not immune to the widespread systems collapse that occurred throughout the ancient Near East, though it was affected to a far lesser degree than the civilizations along the Mediterranean coast. It appears that the "heartland" remained intact and under control of the city of Assur. In this section we will sketch the political history of the creation of the Neo-Assyrian Empire, achieved largely through regular military campaigns carried out by the Assyrian kings.

On a broad scale, the Neo-Assyrian Empire dominated much of the ancient Near East. Beginning at the end of the 10th century, the Assyrian kings were able to secure the heartland and expand to the west and south. This ultimately resulted in the practice of annual campaigning by the Neo-Assyrian king; in order to display their power, ensure payment of tribute, and dissuade rebellion, the king would annually march his army through the conquered regions.

The Neo-Assyrian boundaries were not constant; the empire would expand and contract based on the relative strength of the current king. However, the second half of the 8th century was a time of a great resurgence for the Neo-Assyrian Empire, particularly under Tiglath-Pileser III. Prior to Tiglath-Pileser III's rule, Assyria had been unable to conduct regular military campaigns, and local officials in the west had gained power, greatly reducing Assyrian influence.[87] This was halted by Tiglath-Pileser III, who, along with one of his successors, Sargon II, "restructured the Assyrian state internally, campaigned almost annually outside its borders, and started to incorporate foreign territories into Assyria".[88] By putting down independent local rule and campaigning on a regular basis, Tiglath-Pileser III established a great deal of stability in the region.

This western expansion is referenced in the Old Testament. For example, in 2 Kings 15:19 we read, "Pul [Tiglath-Pileser III] king of Assyria came to the land, and Menahem gave to Pul a thousand talents of silver in order for his support to be with him to strengthen the kingdom by his hand". Similarly, in 2 Kings 15:29:

> "In the days of Pekah king of Israel, Tiglath-Pileser king of Assyria came and he took Ijon and Abel-beth Maacah and Janoah and Kedesh and Hazor and Gilead and Galilee, and all the land of Naphtali, and he exiled them to Assyria" (2 Kings 15:29).

Ahaz submits to Tiglath-Pileser III in the following chapter:

> "And Ahaz sent messengers to Tiglath-Pileser king of
> Assyria, saying, 'Your slave and your son am I. Come up
> and rescue me from the hand of the king of Aram and from
> the hand of the king of Israel, who are rising up against
> me'" (2 Kings 16:7).

It was during the reigns of Shalmaneser V and Sargon II, however, that the political situation deteriorated for Israel in the north (as opposed to Judah in the south).

> "First, Shalmaneser V moved against the cities of the
> central-southern Phoenicia (Sidon, Ushu, Acco: cf. *Ant.*
> 9.283-287), then proceeded against Israel: he imprisoned
> Hoshea and besieged Samaria, which capitulated in 721.
> Soon afterwards Shalmaneser died, and hence the
> conquest of Samaria is described (and claimed) by his
> successor, the great Sargon II, as if it occurred in his first
> year of reign".[89]

At this point of great strength for the empire, Assyria was able to effectively extend its control to the west. Again, however, Assyria's position of strength slowly began to deteriorate.

The Problem with Babylonia

The Neo-Assyrian kings campaigned in the periphery while simultaneously working hard to maintain stability in the heartland. So how did this great empire – with all of its power and reach – come to an end? What events transpired that weakened this mighty nation to the point of collapse?

In 1984, Assyriologist John Brinkman at the University of Chicago published a book entitled *Prelude to Empire*, in which he suggested that the fate of the Neo-Assyrian Empire was greatly influenced by its interactions with its troublesome neighbor to the south: the Babylonians.[90] Brinkman argued that the time and resources the Neo-Assyrian Empire needed to devote to putting down constant rebellions meant that the empire was eventually drained of its resources and left open to attack by the surrounding nations.

Background on Babylonia

Before we examine the reigns of the latter Neo-Assyrian kings and the problems that each faced during his reign, we should take a few moments and understand the makeup of this problem area to the south: Babylonia. Refer to figure 1 for the following discussion. During the 8th century – when Assyria was gaining political momentum – Babylonia was inhabited by three groups: native "Babylonians", the Arameans, and the Chaldeans. While the Babylonian population was native to the area, the Arameans and Chaldeans were tribal groups who had settled somewhat recently and maintained their own distinct culture.[91]

The native Babylonians settled primarily in the northwestern cities like Sippar, Babylon, and Nippur as well as in the southwestern cities of Uruk and Ur.[92] These were important religious and cultural centers, a fact that would play a role in the events that would transpire during the decline of the Neo-Assyrian Empire.

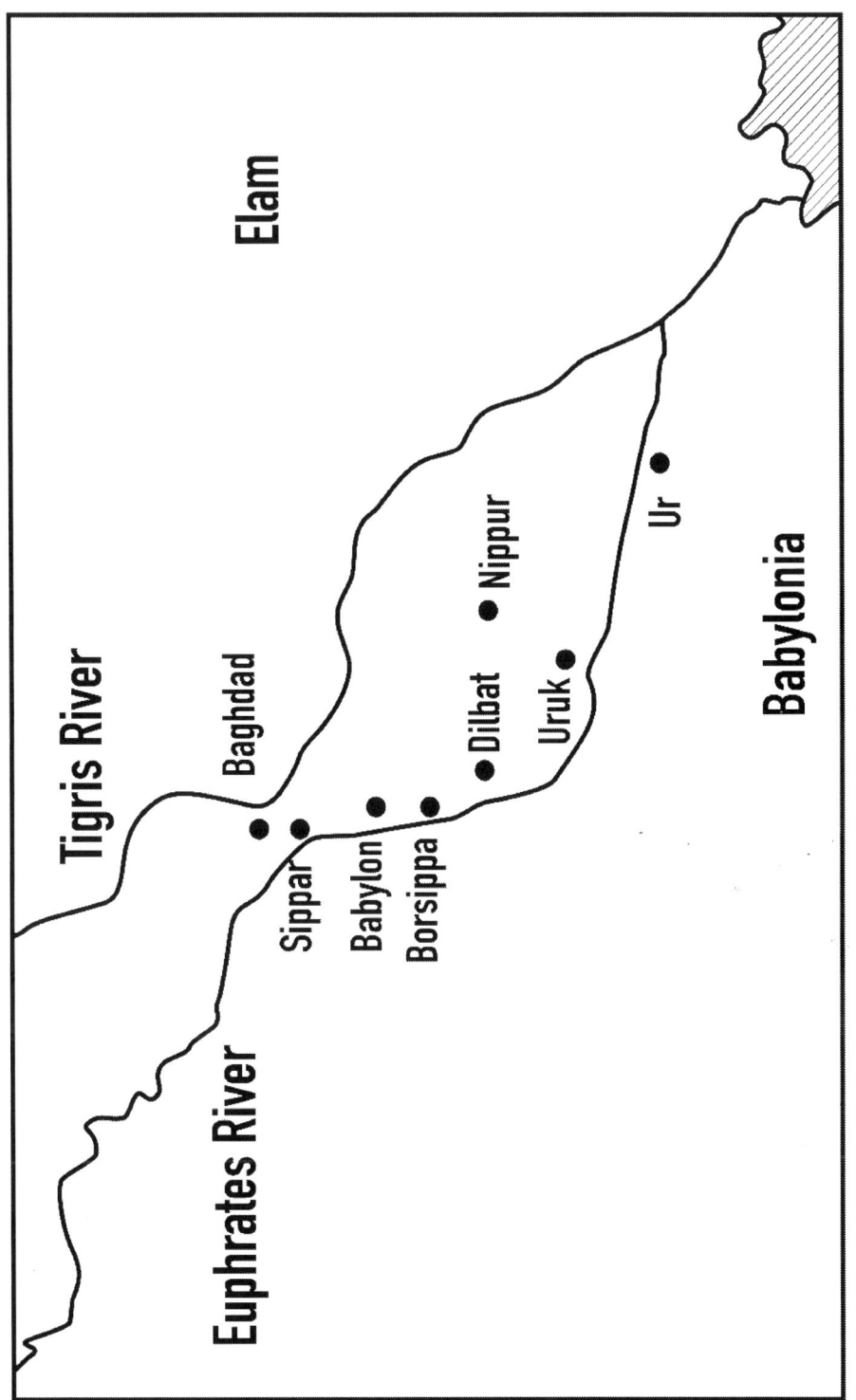

Figure 1. Map of Babylonia with approximate locations of
relevant ancient cities. Modern city of Baghdad shown for context.

The other two groups in Babylonia were the Arameans and Chaldeans. While much could be said about them, it is sufficient at present to note that the Chaldeans were most often responsible for the revolts and rebellions that took place in the south. The Assyrian responses to these revolts led to a development in Babylonian military strategies, particularly with respect to their physical environment in the south. They developed methods for fighting in and from the marshlands, and became skilled at shifting the various watercourses in the region for tactical purposes. [93] This process of Assyrian involvement and Babylonian resistance ultimately led – at least in part – to the rise of the Neo-Babylonian Empire and the downfall of the Assyrians.

Sargon II, Sennacherib, and Merodoch-baladan

Assyria's problems with Babylonia became more pronounced during the reign of Sargon II. In 721, following Sargon II's accession, a figure named Merodach-baladan took the Babylonian throne. Merodach-baladan was responsible for leading several rebellions during both Sargon II's and Sennacherib's reigns, and he proved to be quite a thorn in the side of these two Neo-Assyrian kings. Between 720 and 709, Sargon II had to fight several coalitions in the south.

Things did not improve under Sennacherib, and the king was forced to attempt different methods of rule over Babylonia because of the constant uprisings. For example, he first attempted to govern the south directly; however, this proved ineffective and led him to place a native Babylonian, Bel-ibni, on the throne. When this method failed, he set his own son, Ashur-nadin-shumi, over Babylonia; however, the Elamites captured him and deported him to Elam. All of these frustrations to his rule seem to have enraged the king; in the end, Sennacherib appears to have moved against Babylonia in full force.

His treatment of the south is described by Brinkman as "unexpectedly harsh".[94] Several long campaigns, an expensive siege, and the death of his son all appear to have exhausted the patience of the Neo-Assyrian king, who had the city of Babylon completely destroyed:

> "Assyrian troops were allowed to loot the temples and other local property and to smash the statues of the city's gods. They razed the city, including the residential quarters, the temples, the ziggurat, and the city walls, and dumped the debris into the Arahtu river. They removed even the surface soil from the site, hauling it off to the Euphrates which carried it downstream to the Persian Gulf; the Assyrians also put some of this soil on display in the akitu temple in Assur. To obliterate even the memory of the city, they dug canals to flood the ruins and turned the area into a swamp".[95]

Esarhaddon, His Sons, and the Civil War

Sennacherib was eventually assassinated, and Esarhaddon took the throne in 681. Taking a completely different approach in his policies toward Babylonia, *Esarhaddon treated the south as culturally significant* and *worked to rebuild Babylon.* He was even able to make peace with Elam to the east, bringing about a period of prosperity for the region. This, however, was not to last.

Esarhaddon had two sons: Assurbanipal and Shamash-shum-ukin. Assurbanipal was placed upon the throne of Assyria, while his older brother ruled over Babylonia. As you might imagine, animosity developed between the two brothers, given the lower rank of the older brother compared to the younger. This animosity ultimately developed into outright revolt. Beaulieu writes:

> "In 652 Shamash-shumu-ukin led Babylonian into a rebellion against this brother which lasted until the year 648. Its most likely cause, besides the long standing and widespread opposition to Assyrian rule among Babylonians and Chaldeans, may have been Shamash-shumu-ukin's discontent at his subordinate status".[96]

The ramifications of this civil war are summarized by Brinkman in this way:

> "Shamash-shum-ukin led Babylonia in a full-scale rebellion against Ashurbanipal and won support from Elam, Arabia, and elsewhere in western Asia. *Assyrian military energies were absorbed for four years in dealing with the revolt in urban Babylonia* and then for several additional years in cleaning up pockets of resistance in the Sealand and exacting vengeance from Babylonia's foreign supporters. *These massive military efforts severely strained the resources of the Assyrian empire*" (emphasis mine).[97]

Other Factors

While the "Babylonian Problem" of Sennacherib, as laid out by Brinkman, was very likely a significant factor in the downfall of the Neo-Assyrian Empire, more recently, scholars have postulated additional factors that lead to Assyria's demise. Eckart Frahm summarized three additional hypotheses that have been suggested of late.[98] First, Fuchs put forth the idea that internal instability contributed to the downfall, as there were several contenders for the Assyrian throne from 631-627 B.C.E.[99] Bagg argued that Assyria had become an "empire without a mission" that focused primarily on extracting as much as it could from the nations around them, while not simultaneously investing in them.[100] There was little loyalty to Assyria, therefore, when things began to go awry. Finally, Schneider and Adali pointed to a possible tremendous increase in population in Assyria during the 7th century, coupled with a drought, that left the empire severely weakened.[101] It is likely that several or even all of these factors ultimately led to Assyria's downfall.

The Fall of the Neo-Assyrian Empire

Following the civil war between Assurbanipal and his older brother, Shamash-shum-ukin, there was a state of relative peace and stability in Assyria and Babylonia for approximately two decades. Following Assurbanipal's death, a few fairly insignificant kings ruled, which set the stage for the rise of the first king of the Neo-Babylonian Empire, Nabopolassar, who came to power in 627 B.C.E.

Their ruling practices had earned the Neo-Assyrian Empire few friends, and Nabopolassar was able to find additional support by joining forces with Cyaxares of Media.[102] In 615, the Medes attacked and eventually made their way to Assur, where they desecrated and destroyed much of the city. A near fatal attack came in 612, when both the Babylonian and Median armies laid siege to Nineveh and ultimately killed the Neo-Assyrian king Sin-sharru-ishkun.[103]

Nevertheless, an Assyrian prince held out in the city of Harran and took the throne under the name Assuruballit II. In 610 B.C.E., the Median/Babylonian coalition was able to drive him out of the city of Harran. In the following year, Assuruballit II – aided by the Egyptians, who ostensibly wanted a weak Assyria in power rather than a strong Babylonia – attempted to retake Harran but failed.[104] This was the end of the Neo-Assyrian Empire.

The Neo-Babylonian Period

It is often the case that, during a major empire's final days, the administration is quite weak and unable to maintain control of formerly subjugated peoples in the periphery. Such was the case with the Neo-Assyrian Empire. Toward the end, it had lost control of lands outside its borders, particularly to the west, in the area of Syria-Palestine. As this region was a sought-after buffer zone for the Egyptian rulers, they reasserted their control over this narrow corridor in the power vacuum that existed in the decline of the Neo-Assyrian Empire. Of course, Egypt was no longer the only power that could fill this gap, as the newly established Neo-Babylonian Empire was now on the scene.

Nebuchadnezzar II

Harran was the city where the Neo-Assyrians made their final stand. Immediately after the battle at Carchemish – where Nebuchadnezzar II and his forces defeated the Egyptians in 605 – Nebuchadnezzar received word that his father, the king, had died; he raced home to take the throne. However, his trips to the Levant were far from over.[105]

Nebuchadnezzar II is well known in the Old Testament, particularly because of two major assaults that he launched against the city of Jerusalem. In 597 B.C.E., he besieged the city because of the rebellious acts of the Judean king, Jehoiakim (2 Kings 23:35). Nebuchadnezzar's response to Jehoiakim's behavior are documented a few verses later: "In his days Nebuchadnezzar king of Babylon came up and he [Jehoiakim] became his slave for three years, but he turned and rebelled against him" (2 Kings 24:1).

Cogan and Tadmor explain that, following the battle at Carchemish,

> "Jehoiakim submitted to Nebuchadnezzar and became his vassal for three years (604-602). Despite his initial successes, Nebuchadnezzar suffered a major setback in the winter of 601/600, when he set out to attack Egypt proper . . . Nebuchadnezzar was forced to withdraw all the way to Babylonia. In the following year, he did not campaign; he stayed at home refitting 'his numerous horses and chariots.' *Under these circumstances, Jehoiakim saw a chance to free himself from Babylonian vassalage and so rebelled*" (emphasis mine).[106]

A decade later, in 587/586, Zedekiah, king of Judah, rebelled against Nebuchadnezzar, bringing another siege against the city of Jerusalem (2 Kings 24:20b-25:2). After killing Zedekiah, Nebuchadnezzar's punishment was severe (2 Kings 25:8-11). The second rebellion led to a total destruction and obliteration of the Judean monarchy, as well as the second Babylonian exile. [107] The destruction of Jerusalem was indelibly impressed upon the minds of the Judeans and appears throughout the Old Testament as a critical moment in their past.

Nabonidus and the Fall of the Empire

The other incredibly important and well-known king of the Neo-Babylonian Empire – particularly with respect to the Old Testament – was Nabonidus. Now, you might be thinking, "I've read the Old Testament and I don't remember seeing any Nabonidus in there". Fear not; we will see the connection when we get to the chapter on the dating of the book of Daniel. For now, let's take a quick look at his reign and how it relates to the end of Neo-Babylonian rule.

The reign of Nabonidus has always been a bit of an oddity in Mesopotamian history, as the king left Babylonia in the 3rd year of his reign and remained gone for ten years in the oasis of Teima. His absence was certainly noteworthy, as was his rather unorthodox worship of the moon god Sin. This did not endear him to the priesthood of Marduk, as it was seen as a serious slight to their god and ultimately appears to have caused Nabonidus a number of significant problems.

During his time away from Babylonia, his son functioned as regent in his place. Beaulieu writes,

> "While Nabonidus resided in Tayma his son Bel-sharru-usur stepped in the role of regent, appearing alongside his father in accounts of royal offerings in temples. He is also seen performing a number of official duties. Building

inscriptions, on the other hand, continued to be in Nabonidus's name exclusively".[108]

It would seem that, although Bel-sharru-usur (Belshazzar from the book of Daniel) was able to function in some ruling capacities, many of the prerogatives of the king remained with Nabonidus, even in his absence.

One of these kingly duties was his central role in the New Year's festival. His absence led to the cancellation of this critical event, as it required the physical presence of the king; this cancellation resulted in the disruption of the entire cultic cycle.[109] The animosity that seems to have developed within the Marduk priesthood was seen in later texts about Nabonidus and his role in the fall of Babylonia to the Persians.

When Nabonidus finally returned from his time in Teima in his 13th regnal year, he removed Bel-sharru-usur from his duties as regent and appears to have stationed him in a military capacity on the border (or even outside) of Babylonia. Inscriptions from the last years of Nabonidus's reign place the god Sin definitively at the head of the pantheon, completely ignoring Marduk, and addressing Sin as "'lord of the gods of heaven and the netherworld' and 'god of gods'".[110]

It was into this political situation that Cyrus and the Persian army invaded. It would appear that, without a great deal of resistance, Cyrus was able to march into Babylon and seize control in 539, thus ending the great Neo-Babylonian Empire.

The Persian Period

The Persian or Achaemenid Empire was the largest and most expansive prior to the conquest of Alexander. It was an enormous empire, "covering the entire Near East and regions beyond from the Indus valley to northern Greece, from Central Asia to southern Egypt".[111] Kuhrt writes,

> "It developed around a tiny core in the modern province of Fars in south Iran . . . Its expansion began c. 550, with the astonishing conquests of Cyrus (II) the Great (559-530) and Cambyses (II, 530-522); it was brought to an end by the conquests of Alexander of Macedon between 334 and 323".[112]

In this final section, we will look at some of the highlights of the Persian Empire and how its sweeping conquests were brought to an abrupt halt by Alexander the Great.

Cyrus II, who ruled from 559-530, defeated the Medes relatively early in his reign. A few years later, he marched far to the west and defeated the Lydians who were under the command of King Croesus. As we saw above, in 539, he came to Babylon and appears to have taken it with little resistance, likely due to the disenchantment felt over the rule of Nabonidus.

Following Cyrus's death in 530 B.C.E., his son Cambyses came to the throne. Cambyses ruled from 529-22 B.C.E., and built on his military campaigns during his time as crown prince and co-regent by conquering Egypt in 525 B.C.E.[113] While other kings in the ancient Near East had campaigned against Egypt, Cambyses was intent on *turning it into a part of the Persian Empire*. Kuhrt notes, "Cambyses appears to have been a ruler who not only maintained Persian control of his father's immense conquests, but also extended and consolidated them in crucial areas".[114]

His most famous successor, Darius I (521-486 B.C.E.), also sought to expand his reach. He is perhaps best known for his attempt "to invade Greece itself, but was rebuffed in 490 at the battle of Marathon".[115] A similar move was made by Xerxes.

> "Xerxes is perhaps the figure from Persian history most familiar to us. The reason is, of course, that he is the Achaemenid ruler who invaded Greece in 480, but whose army was defeated and withdrew (479)".[116]

Given the vast expanse of the Persian Empire, one of the recurring themes in its history was the need to put down revolts and rebellions throughout the empire.

We also see contact between the Old Testament and the Persian Empire in several different places. For example, Cyrus is said to have returned the exiles to Jerusalem in Ezra 1:1-4:

> "Now in the first year of Cyrus king of Persia – in order to fulfill the word of Yahweh by the mouth of the prophet Jeremiah – Yahweh aroused the spirit of Cyrus king of Persia and he sent out a proclamation throughout all his kingdom saying, 'Thus says Cyrus king of Persia, "All the kingdoms of the earth has Yahweh, the God of the heavens, given to me, and he appointed me to build for him a house in Jerusalem, which is in Judah. Whoever among you from all his people – may his God be with him – let him go up to Jerusalem, which is in Judah, and let him build the house of Yahweh, the God of Israel. He is the God that is in Jerusalem. And all those who remain from all the places

where he lives, let the men of that place support him with silver and with gold and with property and with cattle with the freewill offering for the house of the God that is in Jerusalem"""" (Ezra 1:1-4).

As you might imagine, there are problems with the historical details of this command; however, it does seem to have some historical correspondence. Collins notes, "The authenticity of this edict has been questioned, but it is certainly the case that Cyrus authorized Judeans to return from Babylon to Jerusalem and to rebuild the temple there".[117] Other references to Persian kings appear in the Old Testament, including Xerxes I (Ahasuerus in the Bible) in the book of Esther, as well as Artaxerxes (likely Artaxerxes I) in the book of Ezra. Given the significance of the return from Babylonian captivity in the Hebrew Bible, it is unsurprising that Persian kings would be spoken of in the Old Testament.

The end of the Persian Empire came rather swiftly at the hands of Alexander of Macedon. As we saw above, previous Persian kings had attempted to invade Greece, but were ultimately unsuccessful. This time, it was Persia who was on the defensive. Van De Mieroop summarizes:

"In 336, the twenty-year-old Alexander became king, and after having reestablished Macedon's control over Greece, he marched his army into Anatolia. A continuous ten-year-long campaign followed in which he led his troops throughout the Persian Empire, annexing all its satrapies. The Persian King Darius III offered fierce resistance in the battles of Issus in north-west Syria (333) and Gaugamela in northern Iraq (331), but was finally defeated".[118]

Conclusion

It has hopefully become clear that the history of the ancient Near East is incredibly important to understand, not only for the study of the Old Testament, but for its own sake. We have looked at the major periods, focusing primarily on Mesopotamia, given its rather central place in the history of the region. As noted in the introduction, volume II of this series will contain a detailed history of ancient Egypt to complete the historical background to the Old Testament.

We began with the 3rd millennium B.C.E., just after the invention of writing, and viewed in some detail the border conflict that took place between the cities of Umma and Lagash. The final ruler of Lagash, Urukagina, was conquered by Lugalzagesi, who served as a transition into the Old Akkadian period. Sargon of Akkad and his grandson Naram-Sin were the leading figures during that period, establishing what was arguably the first empire.

Following the fall of the Old Akkadian Empire and a brief hiatus, the kings of the Ur III dynasty reunited the region and established a highly centralized administrative system. In spite of these advances, the rulers of the Ur III period eventually fell, which brought us to the early 2nd millennium B.C.E. We saw a brief snapshot of international trade that took place in the Old Assyrian period, as traders from the city of Assur brought tin and textiles from Mesopotamia into Turkey. The letters and documents that were found from this period show us not only the trade practices and communications, but also give us some insight into the participants' personal lives.

We then discussed the complex time of the first half of the 2nd millennium, where individual local rulers made alliances and vied for power. The reign of the city of Isin was followed by Larsa, which ultimately gave way to the famous city of Babylon, ruled by Hammurabi, who was able to conquer Elam, Larsa, Eshnunna, and ultimately Mari. After conquering the region, Hammurabi's dynasty had a short-lived success, ending in the sacking of Babylon by the Hittites around 1600 B.C.E.

The Amarna period followed, in which international diplomacy was the characteristic trait. The ancient Near East was then divided into two primary groups: the "Great Powers Club" (Assyria, Babylonia, Egypt, Hatti, Mittani, Alashiya, and Arzawa) and the vassal states of the Syria-Palestine region. Letters from each of these groups showed a created familial relationship between the great kings, while the vassals – as we would expect – took on the role of servants to the king of Egypt.

It was during this period that Assyria began to rise in power. Following several powerful kings, however, there was a regional collapse in the eastern Mediterranean and Assyria went into decline. This power was reestablished in the Neo-Assyrian Empire, particularly during the reign of Tiglath-Pileser III in the middle of the 8th century. The Assyrian kings campaigned extensively to the west but were plagued by problems with their neighbor to the south, the Babylonians. This ultimately led to the fall of the Assyrians and the rise of the Neo-Babylonian Empire.

We looked at two of the more influential Neo-Babylonian kings: Nebuchadnezzar and Nabonidus. Nebuchadnezzar campaigned in the west and was ultimately responsible for destroying Jerusalem and taking the Judeans into captivity in Babylon. The final king, Nabonidus, had an unorthodox absence from Babylon for a decade, alienating many of his subjects, not only by his absence, but by his excessive worship of a deity other than Marduk.

This appears to have set the stage for Cyrus to overthrow Babylon and set up the Persian Empire. The Persian rulers expanded their territory to a greater degree than others had before them, even conquering Egypt under Cambyses, who set up his rule in Egypt itself for much of his reign. As powerful as the Persian Empire was, however, they could not withstand the onslaught of Alexander the Great's military force, which brought an end to the Persian Empire, along with our survey of the history of the ancient Near East.

---

[1] Westbrook 2003: 2, Van De Mieroop 2007: 1.

[2] Van De Mieroop 2007.

[3] Van De Mieroop 2007: 2.

[4] Van De Mieroop 2007: 41.

[5] Beaulieu 2018: 35.

[6] See Pomponio 1994 for more details on the Hexapolis.

[7] Van De Mieroop 2007: 48.

[8] Cooper 1986: 36.

[9] For a discussion of the Stele of the Vultures, see Winter 1985.

[10] The quotes from the various inscriptions in this section will come from Jerrold Cooper's 1986 publication, *Sumerian and Akkadian Royal Inscriptions, Volume 1*. Cooper provides an excellent reconstruction of the events from the inscriptions (pp. 22-37) on which I will rely in this section.

[11] Cooper 1986: 25, La 1.6, r.i-v.

[12] Cooper 1986: 34, La 3.1, iii-iv.

[13] Cooper 1986: 22.

[14] Cooper 1986: 54, La 5.1, i.

[15] Cooper 1986: 54-55, La 5.1, i.

[16] Edzard 2009: 56. "Jedenfalls stimmt En-metenas Formulierung, 'Ningirsu habe das große Fangnetz auf Umma geworfen', hervorragend mit dem Bild der Geierstele überein, das den Gott mit einem überdimensionalen Netz in der Hand zeigt".

[17] Cooper 1986: 55, La 5.1, ii.

[18] Cooper 1986: 29.

[19] Cooper 1986: 55, La 5.1, iii.

[20] Cooper 1986: 78-79, La 9.5.

[21] Cooper 1986: 36.

[22] Beaulieu 2018: 41.

[23] Edzard 2009: 77. "Sargons Herkunft ist dunkel, und sie war schon früh sagenumwoben. Die akkadische Geburtslegende ist eine 'Aussetzungsgeschichte'. Ihr zufolge wurde Sargon von einem Gärtner als Ziehsohn angenommen. Später hätte die Göttin Ištar an dem jungen Sargon Gefallen gefunden und ihm den Weg in eine große Zukunft gebahnt".

[24] Foster 2005: 912, lines 1-10.

[25] Black, Cunningham, Fluckiger-Hawker, Robson, & Zólyomi 1988-2006. ETCSL 2.1.1, *The Sumerian King List*, lines 266-269.

[26] Cooper & Heimpel 1983: 74.

[27] Beaulieu 2018: 42.

[28] Sallaberger & Westenholz 1999: 38.

[29] Sallaberger & Westenholz 1999: 46.

[30] Sallaberger & Westenholz 1999: 52-53.

[31] Frayne 1993: 113-114, E2.1.4.10, lines 5-53.

[32] Sallaberger & Westenholz 1999: 54.

[33] Cooper 1983: 5.

[34] Black, Cunningham, Fluckiger-Hawker, Robson, & Zólyomi 1988-2006. ETCSL 2.1.5, *The Cursing of Agade*, lines 104-118.

[35] Sallaberger & Westenholz 1999: 55.

[36] Beaulieu 2018: 52.

[37] Van De Mieroop 2007: 75.

[38] Roth 1997:15-16, LU A iii 114-124.

[39] Roth 1997: 16, LU A iv 162-168.

[40] Roth 1997: 17, LU A iv 170.

[41] Beaulieu 2018: 55.

[42] Van De Mieroop 2007: 78.

[43] Van De Mieroop 2007: 95.

[44] These numbers do not necessarily reflect realistic profits; they are simply for illustrative purposes. Van De Mieroop 2007: 91 notes, "The profit margins in this trade were high, however: tin cost at least double in Anatolia what it cost in Assur, and textiles tripled their value. A merchant could easily make a 50 to 100 percent profit in a year".

[45] Van De Mieroop 2007: 96.

[46] Veenhof & Eidem 2008: 131.

[47] Van De Mieroop 2007: 97.

[48] Van De Mieroop 2007: 97.

[49] Van De Mieroop 2007: 97-98.

[50] Van De Mieroop 2007: 85.

[51] Beaulieu 2018: 62. For an introduction to how Sumerian was used in the education of students during the early second millennium, along with extensive citations to additional resources, see Bowen 2020b.

[52] Roth 1997: 25, LL i 20-37.

[53] Roth 1997: 26-27.

[54] Roth 1997: 31-32.

[55] Beaulieu 2018: 64.

[56] Van De Mieroop 2007: 108.

[57] Heimpel 2003: 54.

[58] Van De Mieroop 2005: 16.

[59] Van De Mieroop 2005: 18.

[60] Beaulieu 2018: 83.

[61] Van De Mieroop 2005: 35.

[62] Van De Mieroop 2005: 75.

[63] Van De Mieroop 2007: 111. The Old Babylonian period is used in different contexts and can specifically refer to the time following Hammurabi's dominance over Mesopotamia (beginning in the middle of the 18th century) or can more broadly include the Isin-Larsa period, extending back to the beginning of the 2nd millennium.

[64] Beaulieu 2018: 88.

[65] Roth 1997: 72.

[66] Roth 1997: 76-77.

[67] Roth 1997: 80-81.

[68] Roth 1997: 84.

[69] Roth 1997: 103.

[70] Roth 1997: 103.

[71] Edzard 2009: 141. "Der Hethiterkönig Muršili (um 1600 v. Chr.) soll im 32. Und letzten Jahr des babylonischen Königs Samsu-ditāna Babylon erobert und damit die gut dreihundertjährige von uns so genannte I. Dynastie von Babylon beendet haben".

[72] Van De Mieroop 2007: 129.

[73] Moran 1992: xiii.

[74] Van De Mieroop 2007: 134-135.

[75] Moran 1992: 1, el-Amarna (EA) 1, lines 1-9.

[76] Moran 1992: xxvi.

[77] Moran 1992: xxvii.

[78] Moran 1992: 127, EA 55, lines 1-9.

[79] Moran 1992: 142, EA 74, lines 1-4.

[80] Moran 1992: 7, EA 3, lines 18-22.

[81] Van De Mieroop 2007: 181.

[82] Van De Mieroop 2007: 181.

[83] Foster 2005: 313-314, *Tukulti-Ninurta Epic*, lines 31'-42'.

[84] I highly recommend Eric Cline's immensely popular 2015 book, *1177 B.C.: The Year Civilization Collapsed*, for more information on this collapse and the events leading up to it.
[85] Van De Mieroop 2007: 201.
[86] Van De Mieroop 2007: 206.
[87] Van De Mieroop 2007: 248.
[88] Van De Mieroop 2007: 248.
[89] Liverani 2003: 145.
[90] Brinkman 1984.
[91] Brinkman 1984: 11.
[92] Brinkman 1984: 11.
[93] Brinkman 1984: 24.
[94] Brinkman 1984: 67.
[95] Brinkman 1984: 67.
[96] Beaulieu 2018: 214.
[97] Brinkman 1984: 93.
[98] Frahm 2017: 192-193. The next three citations from Frahm's chapter.
[99] Fuchs 2014: 35-36; 54-58.
[100] Bagg 2011: 305-308.
[101] Schneider & Adali 2014.
[102] Frahm 2017: 192.
[103] Frahm 2017: 192.
[104] Van De Mieroop 2007: 250.
[105] Beaulieu 2018: 227.
[106] Cogan & Tadmor 1988: 308.
[107] Beaulieu 2018: 228.
[108] Beaulieu 2018: 240.
[109] Van De Mieroop 2007: 280.
[110] Beaulieu 2018: 243.
[111] Van De Mieroop 2007: 286.
[112] Kuhrt 2007: 1.
[113] Van De Mieroop 2007: 287.
[114] Kuhrt 2007: 106.
[115] Van De Mieroop 2007: 289.
[116] Kuhrt 2007: 238.
[117] Collins 2018: 407.
[118] Van De Mieroop 2007: 299-300.

CHAPTER THREE
Biblical Archaeology

It was hot... well, it was always hot. Summer days in Syria were not known for their mild temperatures. It was almost time for the dig team to return to the village, when one of the workers pulled his hands from the dirt pile he was sifting to reveal a small clay bull figurine. From the edge of the *tell* (the mound where we were excavating), I called out to the dig director, Glenn Schwartz, who made his way over from the center of the site. "Glenn! Glenn! Look what we found!" I shouted as he came close enough to catch sight of my amazing discovery. His response was, perhaps, less enthusiastic than I had anticipated: "Shut everything down", he said in a flat, sarcastic voice, his tongue firmly set in his cheek, "we found what we've been searching for".

Of course, you might be wondering why a small clay bull figurine might instill so much excitement in me; certainly this was not the find of the century. However, as with many who have excavated at an archaeological site for the first time, I had visions of grand discoveries – a cache of tablets written in Akkadian or Sumerian, perhaps. To my chagrin, after weeks of excavating day in and day out, I had found little else but pottery. Lots and lots of pottery. And not whole pots, mind you. No complete jars, bowls, or plates with elaborate decorations. Just fragments of pottery. In fact, I was excited when I found a pottery sherd that contained a part of a rim or base, or – be still my fluttering heart – a design of some kind.

As I learned that summer excavating at the Syrian site of Umm el-Marra, archaeology is not at all like what I had seen in the Indiana Jones movies. No secret caves with elaborate booby traps, no heads of gold, no spirit-filled arks or crystal alien skulls. For me it was just lots and lots of pottery sherds. From time to time, in an ironic fashion, one of the seasoned archaeologists would hum the Indiana Jones theme song as we made our way out to the *tell* at 4:30 in the morning.

While the science of archaeology might not be as flashy as some might think, it is a field that is absolutely essential to the proper understanding of our past. While ancient written sources can certainly provide us with critical historical information, archaeological finds are able to provide data that do not suffer from the same types of biases that written sources do. Dever writes,

> "The argument is that these data are primary by offering contemporary eyewitness information, whereas the biblical accounts were often written centuries later than the events that they purport to describe. Furthermore, the archaeological data, when they first come to light after being hidden for centuries, are unbiased. That is, they are unedited, in contrast to the biblical texts, which have been edited and reedited for twenty centuries or more".[1]

But how does archaeology work? And how can it help us understand the ancient world and – especially for our purposes – the Old Testament?

Perhaps the question on everyone's mind is, "Do the archaeological data actually confirm what the Old Testament presents in its narrative?"

This chapter will present the reader with a brief introduction to the practice of archaeology, including things like excavation methods, the tools of the trade, and how archaeologists record and analyze the data. We will then narrow our focus to "biblical archaeology", looking at how the discipline began and how it has developed up to the present. We will then turn our attention to the controversial period that frequently appears when atheists debate Christians: Iron Age I (roughly 1200-1000 B.C.E.). It was around or during this period that so many critical events were supposed to have taken place, including the Exodus from Egypt and the conquest of Canaan. This was also a time that involves the Canaanites and the Philistines, both of which will be discussed in this chapter as test cases for biblical archaeology. Volume II of this series will delve into what archaeology can tell us about the early formation of Israel, including the historicity of the Exodus account and the supposed conquest of the promised land by the Israelites.

An Introduction to Archaeology

The field of archaeology has come quite a long way in the last century. Methods for choosing where to excavate, how to excavate, and how to record your findings have all developed significantly. This section will provide the reader with a brief overview of the basics of archaeological methods, including how archaeologists decide where, what, and how to dig, and what they do with the material once it comes out of the ground. An excellent introduction to archaeology can be found in Fagan and

Durrani's *Archaeology: A Brief Introduction*, on which we will lean heavily in this section.[2]

Where to Dig?

When I decided to write my dissertation on a collection of Sumerian cuneiform tablets that were found at the Mesopotamian city of Kish, I realized that I would need to write a section on the archaeology of the site. After all, these clay tablets did not magically appear in a museum somewhere; they had to be dug out of the ground. Knowing exactly where in an excavation site they were uncovered, along with what other objects they were found with (the "archaeological context"), is incredibly important when it comes to fully understanding how ancient objects were used. During a conversation with a seasoned archaeologist, I happened to mention that I would be writing on the excavations of Kish, which elicited the response "Good luck with that". I soon found out why.

In 1912, the French archaeologist Henri de Genouillac excavated at the city of Kish for one season. Parts of the site had been looted, leading de Genouillac to think that, because looters were finding objects in those areas, they were probably good areas in which to dig. He removed approximately 1,400 tablets from the ground, *but he didn't record any of the specifics about where they came from*. Instead, what we have is a topographical map that indicates that the tablets were found to the west of a large structure that was on the site, marked by the shaded areas in figure 2 below. In other words, if someone were to ask, "Where did this legal document come from?" or "Was this letter found in a house or outside in a trash pit?", I was out of luck. The "find spots" of the tablets were not recorded with any kind of precision.

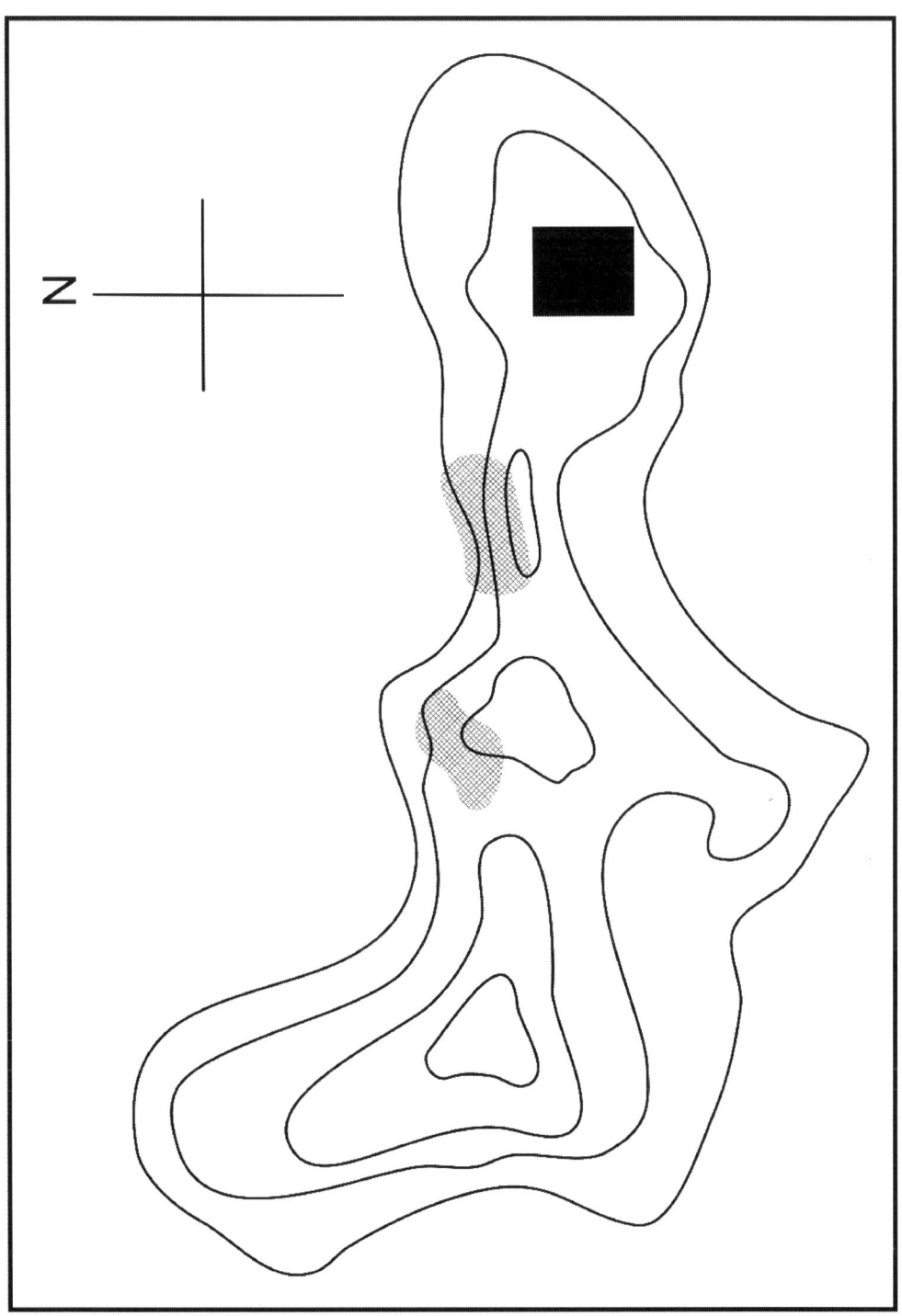

Figure 2. Topographical map of the site of Kish. Shaded areas
indicate findspots of tablets.

A little over a decade later, the British archaeologist Stephen Langdon began his own excavations at Kish. Again, a significant number of clay tablets were found at the site. While the excavation and recording methods had improved beyond a shaded area on a map, they were certainly not ideal. Citing McGuire Gibson in my dissertation, I wrote:

> "Gibson describes the methods employed in the excavation of these trenches as 'a simple matter of treating the mound as something to be sliced in blocks that were five meters wide, five meters high or deep, and as long as the mound was wide.' It is, therefore, difficult to speak with any specificity about the provenance of tablets excavated at these trenches".[3]

Five meters by five meters by the length of the *tell* (the entire archaeological site)... yeah, that doesn't narrow it down much, does it?

Today, these types of practices would be unacceptable in the field. When I excavated at Umm el-Marra, we excavated two-meter squares that were twenty centimeters deep, digging one square at a time. Each square had a specific designation and all pottery sherds (and anything else that was found in that square) were labeled with that designation. If we found a wall, we would identify where the sherds were found in relation to that wall. All of this information was meticulously documented in my excavation notebook, along with a detailed drawing of the square itself. In other words, if you wanted to know today where something was found in the area that I was excavating, you could narrow it down to where in that particular two-meter by two-meter square it was excavated from.

One of the reasons that this type of precision is so important in an archaeological excavation is that *you only get one bite at the apple.* Archaeological excavation is an inherently destructive process; once you excavate a site, that's it. You can't put the materials back in place for someone else to come along and try again. If you don't excavate properly and record your findings well, it will make it very difficult for those who follow you to properly understand and interpret the data from your site.

Because of this reality, archaeologists must be careful and intentional in determining which sites and areas they will excavate. Fagan and Durrani describe excavation as "the strategy of last resort because it destroys the archaeological record".[4] They continue:

> "The first principle of excavation is that digging is destructive. As archaeologist Kent Flannery once remarked, we are the only scientists who murder their informants (our sites) when we question them! The archaeological deposits so carefully examined during a dig are destroyed forever".[5]

Once it is determined that excavation is necessary, the archaeologist must choose the place to dig. As we saw above, Henri de Genouillac began to excavate in the place that looters had been digging holes in the mound and pulling out objects to sell illegally. Because these looters found several objects in this area, he surmised that there might be more substantial remains beneath. This is similar to using a "surface survey", where the archaeologist walks around a large area on the site, looking for things like pottery sherds lying on the surface of the ground, to determine if there is a particular concentration of settlement on the mound.

Another way that archaeologists attempt to confirm the presence of remains is by digging "test pits".

> "The test pit remains the most useful way of obtaining preliminary information on stratigraphy and culture history in advance of a larger-scale excavation . . . More often, test pits are laid out in lines and over considerable distances to establish the extent of a site and the basic stratigraphy in different areas".[6]

In effect, this is a way for the archaeologist to "dip their toe in the water" before jumping in headlong.

Excavation Methods

There are several ways in which responsible and effective excavation can be done at a site. As described above, the method that we used at Umm el-Marra was to dig two-meter squares, twenty centimeters deep, one at a time. This method allows the archaeologist to excavate enough of a particular area to make sufficient progress during the (often) little time they have at the site, but controls the speed of the excavation so that the material culture (i.e., the things that are found during the excavation) can be properly identified, recorded, and processed.

Fagan and Durrani note two general ways in which archaeologists excavate: vertically and horizontally. Vertical excavation focuses more on digging *down* in one particular area, while horizontal excavation involves digging *across* (usually) larger areas of a site. Each method has distinct advantages and disadvantages, and each can be suited to particular circumstances.

Let's say that an archaeological team has only a short period of time to excavate a site, and they have a pretty good idea that a particular area on the *tell* was inhabited for an extended period of time. In this scenario, digging deeper into the specific part of the mound might produce greater results than excavating a large but shallow area.

> "Some of the world's most important sites have been excavated on a small scale by vertical excavation, digging limited areas for specific information on dating and stratigraphy. Vertical trenches can be used to obtain artifact samples, to establish sequences of ancient building construction or histories of complex earthworks, or to salvage sites threatened with destruction".[7]

Conversely, if an archaeologist were to come upon an area of the *tell* where several walls were still partially preserved, sticking up out of the ground, it might be a better idea to dig horizontally in order to uncover a much wider area, revealing all of the architecture that is associated with that building. Fagan and Durrani write, "Horizontal, or area, digs are commonly associated with stratigraphic excavation, exposing large areas of a site to uncover house plans or settlement layouts".[8] The appropriate method – whether vertical or horizontal – will depend on the particular circumstances of the excavation.

Stratigraphy

We have seen the word "stratigraphy" appear a few times in the discussion above, although we have not really explained what it means. Grant, Gorin, and Fleming's coursebook on archaeology provides an excellent discussion on this incredibly important topic; much of the following presentation will be based on their material.[9]

Many cities were founded upon natural hills, particularly in Mesopotamia and the Levant. Because buildings were made from perishable materials, structures would eventually break down and require rebuilding. When people live in a particular area for any significant period of time, they leave behind material culture, like pottery, tools, bones, etc. As time goes by, and new structures are built upon older remains, the older materials are covered up and buried. This forms a *layer* – what is often referred to as an "occupation layer" – that is built upon by the people who will create the next "occupation layer".

Later, the people who lived and built upon the earlier occupation layer are eventually superseded by those who come after them, and *that* becomes *another* occupation layer. Again and again, as time goes by, old buildings and materials are torn, broken, or burned down, and new structures and materials are created above them. Thus, each successive occupation ultimately condenses down into an occupation layer, and each subsequent layer is formed upon the last.

When archaeologists excavate a site, they dig down *through* those occupation layers. After digging down, you can view the cross-section of the *tell* by looking at the wall of the exposed hole or trench that you have excavated, revealing each of the occupation layers that have been formed on the site. Grant, Gorin, and Fleming summarize in this way:

> "In any text about archaeological sites you will come across terms such as 'level', 'layer', 'deposit', 'stratum'. They describe the make-up of the excavated ground in terms of deposits. These were created either by people or by nature. Archaeologists attempt to carefully record these strata – the stratification".[10]

As you can probably guess, there is a great deal of information that we can glean from understanding the stratigraphy of a particular site or part of a site. For example, you have probably already figured out that the "higher" the layer/stratum/deposit/level, the "younger" it is or later it is. As archaeologists dig down through each successive layer, they label each stratum with a number: for example, Level I, Level II, Level III, etc. The higher the number, the further down and older it is. The smaller the number, the closer it is to the surface and the younger it is.

By way of example, let's say we are excavating a site that we will call "City X". A guy named John lived in City X around 1000 B.C.E. Eventually John died, and the "version" of City X that he lived in (its buildings, streets, etc.) was renovated and rebuilt. All of the buildings, pottery, animal bones... all of this "material culture" was buried and compressed into a layer that we will call (very creatively) "Layer John". Now, in 800 B.C.E. (200 years later), someone named *Jim* moved into the "version" of City X that was built *on top of* the City X that John lived in ("Layer John"). Jim eventually died, and City X was again rebuilt, depositing him, his city, and all of the things associated with the people that lived there in 800 B.C.E. into their own occupation layer: "Layer Jim".

If we were to go to City X today and dig down (vertical excavation) through both layers ("Layer Jim" and "Layer John"), which layer would be on top? Correct: "Layer Jim". Because we reached "Layer Jim" first (digging down from the surface), we would label it "Level" or "Stratum I". "Layer John" would be labeled "Level II", since we dug down through it *after* Level I. Which layer would be older and which would be younger? Because Level II ("Layer John") was *laid down* first (in 1000 B.C.E.), and Level I ("Layer Jim") was *laid down on top of* Level II (in 800 B.C.E.), we would know that the "higher" layer would be the younger layer.

Being able to identify the individual occupation layers is incredibly important for interpreting the archaeological data from a site. For example, let's say that we have excavated City X and have identified which layer is "Layer John" and which is "Layer Jim". If we look in "Layer Jim" and find several documents that are dated to what we know is 800 B.C.E., we can then date "Layer Jim" to around 800 B.C.E.[11] Furthermore, if we dig down in one area of the mound and find "Layer Jim", and we dig in *another* area of the mound and find "Layer Jim", we can begin *to tie different parts of the site together*. What's more, if we go to *another mound* and find "Layer Jim" (based on evidence from the material culture that we find in that layer), we can then draw conclusions about the other mound. Grant, Gorin, and Fleming note, "It is within the deposits that the artefactual, environmental and dating evidence is located. Deposits are a time capsule which hold the clues to the immediate context of finds and structures".[12]

Oh, that it were always so simple. There are many circumstances in which the layers get... complicated (refer to the illustration in figure 3 below for the following discussion). For example, let's say that you want to construct a new building in my city. You will most likely dig down some distance in order lay a firm foundation for the new building. This will probably result in you *digging down through several occupation layers*. Now, if a later archaeologist were to excavate this building, they would find that the bottom of the foundation is actually in line with a *much earlier occupation layer*. Does this mean that the building should be dated to the earlier level? No, of course not. But this type of "intrusion" into lower or earlier layers is something that must be carefully considered.

A similar type of intrusion is a trash pit; if someone digs a hole to get rid of rubbish, the rubbish will be in line with earlier levels, but will be associated with the layer at the *top* of the pit. While it would be convenient to be able to assume that objects and features at the bottom of an excavation are always older than those at the top, pits, ditches, and building works from more recent periods can cut down into earlier stratigraphic layers. [13] A proper understanding of stratigraphy can provide the interpreter with a wealth of archaeological information.

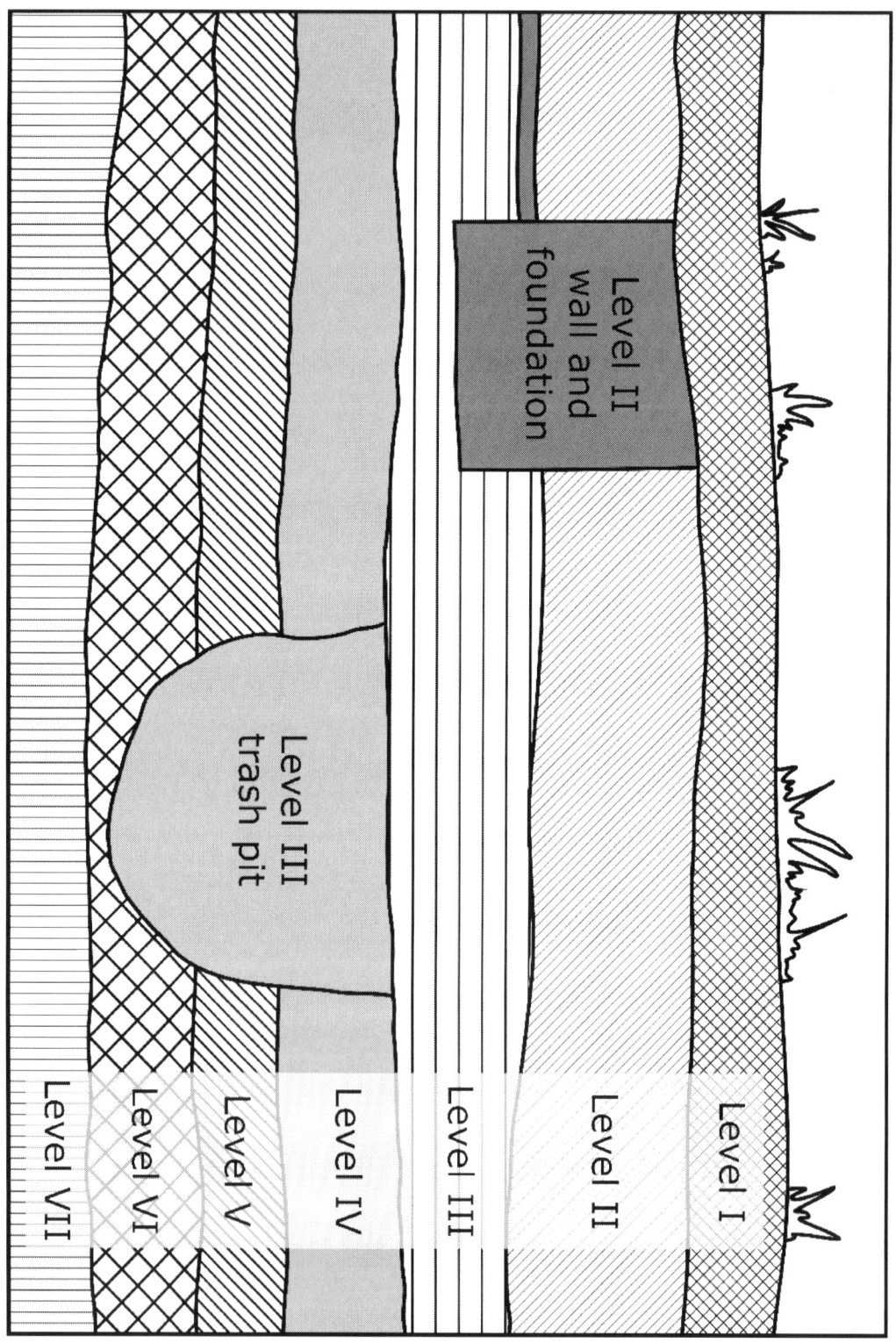

Figure 3. Illustration of how stratigraphy works.

Digging and Recording: The Tools of the Trade

To this point, we have identified methods for choosing where to dig, as well which method to use – horizontal or vertical. We also know what to look for when we dig down. But... how should we dig? And once we dig things up, how should we record and process them? How do we ensure that those who come after us are able to effectively use and interpret the data that we have been entrusted with unearthing?

To begin, there are certainly times – as counterintuitive as this may seem – that it is appropriate to use large excavating equipment. Fagan and Durrani write, "In the hands of an expert operator, a front loader, bulldozer, or backhoe with toothless bucket are remarkably delicate implements for removing sterile soil and surprisingly thin slivers of overburden".[14] When a significant amount of soil sits on top of the strata that need to be reached, these larger pieces of equipment can come in real handy.

The most common tool for the archaeologist, contrary to what we see in Indiana Jones, is not the whip. It is, instead, the *trowel*.

> "Picks, shovels, and long-handled spades carry the brunt of the heavy work. But the most common archaeological tool used in North America is the diamond-shaped trowel with straight edges and a sharp tip. With it, soil can be eased from a delicate specimen or an unusual discoloration in the soil can be scraped clean. Trowels are used for tracing layers in walls, clearing small pits, and other exacting jobs. They are rarely out of the digger's hand".[15]

With recent technological advancements, computers have become an integral part of the archaeologist's arsenal. An important instrument is known as the "total data station", which is used to record the three-dimensional position of any point on a site.

> "Large, open area excavations require accurate recording over considerable distances, made much easier when the positions of the houses and finds can be recorded with a total data station, an electronic distance-measuring device with recording computer, which records data that can be downloaded to laptop computers at the end of the day's work".[16]

Other tools include a variety of brushes – both large and small – as well as buckets, picks, shovels, measuring tapes, and plumb bobs. I remember using a large household broom – without the handle – at the end of each day of excavation. Once the square had been cleared and leveled, there was a thin layer of loose dirt that remained on the top of the square. In order to see the mudbrick, rocks, and other features in the soil, this top layer of loose dirt had to be removed. The broom – used very lightly and intentionally – was able to effectively sweep this dirt aside without damaging the remains or digging down further into the square. As tedious as this process was, it would have been impossible to accurately draw the square without it.

This leads us to recording and processing.

> "No dig is worth more than its records. Excavation notebooks provide a day-to-day record of each trench, of new layers and significant finds . . . It is information from

your records, as well as the artifacts from the dig, that form the priceless archive of your excavation. If the records are incomplete, the dig is little better than a treasure hunt".[17]

Careful attention must be paid to properly documenting your work as the excavation progresses. Thoroughly checking the soil that is being dug out of the ground for material culture, keeping the sides of the trench straight and plumb, ensuring that floors are identified and followed, and bagging and properly labeling all finds are just some of the activities that must be constantly performed and systematically documented. Once the excavation has been completed for the day, the area should be drawn and described in the excavation notebook, and all pottery and other material remains should be properly washed and prepared for further investigation. For example, at Umm el-Marra, after the pottery was washed and dried, we laid out the sherds in their respective groups for the dig director to analyze. After he had examined the groups of sherds, we proceeded to weigh the individual groups and document the results.

Once an area has been sufficiently excavated, it will be necessary to draw the walls that have been created by digging down through the occupation layers. These walls, or "baulks", show the different occupation layers in relation to one another, along with all intrusions, such as pits, foundations, or burrows (see figure 3 above). By clearly delineating and accurately drawing, photographing, and describing the baulks, the information can later be used for review, research, and publication. In the end, by carefully excavating and accurately recording your findings, you allow later researchers to utilize your work in an effective and responsible way.

The History of "Biblical Archaeology"

What exactly is "biblical archaeology"? Is it different from "regular" archaeology? While this is certainly not the place to provide an exhaustive account of the long and detailed developments in the discipline of "biblical archaeology", it is appropriate to provide a brief overview of some of the earlier problematic ideas and methodologies that plagued archaeological investigation in the southern Levant. Perhaps more problematic than anything else was the notion that the purpose of archaeology in this area *was to focus on the Bible*, particularly with the goal of "illuminating" or "defending" it. There are many treatments and summaries of this topic; a particularly thorough and relatively recent discussion can be found in *Shifting Sands: The Rise and Fall of Biblical Archaeology* by Thomas W. Davis.[18] A shorter but more recent summary can be found in William Dever's *Has Archaeology Buried the Bible?*; both of these works will be referenced frequently in this section.[19]

The 19th and Early 20th Centuries

The first archaeological investigations into the area of Palestine started in the mid-19th century with the work of Edward Robinson and Eli Smith.[20] Davis writes that Robinson "combined biblical interest and a strong personal faith with an attempt to be as 'scientific' as possible in his research",[21] something that was continued by subsequent biblical archaeologists. As Finkelstein and Silberman put it:

"Yet there was something much deeper, much more intimately connected with modern religious belief, that motivated the scholarly search for the 'historical' patriarchs. Many of the early biblical archaeologists had been trained as clerics or theologians. They were persuaded by their faith that God's promise to Abraham, Isaac, and Jacob . . . was real. And if it was real, it was presumably given to real people, not imaginary creations of some anonymous ancient scribe's pen".[22]

Faith was constantly in the background (and sometimes even the foreground) of archaeology, and this quite often led to significant problems, not only in interpretating the data, but in the decisions made by archaeologists concerning where and why to excavate. When it came to Robinson, his goals and presuppositions – particularly with respect to the reliability of the Bible – motivated and colored his interpretations. Davis writes:

"Underlying his approach is the search for solid demonstrable evidence of the accuracy of the biblical witness; it is a search for realia . . . Robinson came to Palestine expecting to find support for his conservative views on the Bible. *He came with a closed mind regarding the accuracy of Scripture,* and despite evidence to the contrary, as in the Sinai, *he did not change his views*" (emphasis mine).[23]

In 1865, the British Palestinian Exploration Fund (PEF) was formed, which "aimed for the scientific investigation of the 'Archaeology,

Geography, Geology, and Natural History of Palestine' for its own sake and for the purpose of biblical illustration".[24] Shortly thereafter, in the United States, came the Palestine Exploration Society (PES). Comparing the American PES to its British counterpart, Dever writes:

> "The American Palestine Exploration Society, founded in 1870, had an almost identical statement of purpose. But, significantly, to the goal of 'illustration' it added 'for the *defense* of the Bible.' That would set the trend for American archaeology in Palestine for the next century".[25]

Although archaeological methods had developed "from treasure hunting to true scientific inquiry in Palestinian archaeology",[26] the assumptions and motivations based on the biblical texts were a significant obstacle to overcome. In the late nineteenth and early twentieth centuries, many archaeologists' main aim was to bring the world of the Bible to light, focusing largely on sites that were known from the biblical text.[27]

William F. Albright

Following World War I, there was a development in the archaeology of Palestine; this was brought about by the work of William F. Albright, who "profoundly changed the nature of biblical archaeology".[28] However, Albright maintained that the biblical texts contained a historically reliable account of critical events. Dever explains:

> "These events were: (1) The migration of the patriarch and matriarch from Mesopotamia to Canaan in the early second millennium B.C.E.; (2) the Hebrew exodus from Egypt and the conquest of Canaan ca. 1250-1150 B.C.E.;

(3) the giving of the law and the covenant with Yahweh, Israel's sole god, at Mt. Sinai; (4) the establishment of the united monarchy in the tenth century B.C.E. under Saul, David, and Solomon, a 'divine kingship'; and (5) the development of the nation of Israel and its religion and culture in the subsequent Iron Age as unique and under divine providence".[29]

Albright's "aim was a simple one: to demonstrate the basic accuracy of the biblical depiction of the world of Abraham".[30] This approach was continued by Albright's student, G. Ernest Wright, for whom the historical veracity of the Old Testament stories was essential. Dever aptly sums up the problematic nature of this approach with the following question: "But what happens if the 'central events' – patriarchal migrations, Moses and monotheism at Sinai, exodus and conquest, Israel's unique ethnogenesis – had not occurred?"[31]

The Late 20th Century

Fortunately, within the last 50 years, the field has again shifted, this time toward an approach to the archaeology of the southern Levant that is not focused on the Bible. By the mid-1980s, "biblical archaeology" had given way to a new, secular form of Near Eastern archaeology. Initially known as "Syro-Palestinian" archaeology, it is now more often referred to as "Levantine" or "Southern Levantine archaeology," or simply "the archaeology of Israel" or "of Jordan".[32] Finkelstein and Silberman concur: "By the 1970s, however, new trends began to influence the conduct of biblical archaeology and eventually to change its major focus and completely reverse the traditional relationship between artifact and biblical text".[33]

While there are many factors that have been involved in this transition from a biblical to a secular focus, one of the significant catalysts has been the various historical problems with the biblical account that have been brought to light by the archaeological data. In spite of Albright's efforts to demonstrate the Bible's historical veracity, "all of his achievements have been undermined. The archaeological search for the historicity of the events in question *has been all but abandoned*" (emphasis mine).[34] Finkelstein and Silberman note:

> "By the end of the twentieth century, archaeology had shown that there were simply too many material correspondences between the finds in Israel and in the entire Near East and the world described in the Bible to suggest that the Bible was late and fanciful priestly literature, written with no historical basis at all. But at the same time there were too many contradictions between the archaeological finds and the biblical narratives to suggest that the Bible provided a precise description of what actually occurred".[35]

As we move into the next section, we will examine a few of these historical inconsistencies and contradictions that have been brought to light by archaeology.

Some Historical Problems in Israel's Early Period
(Iron Age I)

I remember my first semester at Johns Hopkins rather well, as it was the time that I left fundamental evangelical Christianity. I remember sitting in class with Kyle McCarter, who was teaching us about the history of Syro-Palestine, and thinking to myself time and again, "Wait… that can't be right". My experience was certainly not unique; many sincere believers have been confronted with the historical and archaeological data from the ancient world and determined that their interpretation of the Bible was no longer tenable.

What are these problems? Obviously, this is not the place to list and develop all of the historical problems with the Old Testament. There are other excellent publications that go into great detail concerning this issue (see bibliography). This section will instead focus on a particular period in Israelite history: Iron Age I (ca. 1200-1000 B.C.E.). It is in this period that we are confronted with a myriad of historical problems, including matters related to our two "test cases": the Canaanites and the Philistines. In each case, what we see in the biblical texts does not conform to what we know from history and archaeology.

The Canaanites

Few other groups in the Old Testament have been as vilified as the Canaanites. The object of the wrath of the ancient Israelites and their god, Yahweh, the Canaanites were to be utterly destroyed and driven out of the land. Tigay writes in his commentary on Deuteronomy 20:

"According to verse 18, the aim of this harsh policy is to prevent Israel from being influenced by the Canaanites to adopt their abhorrent practices . . . To Deuteronomy, the Canaanites' guilt in practicing child sacrifice – that is, ritual murder – underscored the necessity of forestalling their influence and eliminated any doubt that they deserved annihilation".[36]

But who were the Canaanites? Were they this malevolent group sacrificing children and practicing some of the most wicked activities imaginable? Did they live in the large, fortified cities that the Old Testament describes, from which Joshua had to expel them? Fortunately, we are not beholden to the presentation of the Canaanites in the Pentateuch; we have a fair amount of information concerning the groups who lived in Canaan prior to Israel "entering" the land. In this section, we will look at the history of the Canaanites in the region, focusing particularly on the period leading up to and during Iron Age I. This section will be structured upon Mary Ellen Buck's recent publication *The Canaanites*.[37]

Historical Background

Before we discuss the people who lived in the area known as Canaan, it would be good to define its geographical limits. "Canaan" was used to describe the coast of the southern Levant – what is today parts of Syria, Israel, Palestine, and Jordan – and "Canaanite" was used between around 1800 B.C.E. to roughly 400 C.E. to refer to those individuals living in that area.[38] More specifically, Buck writes that:

"[T]he territory of Canaan extended from the Lebanon and Anti-Lebanon mountain ranges in the north, to the Negev desert in the south. From east to west, the land of Canaan was bordered by the natural boundaries of the Ard as-Sawwan Desert in modern-day Jordan and the Mediterranean Sea" (see figure 4).[39]

Although questions of ethnicity – who would have considered themselves to be a Canaanite during a particular period – are important and intriguing, given the introductory nature and goals of this section, we will largely leave them aside. We will focus, therefore, on the populations that inhabited this area.

According to archaeological evidence, the southern Levant was continually inhabited from roughly the 3rd millennium B.C.E. on, and Buck notes that this suggests that the local people stayed in the area, regardless of the changing political or ecological situation.[40] Let's briefly take a look at the overall occupation history of the region.

The area of Canaan was continuously inhabited at least from the 3rd millennium into the 1st millennium B.C.E. During this period, we see a recurring pattern in the settlement strategies of the local populations, generally speaking. We begin in the 3rd millennium (Early Bronze Age III – 2500-2200 B.C.E.), when the cities were larger and were known for their monumental architecture and urbanization.

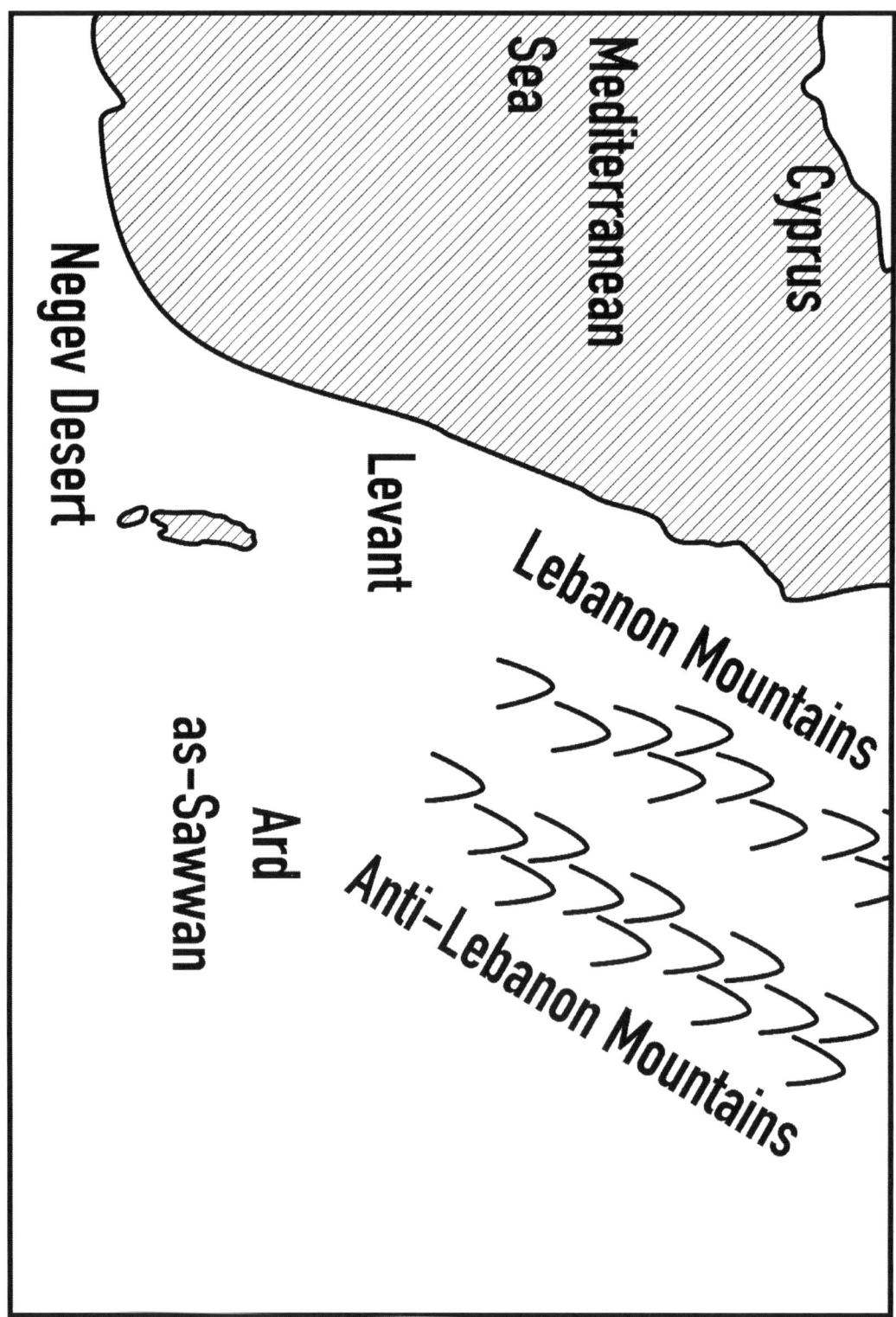

Figure 4. Boundaries of Canaan.

"Archaeological remains from the Early Bronze Age II-III period of the southern Levant tell of a flourishing society responsible for constructing massive structures . . . The Early Bronze III period marks the pinnacle of the Canaanite civilizations in the pre-historical period. Sites are characterized by monumental architecture and expansive fortifications".[41]

In other words, it was a time of urbanization; settlements housed increased populations and were subject to large-scale building works.

During the following period, known as Early Bronze Age IV (2200-1800), there was a significant change in the climate of the region; "Northern Syria and the northern and southern Levant witnessed a three-hundred-year period of dramatically low precipitation". [42] With a significant decrease in precipitation came greater difficulty in effectively farming and remaining sedentary; this caused many people to leave the cities and take up pastoral nomadism (migrating with their herds to find land for grazing). Buck writes, "Most cities were abandoned and the populations appear to turn to more nomadic lifestyles".[43]

However, when the climate stabilized during the Middle Bronze Age (1800-1550), people returned to the cities, and we once again see the construction and renovation of monumental architecture, large fortifications, etc. This process apparently had additional stimulations; Buck notes that a group of people known as the Amorites migrated into the northern Levant and gradually spread down into the south. The Amorites probably didn't take over the region as a whole, but settled in areas that allowed access to pre-existing trade routes, including Megiddo, Hazor, and Shechem.[44]

In the following Late Bronze Age (1550-1200), however, the land of Canaan fell under the control (primarily) of Egypt, and its local Canaanite rulers were subject to the Egyptian pharaohs. This is the famous Amarna period, when nations like Egypt, Hatti, Mitanni, Assyria, and Babylonia were engaged in international relations. The "middle ground" that connected Egypt to the rest of these nations was Canaan, which was made up of these subservient local kingdoms.[45] Egypt established several forts and outposts in Canaan in order to maintain control over the region.

Finally, around 1200 B.C.E., there was a major collapse throughout the eastern Mediterranean, and the local Canaanite groups were able to reassert control of their own individual kingdoms. This collapse, brought about in part by the Sea Peoples, was a significant catalyst in the later development of the political structure in Canaan. With Egypt no longer in control of the region, these individual kingdoms had the ability to establish their own rule free from domination. Nations like the Moabites, Edomites, Ammonites, Phoenicians, and *Israelites* were the product of this political development.

Simply put, control of the region shifted from autonomous Canaanite territories in the Middle Bronze Age to Egyptian hegemony in the Late Bronze Age, and then back to local Canaanite control after the arrival of the Sea Peoples and the Bronze Age collapse.[46] In the Iron Age, these local Canaanite groups who had lived in the region for centuries arose as "localized kingdoms, including the Phoenicians, *Israelites,* Moabites, Ammonites, and Edomites" (emphasis mine).[47]

Child Sacrifice: A Test Case

As you were reading through the historical background to the Canaanites, you might have been asking yourself, "So what? Why am I reading this?"

One of the things that stands out to me in discussions with apologists is their overt (and perhaps unconscious) reliance on the narrative of the Old Testament for historical purposes. A common assertion is that the Canaanites were grossly immoral and abominable people, which is why God had to wipe them out. The most common example given is that of child sacrifice.

Now, it is not my goal here to provide a thorough discussion on the issue of child sacrifice in ancient Israel and Canaan; if you are interested in that topic, you should read Heath Dewrell's *Child Sacrifice in Ancient Israel* (2017) and Francesca Stavrakopoulou's *King Manasseh and Child Sacrifice* (2004).[48] Instead, we will use child sacrifice as a test case to illustrate how the Old Testament often describes events or people groups in ways that conflict with what we know from other, more reliable sources. Heath Dewrell's book on child sacrifice will inform the structure of the discussion below.

> "And Yahweh spoke to Moses, saying, 'Speak to the children of Israel and say to them, "I am Yahweh your God. According to the works of the land of Egypt, where you dwelled, you shall not do. And according to the works of the land of Canaan, where I am about to bring you, you shall

not do, and you shall not walk in their statutes"""" (Leviticus 18:1-3).

Among those wicked practices was child sacrifice:

> """"And from your seed do not give to offer as a *mlk* sacrifice [more on this below], and do not defile the name of your God, I am Yahweh . . . Do not defile yourselves with any of these things, because with all of these things the nations were defiled, whom I am about to cast out before you. And the land has become defiled, and I have visited its iniquity upon it, and the land has spewed out its inhabitants"""" (Leviticus 18:21, 24-25).

Only two chapters later we read more about the practice of child sacrifice and the severe punishments that would come should the Israelites practice it (Leviticus 20:1-5). But what is the connection between this behavior and the Canaanites? At the end of chapter 20 (after describing many more practices that God condemns) we read:

> """"And keep all my statutes and all my judgments and do them, so that the land will not spew you out, where I am about to bring you to dwell in. And do not walk in the statutes of the nations, whom I am about to cast out before you, because they did all of these things, so that I have become disgusted with them"""" (Leviticus 20:22-23).

There is no question that the Old Testament writers viewed the previous inhabitants of the land of Canaan as wicked, detestable people, worthy of extermination. Much of their condemnation focused on child sacrifice.

But what evidence do we have that there was the widespread ritual practice of child sacrifice throughout Canaan in the centuries leading up to the Israelite "conquest"?[49] As it turns out, we have very limited archaeological evidence for the practice of child sacrifice on the whole, and it would appear from the available data that the Israelites themselves were participating in this practice, sacrificing their children, not to a foreign Canaanite deity, but *to Yahweh*.

Let's begin by examining what it means to sacrifice "to Molek". Again, without going into a great deal of detail, the Hebrew that is translated "to Molek" is the form *lmlk*. The first letter "*l*" represents a preposition, which is usually translated "to" or "for". However, like so many prepositions (even in English), the Hebrew preposition *l* can take on a wide range of meanings, depending on the context. A number of Punic inscriptions have been found that speak of a *mlk* sacrifice being made to Baal Hammon. For example, "To the Lord, to Ba'l Hammon, a *mlk 'adm*, the vow which Ba'l-Pado' son of Magon vowed. He heard his voice; he blessed him".[50]

The Punic colonies were founded by Phoenicians who had left the mainland. If you remember from our discussion above, the Phoenicians were part of the area known as Canaan. Thus, one could make the connection (potentially) between the practices in the Punic colonies and those in the Phoenician homeland, which could make them Canaanite practices. Returning to the Punic inscription, the *mlk* sacrifice was not a sacrifice made to a deity named *mlk*, but rather to Baal Hammon. That means that the word *mlk* did not refer to a deity, but to a *type of sacrifice*. This was confirmed by the appearance of *'adm* following *mlk* (see the inscription above); the word *'adm* means "man" or "human". The word *'mr* means "sheep", so a *mlk 'mr* means "a sacrifice of a sheep". Thus – as we see above – a *mlk 'adm* would ostensibly mean "a sacrifice of a human".[51]

In the Punic colonies, therefore, we see that the *mlk* sacrifice was a *type of sacrifice*, not the *deity to whom a sacrifice was made*. It was often connected with the object being sacrificed, such as a sheep or human. A scholar named Eissfeldt determined, based on this evidence, that the Hebrew phrase *lmlk* did not mean "to Molek" (Molek being a deity), but rather "as a *mlk* sacrifice". The preposition *l* is used in other similar contexts in the same way; for example, in Genesis 22:2, Abraham is commanded to "take your only son, whom you love – Isaac – and go to the land of Moriah, and offer him up there ***as*** *a whole burnt offering* upon one of the mountains that I will show you" (emphasis mine).

The next question that we need to ask is, "When does this archaeological evidence date to?" If you would like to read a detailed overview of the archaeological evidence concerning child sacrifice in the region during this period, see chapter two of Dewrell's book.[52] There you can see that the primary evidence for the practice of child sacrifice among the Canaanites – the Punic material – *comes from the 1st millennium B.C.E., from the 7th through the 1st c. B.C.E.*[53] In other words, the Punic evidence for child sacrifice is far too late to be considered evidence for the practice of child sacrifice in the early to mid-2nd millennium B.C.E., when the practice would have been required to fit the biblical timeline.

While it is certainly not a settled issue as to whether there was a deity named Molek to whom child sacrifices were offered, or whether child sacrifice was practiced on the Phoenician coast in the 1st millennium

B.C.E., what we *can* say is that there is insufficient extra-biblical evidence to support the biblical claim of grossly immoral population groups that practiced child sacrifice in Canaan during the 2nd millennium B.C.E. Dewrell writes:

"There is as yet no unambiguous material evidence from Syria-Palestine itself that corroborates the claims of the Hebrew Bible. The fact that the Punic evidence supports the conclusion that children were sacrificed as part of a *mlk* ritual makes it tempting to connect these sacrifices with Hebrew מֹלֶךְ sacrifices, as Eissfeldt did nearly a century ago, but making this connection probably requires assuming that the rite also took place on the Phoenician mainland in order to provide the necessary link between Judah and Carthage. Unfortunately, there is as yet no strong material evidence for child sacrifice in Phoenicia proper, or Syria-Palestine in general, apart from the possible exception of the third-millennium equid burials at Umm el-Marra, which are largely irrelevant to this discussion, given their early date and specific connection with equid funerary rites".[54]

In short, while the people in Canaan in the 1st millennium were likely practicing child sacrifice infrequently, the biblical portrayal is not historically reliable. It does, however, seem reasonable to conclude that child sacrifice was being practiced – albeit to a limited degree – in the land of Canaan *and among the Israelites.* Furthermore, it would seem that these Israelite child sacrifices were not originally being made to other deities, *but to Yahweh himself.*

Dewrell isolates three different types of child sacrifices that were very likely made to Yahweh. The first was a general firstborn sacrifice, which can be seen in Exodus 22:29-30: "Do not hold back from your harvest and your wine vat. The firstborn of your sons you will give to me. Thus you will do with your oxen and sheep: seven days it will be with its mother, and on the eighth day you will give him it to me". Dewrell argues that these verses show

> "[T]hat at least some Yahwists viewed the literal sacrifice of a firstborn child as the appropriate means of acknowledging Yahweh's claim to firstborn children. These sacrifices, like firstfruit offerings in general, served to ensure bounty and prosperity, and failing to give Yahweh his due would result in calamity and destruction".[55]

A second type of child sacrifice likely practiced in Israel was that which was done in times of distress. This can be seen, for example, in 2 Kings 3:27, where Mesha, the Moabite king, offered his firstborn son in order to avoid annihilation: "And he took his firstborn son, who would reign after him, and he offered him up as a whole burnt offering upon the wall. And a great wrath was against Israel, and they went out from him and they returned to their land". As noted by Dewrell, the very fact that this sacrifice is shown to be successful in removing the military threat, in combination with the reference to child sacrifice in Micah 6:1-8, shows that "firstborn children were also perceived by at least some Israelites as appropriate sacrificial victims during times of distress".[56]

The third and final type of child sacrifice was the *lmlk* sacrifice that was discussed above. This would have been, most likely, late and of foreign origin. As identified by Dewrell, there are then three different types of child sacrifice referenced in the Hebrew Bible:

> "Two appear to have relatively old roots in the Israelite cult, while the third was likely the result of syncretistic borrowing. Each had a different function and purpose, and none of the various types of child sacrifice can be subsumed to another . . . There must have been some variety of practice among different Yahwistic groups, some of whom may have participated in one or more of these rites, while others may have participated in none".[57]

What does this mean for us if we are using child sacrifice as a test case? First, as we saw in the section above, we have a fair amount of evidence that helps us understand Canaanite culture from the 2nd millennium B.C.E., the period described in the Old Testament as one of gross immorality and child sacrifice. The land of Canaan – during the Late Bronze Age (1550-1200 B.C.E.) – was firmly under the control of the Egyptians and does not reflect the descriptions of the Canaanites given in the Old Testament. More specifically, however, the archaeological evidence that we have for child sacrifice does not come from the 2nd millennium, but from the middle and latter portions of the 1st millennium B.C.E. The evidence itself also does not come from the land of Canaan, but from Carthage and the Punic colonies. Thus, we have no solid evidence of child sacrifice in Canaan proper, and what evidence we have comes from the 1st millennium B.C.E.

Finally, we saw that, while child sacrifice was very likely performed sporadically during the 1st millennium, it was not only practiced by the

Canaanites, but also by the Israelites. These child sacrifices were offered to Yahweh, not to other deities. In short, the depictions of the Canaanites presented in passages like Leviticus 18 and 20 do not reflect historical reality and clearly functioned as a form of anti-Canaanite propaganda.

The Philistines

> "Then there is the issue of the Philistines. We hear of them in connection with Isaac's encounter with 'Abimelech, king of the Philistines,' at the city of Gerar (Genesis 26:1). The Philistines, a group of migrants from the Aegean or eastern Mediterranean, had not established their settlements along the coastal plain of Canaan until sometime after 1200 B.C.E."[58]

The book of Genesis speaks often of the Philistines as having been in the land long before archaeology can detect their arrival around 1200 B.C.E. Is the Old Testament historically correct, or did the Philistines arrive at the end of the 2nd millennium as part of a group known as the Sea Peoples, settling in Canaan and providing a catalyst for the formation of the nation of Israel?

Among the variant people groups found in the Levant, few are as intriguing and elusive as the Philistines. While the Hebrew Bible and Egyptian sources provide detailed information concerning the origin and culture of these foreign invaders, debate continues on the original homeland of these "peoples of the sea". Written sources, along with much of the archaeological record, indicate that the Philistines came to southern Palestine from somewhere in the Aegean. However, some have contended that no such infiltration or invasion occurred. Instead, the "Philistines" were either an endogenous group in Palestine, or mercantile traders who settled in Palestine over a long period of time. An examination of the available written sources and material culture can help us determine the most likely origin of the Philistines.

Philistines as Part of the Sea Peoples

The common view among scholars today is that the Philistines were a part of the Sea Peoples invasion which occurred at the beginning of the Iron Age.[59] They would have settled in the land of Canaan, along the Coastal Plain (from the Brook of Besor in the south to the Valley of Sorek in the north) between 1180 and 1150 B.C.E. It is argued that this branch of the Sea Peoples brought its own material culture from the Aegean region but quickly assimilated many Egyptian and Canaanite cultural motifs. Evidence supporting this conclusion comes from both textual sources (Hebrew Bible, Egyptian records, a Canaanite inscription) as well as material culture, both inside and outside of Palestine.

Textual sources

The biblical writers seem to continue an Israelite tradition that sets the Philistine place of origin in Caphtor. The prophet Amos writes, "'Are you not like the Cushites to me, O children of Israel', says Yahweh. 'Did I not bring up Israel from the land of Egypt, and the Philistines from Caphtor, and Aram from Kir?'" (Amos 9:7). Similarly, the prophet Jeremiah cries, "On account of the day that is coming to destroy all the Philistines, to cut off from Tyre and Sidon every surviving ally. For Yahweh is about to destroy the Philistines, the remnant of the island of Caphtor" (Jeremiah 47:4). Though less clear, Genesis 10:14 also identifies Caphtor as the Philistine homeland.[60] Thus, there is general continuity in the biblical tradition concerning Philistine origins.

But where is Caphtor? Known variously as *kftyw* ("Keftiu", Egyptian), *Kaptaru* (Akkadian), and *kaphtor* (Hebrew), the fields of Biblical studies, Assyriology, and Egyptology, all identify it with the island of Crete, located in the Mediterranean Sea.[61] The Septuagint (Greek translation of the Old Testament) translates Hebrew *kaphtor* in Amos 9:7 as *kappadokias*, "Cappadocia".[62] However, the prophet Ezekiel seems to equate the Philistines with the Cherethites who dwell along the Coastal Plain (Ezekiel 25:16). Here, the Septuagint translates Cherethites as *kretas*, "Crete" (see also Zephaniah 2:5). And while the Septuagint of Amos equates *kaphtor* with "Cappadocia" (as does Deuteronomy 2:23), Jeremiah states that *kaphtor* is an island (Jeremiah 47:4), which Cappadocia is clearly not. It would appear that the biblical writers identify the Philistines with the Cherethites (Ezekiel 25:16; Zephaniah 2:5), claiming that they originated in Crete, that is, Caphtor.[63]

Even earlier than the biblical text are the inscriptions at Medinet Habu, a mortuary temple in Egypt. On its second pylon, commemorating the battles of the eighth regnal year of Ramesses III, is an inscription concerning the travels and invasion of the Sea Peoples. This marauding band, according to the inscription, was comprised of different groups of people, including the Philistines, Tjekker, Sheklesh, Denyen, and Weshesh. Perhaps most important for this discussion is the path of conquest described in the text: Hatti, Kode, Carchemish, Arzawa, Alashiya, Amurru, and Egypt. In other words, the inscription depicts the Philistines, a member of the invading Sea Peoples, *moving east and south through the Mediterranean*, finally arriving at Egypt. If accurate, this would clearly argue for a Philistine origin, not in Canaan, but *at least* in the western part of Anatolia or in the Aegean.

A set of reliefs accompanies the Sea Peoples inscription at Medinet Habu, on the outside of the northern wall of the inner temple. The Egyptian enemies are ichnographically distinguished by salient features that might indicate their origin. The invaders wear a distinctive type of plumed headdress. Dothan observes, "Sailors along the Aegean coasts of Asia Minor were long known for their 'feathered crests'".[64]

Further investigation of the Medinet Habu reliefs shows the sea invaders carrying women in ox-drawn carts. Dothan argues that in the relief, "A spokeless-wheeled wagon harnessed to a team of four oxen is caught up in battle while carrying women and children to settle in territories conquered by Sea People warriors".[65] By this understanding, the passengers would have been the families of the Sea Peoples, traveling to their final destination of settlement. Gertzen, however, argues that these are not family members, but captives taken during the Syrian portion of the conquest.[66] Thus, they may not indicate a migration at all.

Finally, the ships in which the Sea Peoples arrive possibly resemble those used in Mycenaean prototypes.[67] The design of the vessels is reminiscent of those used to the north. Overall, the iconography of the reliefs seems to indicate that the warriors came from the Aegean region and would later be associated with the Philistines.

Further information on the settlement of the Philistines comes from the Harris Papyrus, an Egyptian document discovered in the 1870s. In the text, Ramesses III (the purported writer/speaker) says that he not only defeated the Denyen, Tjekker, Philistines, Sherden, and Weshesh, but settled them in his own lands (including Canaan). [68] Because the archaeological record (as will be further discussed below) argues for a Sea Peoples settlement in the Coastal Plain of Palestine, the Harris Papyrus seems to support the view that an invading group of marauders ultimately settled in Canaan.

Finally, the recent discovery of a Canaanite inscription at Gath appears to support an Aegean origin of the Philistines. The inscription is dated to the last phase of Iron I and to the early phase of Iron II. [69] The short inscription (the earliest known Philistine inscription in alphabetic script) appears to include two Philistine names that are Greek or Anatolian in origin. [70] Demsky writes, "The names . . . are identified as non-Semitic names, known from the Greek or Anatolian onomastica (Mycenaean, Lydian, and possibly others)". [71] This retention of Greek or Anatolian names argues for an Aegean origin for the Philistines.

In summation, the written sources ostensibly support the theory that the Philistines, an ethnic group of the Sea Peoples, migrated to the Coastal Plain of Canaan from somewhere in or around the Aegean. The Hebrew Bible places their origin in Caphtor, most likely to be identified with Crete. The inscriptions of Medinet Habu and the Harris Papyrus describe an invasive group of marauders coming from the north and west, eventually settling (or being settled) along the coast of Canaan. The reliefs accompanying the Medinet Habu inscriptions portray Aegean and later Philistine styles and motifs, seemingly connecting the Sea Peoples with the Philistines. Finally, the Canaanite inscription found at Gath shows Greek or Anatolian influence, arguing for an Aegean origin of the Philistines at Gath.

Material Culture in Palestine

The material culture found in the land of Palestine dating to the Iron I and II periods seems to support a Philistine migration from the Aegean region. Two aspects of the archaeological assemblages point to such a conclusion: pottery (and pottery technology) and cultic objects. In each case, characteristics and features of the material culture appear to be *locally made* yet *have their stylistic origin in the Aegean.* The abundance of distinct Philistine material culture that appears in the Levant during the 12th c. B.C.E. provides "a case study par excellence of the material manifestation of immigration in the archaeological record".[72]

Pottery. In the study of archaeology, different pottery styles are thought to show developments within a culture or people group, as well as to differentiate between different groups. Two different types of pottery are used to identify the presence of the Philistines: Mycenaean III C:1b and Philistine bichrome wares. As a case study, the pottery remains from Tel Miqne can be used to show:

1) the end of a culture;

2) the beginning of a new culture; and

3) the development of that new culture through time.

This section is very data-heavy, so please see table 1 for a helpful summary.

Chronology	Ekron Stratum	Pottery present	Interpretation
Late Bronze	VIII	Late Helladic IIIB	Imported, indicates presence of international trade between local Canaanites and Mediterranean peoples.
Iron I	VII	Mycenaean III C:1b	Locally made wares, Aegean style. Indicates the presence of a new people group from the Aegean (Philistines).
Iron I	VI (early)	Mycenaean III C:1b AND Philistine bichrome	Locally made wares, Aegean style with local influences. Indicates contact between new people group and local culture.
Iron I	VI (late)	Philistine bichrome	Locally made, highly influenced by Egyptian and Canaanite traditions. Indicates continued contact between Aegean migrants and local cultures.

Table 1. Table showing chronological pottery transitions at Ekron.

The Late Bronze Age (1550-1200 B.C.E.) was a time of international trade and complexity. Due to this international trade, Cypriote and Mycenaean pottery was found throughout the Mediterranean dating to this period. However, at the end of the 13th century and into the 12th century, Palestine discontinued importing many goods, including Mycenaean wares. Dothan notes, "The absence of Mycenaean and Cypriote imports signals the end of the Canaanite settlement at the site".[73] At Ekron, Stratum VIII (a Late Bronze Age level) contained *imported* pottery (Late Helladic IIIB), indicating continued international trade with the Aegean.[74] Yet the two principal levels of Iron I at Ekron (Strata VII and VI) contain *locally made* wares in Aegean style. In other words, in the earlier Late Bronze Age level (Stratum VIII), we see evidence of trade. However, in the later Iron Age I levels (Strata VII and VI), the pottery is no longer imported, but *locally made* – and *in an Aegean style.*

Stratum VII, dated to the early 12th c. B.C.E., contains a specific type of pottery style that archaeologists have labeled "Mycenaean III C:1b".[75] Decorations in this style are typically monochrome, utilizing a red or dark brown paint. The pottery found in Stratum VII were not imports, but were instead locally manufactured, evidenced by Neutron Activation Analysis.[76] Further evidence for local manufacture can be seen in the analysis of asphalt (bitumen) found at Ekron, used for waterproofing pottery, which was found to be from the Dead Sea.[77]

Ann Killebrew, after surveying the materials, methods, and technology (kilns, slow wheel) used to create the Mycenaean III C:1b pottery at Ekron, concluded that the potters working in Tel Miqne during the 13th c. B.C.E. "practiced an entirely different craft" from those working during the 12th c. B.C.E.[78] In short, this pottery was made locally, using local materials, but the way in which pottery was made during the Iron Age I period was very different from what we see in the period just before (Late Bronze Age). *Something changed*; namely, a new group of people moved into the area, bringing entirely new pottery production practices. These people are associated by many archaeologists with the Philistines.

In Stratum VI, the pottery types transition from Mycenaean III C:1b to Philistine bichrome wares. Philistine bichrome is characterized by – you guessed it – a two-toned style, which often contains a more stylized form of bird and fish motifs that only infrequently occurred on the Mycenaean III C:1b ware.[79] Mycenaean III C:1b vessels appear initially *alongside* the new Philistine bichrome style, but the bichrome eventually *supplants* the early Mycenaean ware.[80] Philistine bichrome is a complex style of pottery, influenced not only by Aegean tradition, *but by Canaanite and Egyptian as well*. Mazar writes, "The eclectic nature of this pottery . . . must have been a result of a *rather long period of exposure to local Canaanite and Egyptian traditions*" (emphasis mine).[81]

In summary, the initial phase of Philistine settlement in the city of Ekron (Stratum VII) was a time when the Philistine settlers *continued their pottery traditions brought from their Aegean homeland*. Pottery is not imported, but locally manufactured in the Mycenaean III C:1b style. Asphalt collected from the Dead Sea region was sometimes used to seal the vessels. The kilns used to fire the pottery were unknown in Canaan, indicating that the group utilizing them was not endogenous to the region. However, during the second phase of occupation (Stratum VI), the Philistines *began to assimilate aspects of the local culture*, their pottery taking on local styles *while still maintaining a close connection with the Aegean.*

Cultic objects. At both Tel Qasile (a Philistine port city in Tel-Aviv) and Tel Miqne-Ekron, Philistine buildings were excavated which may be interpreted as temples. At Ekron, for example, one of the two public buildings found in the central part of the city provided a number of cultic objects similar in style to those found in the Aegean. In addition, three buildings at Tel Qasile contained the same types of Aegean-style cultic objects, suggesting a possible or likely connection between the Philistine temples and the Aegean.

The public buildings that were found at Tel Miqne-Ekron were labeled by the archaeologists "Building 351" and "Building 350". Building 350 (which was built upon the older Building 351) contained several features and objects that suggested to the archaeologists that those who used the building were of Aegean origin.[82] These objects include hearths, wheels of a decorated cult stand, a linchpin, mudbrick offering platforms (called *bamot*), and knives. While the evidence is sometimes only suggestive, cumulatively it seems to indicate that these temples and the people that utilized them were of Aegean origin.

Round hearths with pebbled surfaces were excavated from a hall in Building 350.[83] As animal bones were found in and around the hearths, the function of the hearths was determined to be cultic. These hearths, and their positioning, were interpreted by Trude Dothan to be Aegean in style. She observes, "Hearths are an important cultic feature in Cypriote and Aegean architecture, particularly in the megaron plan, where they constitute the central architectural element".[84]

Also found in Building 350 were three bronze wheels, each containing eight spokes. The wheels were small (a diameter of only 6 cm.).[85] Along with the wheels, excavators found a corner of a frame along with decoration, each made of bronze. It is theorized that these pieces belonged to a small model of a cultic stand similar to that which was described in 1 Kings, constructed by King Hiram of Tyre:[86]

> "And he made ten stands of bronze; four cubits was the length of each stand, and four cubits was its width and three cubits its height. And this was the design of the stand: they had borders, and borders between the frames. And upon the borders that were between the frames were lions, oxen, and cherubs. And upon the frames was a pedestal above and below the lions and oxen was a wreath of hanging design. And each stand had four wheels of bronze, and axles of bronze, and its four feet had supports. Beneath the basin were cast supports with wreaths at either side" (1 Kings 7:27-30).

Many of these cultic stands have been discovered *on the island of Cyprus* dating to the 12th century.[87]

In Room C, a linchpin was discovered that bore a decorative motif found in the Aegean. A face was carved on either side of the top of the pin with a hole drilled between them, presumably for the insertion of a cord. Dothan concludes, "This representation [the two faces] can be interpreted as two sphinxes—similar in style to those from Aegean and Cypriote bronzework".[88]

Finally, an iron knife, attached to an ivory handle by three bronze rivets, was discovered on the floor in Building 350. Dothan argues that, because the knife was constructed of different metals, it should be considered a luxury item.[89] The knife was found in a pottery-rich context, much of which was Philistine bichrome. Other ivory handles were located in the building and in the surrounding area. These knives, it is argued, are similar to knives found in the Aegean and are support for an Aegean origin of the Philistines.[90]

At Tell Qasile, three temples were discovered in Strata XII-X. In Stratum XI, a secondary shrine was built to the west of the main temple. Building a small shrine in proximity to a large temple *"was unknown in Canaanite religious architecture but had parallels in the Aegean and in Cyprus* during the thirteenth and twelfth centuries B.C.E." (emphasis mine).[91] Of interest in these temples were two types of clay figurines: an "Ashdoda" figurine and a "mourning" woman. The "Ashdoda" figurine shows a woman seated on a chair. Dothan sees a strong connection between the Ashdoda and similar motifs found in the Aegean as she writes, "The Ashdoda is the hallmark of the mother goddess in the Aegean cult". [92] Both the Ashdoda and mourning woman are representative objects originating in the Aegean.[93]

Finally, Tel Nagila, a site 28 km east of modern Gaza, provided excavators with an Iron Age II fire-stand that is also connected to the Aegean. Fire stands were utilized in the Aegean during the Bronze Age.[94] The petrographic analysis of the fire-stand indicates that it was *not an import*, but was *fashioned with soil from the Shephelah or Coastal Plain*.[95] Based on this evidence, it is safe to say that cultic objects from temples in Ekron and Tell Qasile, along with the fire stand from Tel

Nagila, *have strong parallels with the Aegean region*. Their presence is one more indication of Philistines migrating to the area from the Aegean region and using local resources to create their own native material culture.[96]

Material Culture in Cyprus

We have seen that there is strong evidence in Palestine to suggest that the Philistines had their origin in the Aegean region, but is there evidence from the Aegean that supports this conclusion? In his 1984 article, Vassos Karageorghis argues that the island of Cyprus provides crucial and convincing evidence of the origin of the Sea Peoples.[97] He examines two settlements established in the 13th century, Pyla-Kokkinokremos and Maa-Palaeokastro. The time of the sites' establishments, their characteristics, and their abandonment or destruction seem to argue that *Cyprus was a stopping point for refugees from the Aegean and/or Anatolian regions on their way to Egypt and the Levant.*

A breakdown in the Aegean and Anatolian regions drove myriads of refugees from their homes, moving east. Karageorghis argues that settlers from this group came to Cyprus in order to establish secure settlements to ensure protection against other marauding bands of Sea Peoples. Two sites have been identified as such settlements: Pyla-Kokkinokremos and Maa-Palaeokastro. Pyla-Kokkinokremos, established for the first time between 1240 and 1230 B.C.E., sat in an agriculturally unproductive area, but was easily defensible. The walls of the houses on the site formed a casemate wall opening into a center courtyard. The inhabitants were partially Cretan, as evidenced by their Late Minoan pottery and symbols of Minoan religion. [98] Though militarily defensible, the site was abandoned near the end of the 13th century. However, the inhabitants intended to return to their homes in short order, as they hid their valuables (gold, silver, bronze, alabaster vessels) rather than taking them with them. It would seem that an outside force caused them to flee the city.

Further evidence can be gained from Maa-Palaeokastro. As at Pyla-Kokkinokremos, this site was established for the first time in the latter half of the 13th century. Again, Karageorghis argues that the site was chosen for its military advantages, not agricultural possibilities. Rather than the site being abandoned, however, the archaeological evidence shows that it was destroyed by fire around 1200 B.C.E., followed by a resettlement. The people who resettled Maa-Palaeokastro *used locally made pottery of the Mycenaean IIIC:1b type*. These new settlers occupied the site for ca. 25 years before leaving in 1175 B.C.E.

From these two sites, Karageorghis draws several conclusions. First, the pottery of the second settlers of Maa-Palaeokastro shows clear connection with the Aegean, indicating that they were migrants or refugees from the Aegean who adopted a local ceramic style, building the Period II settlement.[99] Secondly, each of the groups mentioned (the original settlers of Pyla-Kokkinokremos, Maa-Palaeokastro, and the new settlers of Maa-Palaeokastro) were part of the migration of refugees known as the Sea Peoples.[100] That they were ethnically related apparently did not hinder them from attacking one another during this time of survival. Finally, he concludes that the Philistines, part of the Sea Peoples movement, departed from Cyprus and finally reached Egypt and the Levant.[101] Therefore, it appears that Cyprus provides evidence for a stopping point for Philistine immigrants leaving the Aegean as they eventually made their way to the coast of Palestine.

A great deal of archaeological and textual evidence seems to indicate that the Philistines had their origin somewhere in the Aegean. First, written sources, including the Hebrew Bible, Medinet Habu, the Harris Papyrus, and the Gath Canaanite inscription all seem to argue for an Aegean origin. Second, the material culture from the land of Palestine, including pottery, temples, and cultic objects, shows a strong connection with the Aegean region. Finally, settlements on the island of Cyprus seem to fit well with the hypothesis that Philistine immigrants or refugees from the Aegean settled briefly in Cyprus before making their way to the coast of Palestine.

Philistines as an Endogenous Group

Although a great deal of evidence seems to support an Aegean origin for the Philistines, Schlomo Bunimovitz instead identifies the Philistines as an endogenous group from Palestine.[102] His argument rests primarily on a re-evaluation of the material culture found in the area of Palestine, specifically in the Philistines' pattern of settlement, their pottery, and their cultic practices. If correct, the Philistines would not have emigrated from a distant shore, but rather would have developed as an ethnic group from within the land of Canaan.

Bunimovitz contends that the pattern of Philistine settlement was not indicative of an outside infiltration.[103] First, the Philistines settled in a region that was already populated and influenced by Egyptian and Canaanite culture. Thus, the Philistines did not enter a "culturally neutral" area, but one that had ethnic and cultural complexity. Second, the Philistines settled in areas that had been occupied similarly in the Late Bronze Age. He argues that there was continuity between the socio-political systems of the Philistines and those of the Late Bronze Age. Finally, the Philistines were a minority in the overall population of the coastal plain.

Philistine pottery could also argue against an outside origin. Bunimovitz emphasizes that the Philistine assemblage does not comprise all the necessary types for a full range of cooking. Because much of the Philistine cooking ware is in fact supplemented with Canaanite types, he argues that "the Philistine vessels constituted the luxury tableware for the entire heterogeneous population of Philistia during the 12th and 11th centuries B.C.E."[104] In other words, beginning with the "dark age" of trade in Philistia, the normally imported fine ware was replaced by locally made vessels. Because of this, "Philistine" pottery cannot argue for an ethnic distinction in any context in which it is found; the pottery does not *necessarily* indicate Philistine ethnicity in any given context.

Finally, the Philistine cultic practices may not indicate foreign Philistine origin. Bunimovitz concludes that the temples found at Tell Qasile are not associated with the Aegean region, suggesting that any similarities between Aegean and Philistine temples reflect "Levantine influence on the west and not the other way around".[105] Additionally, because he concludes that Philistine pottery does not indicate ethnicity, the fact that such pottery was found at the Tell Qasile temples indicates nothing. He writes, "Its presence in the assemblages excavated in and around the Tell Qasile temples . . . is irrelevant to the question of their Philistine attribution".[106]

Although Bunimovitz raises interesting arguments concerning the level of certainty scholars may have concerning certain aspects of Philistine culture, it does not seem that he has answered fundamental questions concerning the majority of the evidence. The locally manufactured Mycenaean IIIC:1b pottery argues strongly for an outside origin, as does the archaeological evidence from Cyprus, while independent textual sources indicate an Aegean origin of the Philistine ethnic group. Thus, it seems less likely that the evidence points to the Philistines being solely an endogenous group.

Philistines as a Mercantile Group

The final interpretation of the archaeological and textual evidence is that the Philistines were a mercantile group that eventually settled along the coast of Palestine to solidify their trade network. One proponent of this view is Alexander Bauer.[107] This hypothesis argues that a group of independent maritime traders operated outside of the control of the Egyptians and Hittites during the Late Bronze Age. The hub of their trade network was established at Cyprus. It is theorized that this mercantile group, by trading Mycenaean wares, would have either benefitted from or even caused the downfall of Mycenaean trade.

Eventually, this unified group would have settled in the coastal trading areas of the Levant in order to solidify their trade network. Bauer notes, "It would make sense that these merchants would try to stabilize their threatened network by settling in the very cities that acted as trading gateways".[108] In other words, the sites on the coast that the Philistines occupied were involved in Late Bronze Age trade. That the Philistines would choose these sites accords well with the theory that they desired to continue their mercantile activities from permanent settlements.

Several problems arise, however, when attempting to reconcile the evidence with the mercantile theory. First, the textual sources indicate foreign immigration. Bauer explains this as the Egyptians simply trying to explain them in a manner compatible with their own worldview,[109] but this doesn't explain why the biblical texts also argue for an Aegean origin.

Additional problems concern the location of Philistine settlements; why are they restricted to the southern Levant, and why are there inland Philistine cities if their object was to control maritime trade. Concerning the first objection, Bauer argues that the southern Levant saw a great deal of trade, and the Philistines "would not try to sustain the entire trade network, but only that part from which they directly benefited".[110] In response to the second question, he argues that the market eventually turned inland (e.g., the Arabian trade). Thus, inland cities were established to exploit those markets. These conclusions appear plausible, but not probable in light of the immediacy with which the inhabitants of the Philistine cities began to manufacture Mycenaean wares locally.

What Can We Say About the Philistines' Origin?

Having examined the evidence relevant to identifying the origin of the Philistines, several conclusions may be drawn. First, much of the evidence, both textual and archaeological, appears to indicate an Aegean origin for the Philistines. The textual sources identify the Aegean region generally, or Crete specifically. The material culture in Palestine, from the locally made Mycenaean wares to the cultic architecture and objects, seems to support an Aegean origin. Finally, the evidence from Cyprus points to the Philistines temporarily residing on the island, finally reaching the shores of Palestine. However, some evidence does suggest that the Philistines were either an endogenous group from within Palestine, or a group of traders who eventually settled along the coast to establish a firm trade network. While the evidence cannot be considered conclusive, it seems likely that the Philistines began their journey from the Aegean region, moving to Palestine as refugees who would ultimately shape the course of history in the eastern Mediterranean.

In the end, we will likely discover (I suspect) that the solution is complex. As with Israelite formation, there may have been some who came from outside of Palestine, while the majority were Canaanites who established a new ethnicity. Something similar may be the case for the Philistines: although most came from the Aegean during the movement of the Sea Peoples, there may have been an endogenous population – however small – that joined to the new inhabitants. Whatever the case may be, one thing is clear: the biblical portrayal of the Philistines having inhabited the land of Canaan for many centuries as seen in the book of Genesis is not in line with archaeology. The Philistines arrived at the end of the Late Bronze Age, around 1200 B.C.E., and this is when they appear in the archaeological record.

Conclusion

How many times have you heard, "The more we dig up in the Middle East, the more we prove the Bible to be true" or "Archaeology has never produced a single find that was not in line with what the Bible says"? Nothing could be further from the truth. The early practice of "biblical" archaeologists – particularly in the 19th and 20th centuries – was very often predicated on a belief in the inerrancy or overall historical accuracy of the Old Testament. Henry Jones may have said it best: "You call THIS archaeology?"[111]

In this chapter, we looked at archaeological methods, examining a variety of excavation techniques and comparing them to see their strengths and weaknesses. The discussion then turned to stratigraphy: what it is, how it works, and how it can help archaeologists tell us about the site, the material culture, and what transpired throughout time. We looked at the various tools that archaeologists use in fieldwork and how important meticulous excavation and recordkeeping is to contemporary and future interpreters.

The next section dealt with "biblical archaeology". After overviewing a history of biblical archaeology and its development, we saw that the faith-based excavations and interpretations of the 19th and 20th centuries gave way to the archaeology of the late 20th century, which was no longer grounded in illuminating and/or proving the historical validity of the biblical texts, but in the scientific investigation of the region's archaeology. We then turned our attention to two oft-discussed people groups that appear in the Hebrew Bible: the Canaanites and the Philistines.

We hear a lot about the Canaanites in the Old Testament, primarily when it concerns how wicked and deplorable the inhabitants of Canaan were before the Israelites arrived and killed them or drove them out. To gain a clearer picture of who the Canaanites were, we looked at the historical background of the land of Canaan and the people that populated it. To test the validity or accuracy of the Old Testament with respect to the Canaanites, we used the practice of child sacrifice. We saw that the evidence we have for Canaanite culture from the 2nd millennium B.C.E. does not provide support for the picture painted by the Old Testament.

Furthermore, with respect to child sacrifice, the only convincing evidence that we have for the practice comes from the mid- to late-1st millennium B.C.E., long after the time depicted in the Hebrew Bible. Furthermore, the evidence does not come from Canaan, but from Carthage and the Punic colonies. In fact, we determined that, while child sacrifice was likely sporadically practiced in 1st millennium Canaan, it was also very likely sparingly *practiced by the Israelites, who sacrificed their children to Yahweh.* Thus, passages like Leviticus 18 and 20 cannot be considered historically reliable sources when reconstructing the practices of the period.

Finally, we looked at the origins of the Philistines, a people group that very likely came from the Aegean region at the end of the Late Bronze Age and settled along the coast, becoming a catalyst for the ethnic development of the early Israelites. We saw that the material culture from Philistine sites, including pottery, kilns, and cultic paraphernalia, all point to a group of foreigners who eventually settled in Canaan. This, however, contradicts the biblical account, which has the Philistines inhabiting the land of Canaan long before the Israelites arrive, as described in the book of Genesis.

In the end, we saw that the field of biblical archaeology went through a significant and necessary transition from the early 19th century until the late 20th century. Faith went from being a foundational motivator and interpretive lens to being an irrelevant and even problematic interpretive feature, as well as a recognized bias to be filtered out when practicing archaeology. How thankful we should all be that we have moved beyond archaeological methods that are predicated on faith, leaving Walter Donovan's famous challenge moot with respect to archaeology: "It's time to ask yourself what you *believe*".[112]

---

[1] Dever 2020: 6.
[2] Fagan & Durrani 2016. See also Grant, Gorin, & Fleming 2015 for another excellent introduction to archaeology and its methods.
[3] Bowen 2017: 19.
[4] Fagan & Durrani 2016: 156.
[5] Fagan & Durrani 2016: 157.
[6] Fagan & Durrani 2016: 162.
[7] Fagan & Durrani 2016: 165.
[8] Fagan & Durrani 2016: 166.
[9] Grant, Gorin, & Fleming 2015: 52-56.
[10] Grant, Gorin, & Fleming 2015: 52.
[11] Obviously, dating strata is vastly more complex than this, but I am simply trying to provide a general example for the reader.
[12] Grant, Gorin, & Fleming 2015: 53.
[13] Grant, Gorin, & Fleming 2015: 52.
[14] Fagan & Durrani 2016: 170.
[15] Fagan & Durrani 2016: 170.
[16] Fagan & Durrani 2016: 167.
[17] Fagan & Durrani 2016: 170.
[18] Davis 2004.
[19] Dever 2020: 1-10.
[20] Davis 2004: 4.
[21] Davis 2004: 4.
[22] Finkelstein & Silberman 2001: 34.
[23] Davis 2004: 10.
[24] Davis 2004: 13.
[25] Dever 2020: 1.
[26] Davis 2004: 27.
[27] Dever 2020: 1.
[28] Davis 2004: 47.
[29] Dever 2020: 3.
[30] Davis 2004: 85.
[31] Dever 2020: 4.
[32] Dever 2020: 3.

[33] Finkelstein & Silberman 2001: 21.
[34] Dever 2020: 3.
[35] Finkelstein & Silberman 2001: 19-21.
[36] Tigay 1996: 189.
[37] Buck 2019.
[38] Buck 2019: 3.
[39] Buck 2019: 5.
[40] Buck 2019: 13.
[41] Buck 2019: 16.
[42] Buck 2019: 17.
[43] Buck 2019: 17.
[44] Buck 2019: 21-22.
[45] Buck 2019: 32.
[46] Buck 2019: 57.
[47] Buck 2019: 57.
[48] Dewrell 2017 and Stavrakopoulou 2004.
[49] I put "conquest" in quotes, as there was no conquest of the land of Palestine by the Israelites. We will discuss this issue in volume II.
[50] Dewrell 2017: 14, translating *RES* 339 (=Costa 93).
[51] Dewrell 2017: 16.
[52] Dewrell 2017: 37-71.
[53] Dewrell 2017: 45.
[54] Dewrell 2017: 68-69.
[55] Dewrell 2017: 144.
[56] Dewrell 2017: 145.
[57] Dewrell 2017: 146.
[58] Finkelstein & Silberman 2001: 37.
[59] For a recent detailed examination of the evidence for the Philistines and the Sea Peoples in general, see Killebrew 2013.
[60] See Rendsburg 1987: 89-96 for a detailed argument concerning the relationship between Casluhim and Caphtor.
[61] Rendsburg 1987: 90 fn.3.
[62] Rahlfs 1979: 511.
[63] Strange 1980. Strange argues that Caphtor should be associated with Cyprus, not Crete. For a thorough critique of his arguments, see Knapp 1985: 231-250. Note that, whether Caphtor is to be equated with Crete or Cyprus, the biblical text argues for a population that is intrusive, not endogenous.
[64] Dothan & Dothan 1992: 26.
[65] Dothan & Dothan 1992: 26.
[66] Gertzen 2008: 90.
[67] Gertzen 2008: 90.
[68] Dothan & Dothan 1992: 27-28.
[69] Demsky, Maier, Wimmer, & Zukerman 2008: 47.
[70] Demsky, Maier, Wimmer, & Zukerman 2008: 57-59. Though the authors "strongly caution against" it, one of the names ('alwt) may be connected with the proper name "Goliath" of Gath.

[71] Demsky, Maier, Wimmer, & Zukerman 2008: 62.

[72] Killebrew 2013: 119.

[73] Dothan 1990: 26.

[74] Dothan & Zukerman 2004: 43.

[75] Dothan 1990: 26.

[76] Dothan, Gitin, Gunneweg, & Perlman 1986: 15. "Myc.IIIC:1b pottery at Miqne was locally manufactured and the calcareous Myc.IIIC:1b wares from Ashdod may have come from Miqne".

[77] Connan, Imbus, Macko, Nissenbum, & Zumberge 2006: 1785.

[78] Killebrew 1998: 401.

[79] Dothan 1990: 26.

[80] Dothan 1990: 28.

[81] Mazar 1985: 106.

[82] Dothan 1990: 28-29.

[83] Dothan 1990: 33.

[84] Dothan 2002: 3.

[85] Dothan 1990: 30.

[86] Dothan 1990: 30.

[87] Dothan 1990: 30.

[88] Dothan 2002: 11.

[89] Dothan 2002: 14.

[90] Dothan 2002: 20-22.

[91] Mazar 1992: 320-321.

[92] Dothan 1990: 27.

[93] Mazar 1992: 323.

[94] Shai, Ilan, & Kletter 2009: 162.

[95] Shai, Ilan, & Kletter 2009: 164.

[96] Shai, Ilan, & Kletter 2009: 164.

[97] Karageorghis 1984: 16-28.

[98] Karageorghis 1984: 23.

[99] Karageorghis 1984: 27.

[100] Karageorghis 1984: 27.

[101] Karageorghis 1984: 28.

[102] Bunimovitz 1990: 210-223.

[103] Bunimovitz 1990: 211-212.

[104] Bunimovitz 1990: 212.

[105] Bunimovitz 1990: 214.

[106] Bunimovitz 1990: 215.

[107] Bauer 1998: 149-168.

[108] Bauer 1998: 159.

[109] Bauer 1998: 151.

[110] Bauer 1998: 160.

[111] From Indiana Jones and the Last Crusade.

[112] From Indiana Jones and the Last Crusade.

CHAPTER FOUR
Did Moses Write the Torah?
Contradictions in the Pentateuch

Introduction

Atheists will often question Christian apologists on why they consider the Bible to be the inspired Word of God. Some of their answers include fulfilled prophecy, impossible-to-know scientific predictions, and archaeological evidence. However, just as frequently you may hear something like this: "The Bible was written by multiple authors over more than a thousand years... and there are absolutely NO contradictions in it!" Of course, the skeptic will usually identify some of the contradictions or inconsistencies that appear in the first five books of the Old Testament (the Torah or Pentateuch). Sometimes they point out that there seem to be two different creation stories. If this doesn't resonate with the apologist, the atheist will move on through the biblical narrative, pointing out the contradictions in the story of the worldwide flood. You might even find the discussion turning to the multiple times that the patriarchs decided to lie about their wives being their sisters (although this is not strictly a contradiction in the story). In the end, however, the apologist is usually not only unconvinced, but put on the defensive:

> "The attack on the Mosaic authorship of the Pentateuch is nothing less than an attack on the veracity, reliability, and authority of the Word of Almighty God".[1]

Why does pointing out the presence of contradictions in the Pentateuch create such a problem for so many Christian apologists and fundamentalists? Much of the tension centers on the apparent claims in the Bible that the Torah was written by Moses. How could Moses, writing under the divine inspiration of the Holy Spirit, write stories that have contradictions in them? The atheist will argue that Moses (if he even existed) certainly did not write the Torah; rather, the Pentateuch was written hundreds of years after the events it proports to represent. In other words, when Mosaic authorship is challenged by skeptics or biblical scholars in the field, it can be seen as a direct attack on a core Christian doctrine.

Although a non-Mosaic authorship can be a contentious subject for many Christian apologists, it is a position that represents mainstream consensus scholarship among those in the field of biblical studies. What is it, therefore, that caused scholars to reject the Mosaic authorship of the Pentateuch from very early on, and later to reject single authorship as well? Put simply, *it is because of the contradictions and inconsistencies that appear in its canonical (or final) form*. The purpose of this chapter will be to provide a general overview of the problems that we see in the narrative of the Pentateuch, along with a more detailed analysis of several of these contradictions and inconsistencies.

Specifically, we will examine the contradictions that appear in three major sections of Genesis: the two creation accounts in Genesis 1:1-2:4a and 2:4b-25; the flood story in Genesis 6-9; and the story of Joseph in Genesis 37. We will then turn to smaller but still significant issues, including the (re)naming stories of Bethel, the name(s) of Moses's father-in-law, and the inconsistencies between the laws concerning slaves in

Exodus 21, Deuteronomy 15, and Leviticus 25. Although this will cover only a fraction of the contradictions in the Pentateuch (or in the Old Testament as a whole), they will provide the reader with several solid examples upon which to draw during a debate or discussion.

Before we begin, it is important to note that Pentateuchal studies is an entire field of expertise. While I have a fairly extensive background in Hebrew Bible and Semitic languages, I am by no means a specialist in Pentateuchal studies.[2] There are at least two primary theories that specialists in this field hold to that explain the way(s) in which the Pentateuch found its final form. However, the goal of this chapter will not be to argue for a particular approach. The debate is too complex to adequately cover in a general volume such as this. While this section provides a number of reputable, scholarly resources in the bibliography for the reader who is interested in delving into this debate, the intention here will be to demonstrate the difficulties associated with a single Mosaic authorship of the Pentateuch. This will be accomplished by analyzing several of these contradictions in detail, making it clear that they are genuine literary problems in the text that cannot be easily swept away by the apologist. This will arm the reader with the information they need to understand why scholars in the field argue for different theories of multiple authorship of the Pentateuch, along with the literary and linguistic evidence necessary to support their claim.

Perhaps the most effective way to approach this topic is to give a brief chronological overview of the various ways in which the authorship of the Pentateuch has been understood, including Mosaic authorship. Following this, we will look in some detail at several of the textual problems associated with viewing the Pentateuch as the product of a single author.

A Brief History of Scholarship

There are several excellent introductions to the issues surrounding the formation of the Pentateuch. A thorough review of scholarly opinions can be found in Dozeman's *The Pentateuch: Introducing the Torah* and Blenkinsopp's *The Pentateuch: An Introduction to the First Five Books of the Bible*.[3] A fairly brief presentation can be found in John Collins's book *Introduction to the Hebrew Bible*.[4] Dozeman, Blenkinsopp, and Collins all present the general progression of thought concerning the authorship of the Pentateuch since the end of the 1st millennium B.C.E.

One of the primary questions that drives this investigation is, "To whom should we attribute the writing of the Pentateuch?" Early on, tradition attributed its authorship to Moses, the ideal lawgiver and prophet. However, as time progressed, doubts about a single Mosaic authorship grew, until the notion was done away with during the Enlightenment.

There are several early texts that people use to support their claim of Mosaic authorship; some of these can be found in the Hebrew Bible. Outside of the numerous references in the Pentateuch to Moses and the giving of the law – including several in the book of Deuteronomy (1:1, 4:44, 31:24, 32:45) – Collins notes that Leviticus and/or Deuteronomy are called the "law of Moses" in a variety of OT passages (Joshua 8:31-32; 23:6; 1 Kings 2:3; 14:6; 23:5; Nehemiah 8:1, 13-18).[5] Coming from the later Hellenistic period, around 180 B.C.E., Collins cites the writings of Ben Sira: "All this is in the book of the covenant of the Most High God, the law that Moses commanded us" (Ben Sira 24:23).[6] He notes that similar associations are made in the literature of Second Temple Judaism, as well as in the New Testament. He concludes:

> "It seems that this tradition had its origin in the book of Deuteronomy and was gradually extended until Moses was regarded not only as the mediator of the laws but as the author of the whole Pentateuch, although there is no basis for this claim in Genesis or in the narrative portions of Exodus".[7]

Of course, none of these texts actually require that one should conclude that Moses wrote the Torah.

New Testament texts are frequently cited in support of Mosaic authorship, including passages like Mark 12:19: "Teacher, Moses wrote to us that, if someone's brother were to die and leaves a wife but does not leave a child, his brother should take his wife and raise up a descendant to his brother" (see also Mark 12:26). These, and other similar passages, seem to indicate that, during this period, it was understood that at least large sections of the Pentateuch were associated with and likely written down by Moses, particularly the legal portions.

However, problems with this interpretation developed as time went by. In the 12th century, Abraham Ibn Ezra, in his commentary on the Torah, cited verses like Genesis 12:6 – "And Abram crossed over through the land to the site of Shechem, to the oak of Moreh. *Now the Canaanites were then in the land*" (emphasis mine). This verse led to the question, "Why would the writer say that the Canaanites *were then* in the land?" If you remember from chapter one in this volume, Moses led the Israelites out of the land of Egypt and through the wilderness for 40 years. At the end of that period, Moses died, and Joshua was set to enter the land of Canaan – where the Canaanites were – in order to conquer it. Clearly, if Moses had written the Pentateuch – which ends with Joshua *getting ready to enter the land to defeat the Canaanites* – then the Canaanites *must have still been alive and in the land* when he wrote. However, in Genesis 12:6, from the perspective of the writer, *the Canaanites were no longer in the land*; thus, this appears to have been written much later. The same is true with Genesis 36:31 – "Now these are the kings that ruled in the land of Edom *before a king ruled over the children of Israel*" (emphasis mine).[8] Again, the writer seems to indicate that he is writing long after these events. He is saying, "There are kings in Israel *now*, but there were not kings in Israel *then*".

In the 18th century, Jean Astruc saw that the narrative inconsistencies that appeared in the Pentateuch corresponded to the different names for God that appeared in the text, concluding that there were different documents or "sources" that were used to form the Pentateuch. Several scholars during the 18th and 19th centuries discussed these sources, focusing on passages that utilized the divine name Elohim and those that use Jehovah (Yahweh). Although the theory had been in circulation for many years, the scholar who is most often attributed with popularizing it for a wider audience was Julius Wellhausen in the late 19th century. He argued that there are four sources that can be seen in the Pentateuch: JEDP – Yahwistic (J), Elohistic (E), Deuteronomistic (D), and Priestly (P). This was known as the Documentary Hypothesis.[9]

An immense amount of research and debate followed from these early insights into the Pentateuch's authorship, but they are not our focus here. What is important to remember moving forward is that scholars have not come to the Pentateuch and arbitrarily concluded that one person could not have penned the entire (or even the majority of) the text. Instead, it was the result of approaching the stories of the Pentateuch and being confronted with the literary problems that are present throughout the narrative. It is to some of these inconsistencies that we will now turn.

What's the Problem? Contradictions and Inconsistencies

Why is it that people have an issue with attributing a single author to the first five books of the Old Testament? Is it because of religious or atheistic presuppositions? Do scholars simply believe that Moses could not have written it because he didn't exist, leading them to posit arbitrary theories to explain how it could have been composed? Although the way I formed these questions betrays my opinion on the matter, I will say that I have yet to meet a Hebrew Bible scholar who appears to be motivated in any way by some religious conviction against Mosaic authorship. Of course, I cannot read people's minds; however, there is an overwhelming abundance of evidence to support multiple authorship of the Pentateuch – evidence that cannot simply be ignored. Even if certain scholars are in fact motivated by a personal religious or atheistic bias (again, I have yet to see this), ridding oneself of this theoretical bias would in no way do away with the data that causes us to question earlier tradition.

Those who argue for a single Mosaic authorship will likely address each contradiction or inconsistency that is raised in this chapter individually in an attempt to find some way to reconcile these differences. This is necessary if one holds to a particular belief that the biblical texts are without error and that God has preserved his divinely inspired word in such a way that we now possess it today. If the Pentateuch (and the Bible as a whole) *is* the divinely inspired, inerrant word of God, and Moses *did* author these first five books, then these types of contradictions pose great difficulty for the interpreter. Thus, a great deal of effort has been (and will continue to be) expended in an attempt to reconcile these passages to one another.

While some of these explanations could potentially address a few of the problematic passages, the sheer number of contradictions and general inconsistencies strongly suggests that we should seek a model that more adequately accounts for the data. Unfortunately, it is often true that, short of providing a deductive proof (or the like), Christian apologists and fundamentalists will cling to *the mere possibility* of textual cohesion, despite any mountain of evidence to the contrary. In other words, if you begin with the conclusion that the text is inerrant, then providing a possible reconciliation (however unlikely) will often be sufficient for the apologist to maintain their position. In light of this, you should not expect to find in this chapter definitive proofs of contradictions; instead, we will seek to build a case that is supported by the data and held by scholars in the field. In short, there are so many contradictions and inconsistencies in the Pentateuch that it is very difficult to adequately defend a single Mosaic authorship. We must look to other models to make sense of the data.

Finally, there are many topics that are covered in this book that are agreed upon by the consensus of biblical scholars – both "liberal" and "conservative" alike. For example, there is little to no dissent concerning the prophecy of Ezekiel 26, in that everyone agrees that

Nebuchadnezzar was prophesied to destroy Tyre, yet failed to do so. The same is true on the issue of slavery; the consensus agrees that debt- and chattel-slavery were endorsed in the legal sections of the Hebrew Bible. However, issues in the Pentateuch – particularly those in the early chapters of Genesis – cause a much greater divide. However, the scholars that generally argue for unity or continuity in the text are those that come to the text with a particular theological conclusion. Therefore, you should expect to see more disagreement when it comes to passages like the creation and flood stories, particularly among biblical scholars who have particular theological commitments.

"Creating" Problems: Genesis 1 & 2

If someone begins to read the Old Testament for the first time, it probably won't take them long to realize that Genesis 1:1-2:4a sounds quite different from Genesis 2:4b-25. If they are paying close attention to the narrative, chapter two seems to tell the story of creation for a second time. Collins writes, "Whatever the origin of the Adam and Eve story, it stands in sharp contrast to the Priestly account of creation that now forms the opening chapter of the Bible". [10] Not only does the sequence of events differ from the first account to the second, but the writing style is quite distinct. In this section, however, we will only focus on the order of events as described in the two accounts, identifying and explaining how they differ from and are contradictory to one another.

Let's begin with Genesis 1. If we go through the chapter, we see the following order in the events of creation:

Day 1: Light

"And God said, 'Let there be light'. And there was light. And God saw that the light was good. And God divided between the light and the darkness. And God called the light 'Day' and the darkness he called 'Night'" (Genesis 1:3-5a).

Day 2: The Vault (Sky)

"And God made the vault and he divided between the waters that are under the vault and the waters that are above the vault, and it was so" (Genesis 1:7).

Day 3: Dry Land, Seas, and Vegetation

"And God said, 'Let the waters be gathered together under the heavens to one place, and let the dry land appear', and it was so. And God called the dry land 'Earth', and the accumulation of the waters he called 'Seas'. And God saw that it was good. And God said, 'Let the earth sprout vegetation, plants producing seed, fruit trees producing fruit according to its species, whose seed is in it, upon the earth', and it was so" (Genesis 1:9-11).

Day 4: Sun, Moon, and Stars

"And God made the two great lights (the great light to rule the day and the small light to rule the night) and the stars" (Genesis 1:16).

Day 5: Sea Creatures and Birds

"And God said, 'Let the waters teem with swarms of living creatures, and let birds fly over the earth over the surface of the vault of the heavens'" (Genesis 1:20).

Day 6: Land Creatures and Mankind

"And God said, 'Let the earth bring forth living creatures according to their species, beast and creeping animals, and animals of the earth according to their species', and it was so . . . And God said, 'Let us make mankind in our image according to our likeness and let them rule over the fish of the sea and the birds of the heavens and the beasts and all the earth and all the creeping things that creep upon the earth'. And God created humanity in his image, in the likeness of God he created them, male and female he created them" (Genesis 1:24, 26-27).

The narrative in Genesis 2 is not as literarily structured as Genesis 1; nevertheless, we can determine the sequence in which God created and organized:

Event 1: Man Created

"Then Yahweh God formed the man with dust from the ground, and he blew into his nostrils the breath of life, and the man became a living creature" (Genesis 2:7).

Event 2: God Plants a Garden

"And Yahweh God planted a garden in Eden in the east, and he set the man there, whom he had formed" (Genesis 2:8).

Event 3: God Causes Vegetation to Grow

"And Yahweh God caused every tree that is pleasing to the eye and good for food to sprout from the ground, along with the tree of life in the midst of the garden and the tree of the knowledge of good and evil" (Genesis 2:9).

Event 4: God Puts Man in the Garden to Work It

"And Yahweh God took the man and settled him in the Garden of Eden to work and tend it" (Genesis 2:15).

Event 5: God Creates the Animals

"And Yahweh God formed from the ground every animal of the field and every bird of the heavens, and he brought them to the man to see what he would name them, and everything that the man named each living animal, that was its name" (Genesis 2:19).

Event 6: God Creates Woman

"And Yahweh God made a woman from the rib that he took from the man, and he brought her to the man" (Genesis 2:22).

When you view both sets of creative and organizing events, you quickly see that they appear rather contradictory with respect to their order. If we set them side-by-side we see:

Genesis 1	Genesis 2
Light	Man
Sky	Garden
Dry land, seas, vegetation	Vegetation
Sun, moon, stars	Man placed in garden
Creatures and birds	Animals
Land creatures and mankind	Woman

Table 2. Table showing the order of events in Genesis 1 and Genesis 2.

While we will not point out every discrepancy between these two accounts in their canonical forms, let's highlight a few. For example, when was man created? In Genesis 1:26-27, God creates humanity on the sixth day (the end of the creation period). Furthermore, he creates man and woman at the same time: "And God created humanity in his image, in the image of God he created them, male and female he created them". But what do we see in Genesis 2? Man is God's *first* creation in Genesis 2:7: "And Yahweh God formed the man with dust from the ground, and he blew into his nostrils the breath of life, and the man became a living creature". In contrast, woman is his *final* creation after the garden, vegetation, and animals.

And where was humanity supposed to live? In Genesis 1:28-29 we see God's command:

"And God blessed them and God said to them, 'Be fruitful and multiply and fill the earth and subdue it and rule over every fish of the sea and over every bird of the heavens and over every living thing that creeps upon the ground'. And God said, 'Look, I have given you every plant-bearing seed that is upon the surface of the earth, and every tree that has seed-bearing fruit in it is yours for food'".

So God commands humanity to "fill the earth" and to "rule over" all the animals that were created.

In contrast, we read in Genesis 2:15-17:

"And Yahweh God took the man and settled him in the Garden of Eden to tend and guard it. And Yahweh God commanded the man saying, 'From every tree of the garden you may certainly eat, but from the tree of the knowledge of good and evil you must not eat'".

We see that the man and woman do in fact remain in the garden until they are driven out as a result of their disobedience (Genesis 3:23). It seems as though the story in Genesis 1 commands them to go into all the world, while they are expected to remain in the garden in Genesis 2.

With regards to animals and birds, in Genesis 1 we see that birds were created before the land animals, which were created before mankind. In Genesis 1:20 we read, "And God said, 'Let the waters teem with swarms of living creatures, and let birds fly over the earth over the surface of the vault of the heavens'". We then see:

"And God said, 'Let the earth bring forth living creatures according to their species, beasts and creeping things and animals of the earth after their species', and it was so. And God made the animals of the earth according to their species, and the beasts according to their species, and every creeping thing of the ground according to their species, and God saw that it was good" (Genesis 1:24-25).

This all took place on day six, *before* humanity had been created. However, in Genesis 2:19 we read:

"And Yahweh God formed from the ground every animal of the field and every bird of the heavens and he brought them to the man to see what he would call them, and everything that the man called each living creature, that was its name".

Clearly, in Genesis 1, the birds and land animals are created *before* mankind, while in Genesis 2, they are created specifically to try and fill a particular role for the man.

Again, there are many other problems that could be discussed between these two accounts, but these will suffice. It is interesting to see how some scholars have attempted to reconcile these contradictory accounts. For example, Victor Hamilton argues that the creation of animals in Genesis 2 is not the *first* creation of animals, but the creation of a specific group for Adam to name that occurs *after* the creation of animals in Genesis 1:24-25.[11] Of course, this seems to fly in the face of the natural reading of the verse:

"And Yahweh God formed from the ground *every animal* of the field and *every bird* of the heavens, and he brought them to the man to see what he would name them, and everything that the man named each living animal, that was its name" (Genesis 2:19, emphasis mine).

In short, there appear to be contradictions between the account of creation given in Genesis 1:1-2:4a and what we see in Genesis 2:4b-25. We have focused on the contradictions and inconsistencies in the sequence of events that are given in the creation accounts, although that is but the tip of the iceberg. However, our goal here is only to provide a specific contradiction that can be supported by the data and easily demonstrated.

"Flooded" with Contradictions: Genesis 6-9

The story of the flood is a contentious one, for any number of reasons. Some apologists will argue for the historical veracity of the flood, while others will focus on justifying the worldwide genocide that is committed by the deity. In this section, however, our only concern is the narrative consistency of the story.

David Carr lists 16 "doubled elements" that appear in the flood story alone, including things like God's decision to destroy humanity (6:7 & 6:13), his announcement of the coming of the flood (6:13 & 7:4), the command to bring animals on the ark (6:19-20 & 7:2-3), and the drying of the ground (8:13b & 8:14b).[12] While there are clearly many examples in this story of these doublets and contradictions, we will focus only on two: *the number of animals that Noah was commanded to bring on the ark* and *the duration of the flood.*

Let's begin with the number of animals that were to be brought on the ark. In Genesis 6:19-20 we read:

> "'And from every living thing from all flesh, you are to bring two of each to the ark to keep alive with you; they will be male and female. From the birds according to their species, and from the animals according to their species, and from every creeping thing of the ground according to their species, two of each will come to you to be kept alive'" (Genesis 6:19-20).

Seems fairly straightforward: bring two of every species of animal, male and female.

However, four verses later we read:

> "'From every clean animal you will take to yourself seven pairs, a male and its mate, and from the animals that are not clean, a pair, a male and its mate. Also from the birds of heaven seven pairs, male and female, to keep the seed alive upon the surface of the earth'" (Genesis 7:2-3).

Here the command is different; rather than two of every animal, Noah is to take seven pairs of clean animals and birds, and one pair of those that are not clean.

What we have, therefore, is a first set of commands ordering Noah to take two of every species of animal, while the second set instructs him instead to take seven pairs of clean animals and seven pairs of birds, and one pair of all the "not clean" animals. What are we to make of all of this? Again, there is a multitude of data that could be brought to bear concerning the narrative of the flood story. Our only point here is to identify if there is in fact a narrative problem that is likely a contradiction in the story.

As with the creation story, there are many proposed solutions to this issue. For example, it is argued by some that Genesis 6:19-20 represents the number of animals needed to repopulate the earth, while the animals in Genesis 7:2-3 is that number *plus* additional animals required for sacrifice after the Flood.[13] Another argument is that the Hebrew word for "two" used in Genesis 6:19-20 ("*shenayim*") is simply a collective term for "pairs" of animals – Noah is being instructed to bring in seven pairs of clean, and one pair of unclean, animals.[14] In other words, God first gives him the general instruction: "You are going to bring pairs of animals on the ark". Later, God specifies, "Now, I want you to bring *seven* pairs of clean animals and birds, but only *one* pair of each animal that is not clean".

What is the most reasonable solution? For someone with a theological presupposition about the unity, inspiration, and inerrancy of the text, any of the proposed solutions – if possible – will suffice, allowing for there to be no strict "proof" of a contradiction. Many popular commentaries carry these types of reconciliations. Waltke, for example, writes, "In typical Semitic style, the summary injunction to take pairs of animals into the ark is now developed by the more specific injunction to take seven pairs of clean animals".[15] Similarly, Wenham explains, "According to 6:19-20, pairs of all kinds of creatures would come to the ark to preserve life on earth. Here Noah is told specifically to admit additional clean land animals, seven pairs of each, and seven pairs of birds".[16] These are just two examples among many.

The other apparent literary contradiction in this passage is the length of the flood itself. We have two durations that are repeated throughout the story: 40 days and 40 nights (Genesis 7:4, 12, 17) and 150 days (Genesis 7:24; 8:3). Which is it? Again, as we will see, there are several attempts at reconciling these disparate numbers by Christian apologists. The question is, are they reasonable? More reasonable than other readings of the text?

So, how long did the flood last? Was it 40 or 150 days? Hamilton sees these two numbers as two parts of the overall duration of the flood, that is, 190 days overall.[17] Does this hold up under closer scrutiny?

In Genesis 8:6-7, we read "And at the end of the *forty days* Noah opened the window of the ark which he had made, and he sent out the raven, and it went out going back and forth until the waters dried up upon the earth". There seem to be two options for when during the flood period these "40 days" are to be placed. If we are to conclude that these are the same 40 days that it rained upon the earth, and the remaining 110 days were spent floating on the waters at their ultimate height, then Genesis 8:6-7 strains credulity. We would have to assume that the rain stopped, but the waters continued to "increase greatly" for the remainder of the 150 days. It would have been during this tumultuous movement of the ark, which was being swept about by the increasing flood, that Noah would decide to open the window of the ark and send out the raven to find dry land. This seems quite unlikely.

The other option might be to assume that Noah, following the 150 days of the flood – when the ark came to rest on the mountains of Ararat (Genesis 8:4) – waited not only more than two months (when the tops of the mountains became visible), but an additional 40 days before opening the hatch. This seems to be the intent of the canonical version of the story. However, several questions immediately jump out at the reader. How is the ark coming to rest in the mountains of Ararat, but the tops of the mountains are not able to be seen for a further 2+ months? Hamilton writes:

> "I see no credible way of harmonizing the information of v. 5 with v. 4. V. 4 clearly states that the ark rested on one of the mountains of Ararat in the 17th day of the 7th month. Yet v. 5 states that no mountaintop was spotted until the first day of the 10th month".[18]

A more plausible way to understand these passages is to see two narrative traditions. Collins identifies two different versions of the story (J and P) within the text in his *Introduction to the Hebrew Bible and Deutero-Canonical Books*, laying them out so the reader can see how they could be understood to fit together:

> "J: And Yahweh shut him in. [17]The Flood continued forty days on the earth.
>
> P: and the waters increased and raised the ark so that it rose above the earth . . . [22]All in whose nostrils was the merest breath of life, all that was on dry land, died.
>
> J: [23]All existence on the earth was blotted out – man, cattle, creeping things, and birds of the sky; they were blotted out from the earth. Only Noah was left, and those with him in the ark.

P: And when the waters had swelled on the earth one hundred and fifty days, [1]God remembered Noah and all the beasts and all the cattle that were with him in the ark, and God caused a wind to blow across the earth, and the waters subsided. [2]The fountains of the deep and the floodgates of the sky were stopped up.

J: and the rain from the sky was held back; [3]the waters then receded steadily from the earth.

P: At the end of the one hundred and fifty days the waters diminished, [4]so that in the seventh month, on the seventeenth day of the month, the ark came to rest on the mountains of Ararat. [5]The waters went on diminishing until the tenth month; in the tenth month, on the first of the month, the tops of the mountains became visible.

J: [6]At the end of the forty days, Noah opened the window of the ark that he had made".[19]

Notice how, when the narrative is separated in this way, there is continuity between both stories. For example, if you combine the section of the "J" story above, you get:

"And Yahweh shut him in. The Flood continued forty days on the earth. All existence on the earth was blotted out – man, cattle, creeping things, and birds of the sky; they were blotted out from the earth. Only Noah was left, and those with him in the ark. And the rain from the sky was held back; the waters then receded steadily from the earth. At the end of the forty days, Noah opened the window of the ark that he had made".[20]

In this reconstruction, there is no need to reconcile the apparent contradiction with respect to the duration of the flood. The 40 days (and 40 nights) of the flood would not be part of the 150 days, nor would it be time that would follow the 150 days: it would simply be part of another tradition. Dozeman writes concerning the former tradition (the one with the 40 days): "The flood is a rainstorm that lasts for 40 days (7:4), before a wind dries the water (8:2b-3a). Noah investigates the aftermath through a window in the ark".[21]

Concerning the latter version:

> "The waters of the flood are not rain; the flood is caused when the waters of heaven (*mabul*), held back by the firmament on the second day of creation (1:6-8), and the pre-creation chaotic waters of the deep (1:2) break out upon the earth. These waters undo the structure of creation, rising 15 cubits above the highest mountain (7:20) for 150 days (7:24)".[22]

The same is true for the first contradiction: the number of animals that Noah was to take on the ark. If you examine the story closely, you can see that two versions appear in the canonical text; each is consistent on its own. The versions, however, have been brought together in such a way to form a broadly understandable canonical form. Grossman summarizes this point:

"These chapters do contain a double description of the Flood narrative, continuing the double creation accounts of the first two chapters of Genesis. Unlike the creation narratives, however, these threads, each colored with their own emphases and objectives, are woven into a single, cohesive, harmonious account; their narrative components are interdependent, each providing a part of the whole picture".[23]

While the cohesive nature of the text is debatable, Grossman's point still stands. The narrative is understandable, but clearly displays inconsistencies and contradictions in its details.

Where Did You Go (and How Did You Get There)? Joseph in Genesis 37

Another narrative in Genesis that is generally understandable but lacks continuity in the details is the story of Joseph in Genesis 37.[24] If you recall, Joseph was his father's favorite son, a fact that did not go unnoticed by his brothers. In Genesis 37, his brothers capture him with the intention of killing him, but reconsider and sell him into slavery instead. Joseph ends up in Egypt, sold as a slave to a man named Potiphar. The question is, *how exactly did Joseph get there*? Let's take a look at the relevant sections of the chapter to see the problem.

"And each one said to the other, 'Here comes that dreamer. Come on, let's kill him and throw him into one of the pits, and we will say that a wild animal ate him. Then we will see what will become of his dreams!'" (Genesis 37:19-20).

So far so good. Joseph had angered his brothers earlier in the chapter, telling everyone in his family about dreams that he was having in which he ended up ruling over them all. His brothers then plan to kill him and get rid of his body, throwing it into one of the nearby pits.

> "But Reuben heard and rescued him from their hands. He said, 'Let's not murder him'. And Reuben said to them, 'Do not shed blood. Throw him into this pit that is in the desert, but do not stretch out your hand against him'. (He did this) to rescue him from their hands and to return him to his father" (Genesis 37:21-23).

Reuben to the rescue! Hearing of their plot, Reuben convinces his brothers not to murder Joseph, but instead to throw him into one of the pits in the desert and leave him for dead. Reuben's plan was to later return, pull him out, and take him back home safely. Although the repetition of Reuben's suggestion should give us pause, let's give the narrative the benefit of the doubt and say that, in general, it makes sense so far.

> "And when Joseph came to his brothers, they stripped Joseph of his tunic (the decorated tunic that was on him), and they took him and cast him into the pit (and the pit was empty; there was no water in it). And they sat down to eat a meal. And they lifted up their eyes and looked, and there was a caravan of Ishmaelites coming from Gilead, and their camels were carrying ladanum resin, balsam, and mastic, heading down to Egypt" (Genesis 37:23-25).

Okay, Joseph arrives at his brothers' location, but the welcoming party strips him of his special coat and throws him into an empty pit (to die). They then sit down to get a bite to eat, but notice a caravan of Ishmaelites passing by on their way down to Egypt...

> "Then Judah said to his brothers, 'What will be the profit if we kill our brother and cover up his blood? Come on! Let's sell him to the Ishmaelites! Let's not set our hands against him, for he is our brother and our flesh'. And his brothers agreed" (Genesis 37:27).

Okay, new plan. Judah compels his brothers to sell Joseph to this passing caravan of Ishmaelites instead of murdering him. I mean, come on... he *is* their brother. Plus, they'll even turn a profit! But now the story gets a little more complicated.

> "And Midianite merchant men were passing by, and they pulled Joseph up out of the pit, and they sold Joseph to the Ishmaelites for 20 shekels of silver, and they brought Joseph to Egypt" (Genesis 37:28).

Hmm. So, the brothers are eating, they see the Ishmaelites, and they decide to sell Joseph... but a group of Midianites comes along and pulls Joseph out of the pit and sells him to the Ishmaelites before the brothers can get back, apparently. Oh, it gets more complicated.

> "And Reuben returned to the pit, but Joseph was not there! And he tore his clothes. Then he returned to his brothers and said, 'He is not there! And I... where will I go?!'" (Genesis 37:30).

So Reuben returns to the pit. This probably seems a little strange to the reader, as earlier Reuben's plan was to throw Joseph in the pit so that he could later return and rescue him. What was his plan here? According to the story, we would expect one of the brothers to go and pull Joseph out of the pit in order to sell him. Would Reuben have hoped to reach Joseph first, pull him out, and rush him away before his brothers could sell him off? It is possible, I suppose, that Reuben volunteered to go and fetch Joseph so that they could sell him to the Ishmaelites, all the while planning some great escape for him (that the text doesn't tell us about). But it's not actually a contradiction at this point... it's just a little weird.

The following verses (Genesis 37:31-35) describe the brother's response: they take Joseph's tunic, dip it in goat blood, and take it back to their father, who assumes Joseph has been killed by a wild animal and mourns his loss. We then read:

> "And the Midianites sold him to Egypt, to Potiphar, the official of Pharaoh, the head of the guards" (Genesis 37:36).

Wait... what? I thought the Midianites happened upon Joseph in a pit in the desert and sold him to the Ishmaelite merchant caravan? Now the story has the Midianites selling Joseph *to Egypt*, directly to Potiphar, as a slave? What gives? But the fun doesn't stop there. In Genesis 39:1, we see the following background information:

> "Now Joseph had been brought down to Egypt, where Potiphar . . . had purchased him *from the Ishmaelites who brought him down there*" (Genesis 39:1).

In short, the question is: "How did Joseph get to Egypt?" Was he sold into slavery by Ishmaelites, Midianites… both? In verses 25-27, the brothers agree to sell him to Ishmaelites. But in verse 28, Midianite traders come by and pull Joseph up out of the pit. So who sells him to the Ishmaelites? *Is* he sold to the Ishmaelites? The NIV translates verse 28:

> "So when the Midianite merchants came by, *his brothers* pulled Joseph up out of the cistern and sold him for twenty shekels of silver to the Ishmaelites, who took him to Egypt" (Genesis 37:28, emphasis mine).

However, the Hebrew makes no mention of the brothers; it says:

> "And Midianite men who were merchants passed by and *they* pulled and lifted up Joseph from the pit, and *they* sold Joseph to the Ishmaelites..." (Genesis 37:28, emphasis mine).[25]

We would expect the "they" here to refer to the *Midianites*, not the brothers. If this were not complicated enough, in verse 36, we learn that the Midianites sold Joseph to Potiphar in Egypt, but in Genesis 39:1, we see that it was the *Ishmaelites* who had sold Joseph there! What are we to make of all of this?

Ska summarizes the issue (although it is probably already quite clear to you):

> "We encounter the main difficulty of the narrative of Genesis 37 in vv. 28 and 36 (cf. 39:1). We do not know exactly how Joseph was sold. Indeed, many readings of the

passage are possible: Joseph could have been sold to the Ishmaelites by his brothers, or kidnapped by the Midianites who then sold him to the Ishmaelites, or abducted by Midianites who sold him to Potiphar in Egypt".[26]

The problem, of course, is that *all of these options can't be true*, and it is hard to make them fit with one another... although many have tried over the centuries.[27]

Early interpretations involve simply deleting either one or both groups (Midianites or Ishmaelites) from the story. For example, in the book of Jubilees we read:

> "During the seventh year of this week he sent Joseph from his house to the land of Shechem to find out about his brothers' welfare. He found them in the land of Dothan. They acted in a treacherous way and made a plan against him to kill him; but, after changing their minds, they sold him to a traveling band of Ishmaelites. They brought him down to Egypt and sold him to Potiphar, Pharaoh's eunuch, the chief cook, and the priest of the city of Elew" (Jubilees 34:10-11).[28]

Others attempted to maintain the components of the canonical text, which led to some creative reconciliations. Abraham Ibn Ezra determined that the Midianites and the Ishmaelites were actually the same, based on his understanding of Judges 8:24, where the defeated Midianites seem to be equated with the Ishmaelites: "And he said, 'I do have on request, that each of you give me an earring from your share of the plunder'. (*It was the custom of the Ishmaelites to wear gold earrings*)". Baden writes:

> "Ibn Ezra drew on a passage in Judges in which the kings of Midian, defeated by Gideon, are said to wear earrings because they were Ishmaelites (who tend to wear earrings, as the biblical author assumes everyone knows)".[29]

Others saw the two groups as distinct, but working together; while some argued that the brothers must have sold Joseph to the Ishmaelites, who then sold him to merchants, who then sold him to the Midianites... who *then* took him to Egypt![30]

Ska's comments concerning possible reconciliations are useful here:

> "It is not enough, for example, to assert that 'Ishmaelites' and 'Midianites' are two names for one people (cf. Judg 8:24), because insurmountable difficulties remain. I will mention two of them: Why would one use two different names to designate one people in the same verse (37:28) and elsewhere (37:36; 39:1)? In order to solve this problem, some exegetes argue that in the present text the 'brothers' sell Joseph to the Ishmaelites/Midianites. But in this case, we must ask ourselves where Reuben was at that moment. If he was not with the brothers, why does the text not explain this? If he is with his brothers when Joseph is sold, why does he go to look for him in 37:29?"[31]

Can the contradictions in this story be reconciled? Maybe. A better question is, *should they be*? As we saw above in the flood story, contradicting details in a narrative can be indicative of something other than bad storytelling. If you look closely – paying careful attention to the narrative flow – you will find that, as with the flood story, Genesis 37 appears to contain two versions of the Joseph story. Baden writes:

"Each story represents a fully conceived, internally consistent narrative, a distinct historical claim, relating how Joseph was sold and transported to Egypt. Neither has any gaps that are filled by the other; reading them in isolation is, in fact, far simpler than trying to understand them in light of each other".[32]

Whether you conclude that there are two independent sources in Genesis 37, or that the chapter is the product of a main story with layers of redaction, the narrative problems are indicative of something more than single authorship.

What's in a Name? The Story of Bethel

Having examined some of the larger passages that contain contradictory information, we now turn to some of the simpler or more straightforward contradictions. These examples are taken from the long list provided in Baden's *The Composition of the Pentateuch: Renewing the Documentary Hypothesis*. Although we will investigate a few of these examples in greater detail, a fuller list of doublets, contradictions, and inconsistencies can be found in his publication (you should just go buy a copy, if you ask me).[33] We begin with the different explanations for how the city of Bethel got its name.

In Genesis 28, after being blessed by his father Isaac, Jacob flees from his brother to the city of Harran. On the way, he stops to rest; while he sleeps, God comes to him in a dream, promising him that he will be the recipient of all the promises of Abraham and Isaac. We then read:

> "And Jacob awoke from his sleep, and said, 'Truly Yahweh is in this place, but I did not know it!' And he was afraid and said, 'How awesome is this place! It is nothing else but the house of God, and this is the gate of heaven!'" (Genesis 28:16-17).

The dream and its content were so vivid that Jacob knew that this was the house of God.

In response, we see:

> "And Jacob rose up early in the morning and took the stone on which he set his head, and he placed it as a standing-stone, and he poured oil on its top. *And he called the name of that place Bethel ['The House of God'], although Luz was the name of the city formerly*" (Genesis 28:18-19, emphasis mine).

Because of his encounter with God in the dream, the story records that Jacob renamed that city "Bethel", which was formerly called "Luz". This is a rather straightforward etiological story; it explains the origin of the name "Bethel".

The problem is, only a few chapters later, Jacob seems to have *another* encounter with God at this city, and *again* he changes the name to *Bethel.*

"And God appeared to Jacob again when he came from Padan Aram, and he blessed him. And God said to him, 'Your name is Jacob; your name will not be called Jacob any longer, but rather Israel will be your name'. And he called his name Israel. And God said to him, 'I am El Shadday; be fruitful and multiply. A nation and an assembly of nations will come from you, and kings will go out from your loins. And the land which I have given to Abraham and to Isaac, to you I will give it, and to your descendants after you I will give the land'. And God went up from him in the place where he spoke to him" (Genesis 35:9-13).

Here we see a similar encounter with God to what we saw in Genesis 28, as Jacob was leaving Canaan. A similar blessing is given, and emphasis is again placed on the area in which God appeared. We then see a similar ritual being performed by Jacob/Israel:

"And Jacob set up a standing-stone in the place where God spoke to him, a stone pillar, and he poured out on it a libation, and he poured out oil upon it. *And Jacob called the name of the place where God had spoken with him Bethel*" (Genesis 35:14-15).

Thus, Jacob names the place "Bethel" on his way *out* of Canaan in Genesis 28 and *again* on his way back *into* Canaan in Genesis 35. Not only is the naming the same in both events, but the circumstances are quite similar. God appears to Jacob, makes similar promises to him, and Jacob's response is to perform essentially the same ritual. However one addresses the "double-naming" of the site of Bethel, it clearly presents a narrative inconsistency and should move us to investigate literary explanations.

Who's Your Daddy? Moses's Father-In-Law

We now turn to another small but potentially significant contradiction in the story. To reiterate, these types of narrative contradictions on their own are not likely to cause anyone a great deal of distress. However, they are specific inconsistencies to which you can point in order to help a Christian apologist justify taking the multiple-author theories more seriously. Within the biblical text, three different names are given for Moses's father-in-law – Reuel (Exodus 2:15), Jethro (Exodus 3:1), and Hobab (Numbers 10:29a).

Starting in Exodus, when Moses fled from Egypt, we are told that he went to the land of Midian and stopped to rest at a well (Exodus 2:15).

> "Now the priest of Midian had seven daughters, and they came, drew water, and filled the water-troughs to water the flock of their father. And the shepherds came and drove them away, and Moses rose up and rescued them and watered their flock. Then they went to *Reuel* their father, and he said, 'Why have you returned so quickly today?' And they answered, 'An Egyptian man delivered us from the hand of the shepherds, and he even drew water for us and watered the flock!' Then he said to his daughters, 'Where is he? Why did you not help the man? Call to him and let him eat bread'" (Exodus 2:16-20).

Having rescued the daughters of the priest of Midian, Reuel, Moses marries one of his daughters, Zipporah (Exodus 2:21). I can almost hear the reader now… "Yeah? So?" Let's jump forward just five verses to Exodus 3:1: "Now Moses was shepherding the flock of *Jethro, his father-in-law, the priest of Midian*". Excuse me? I thought his name was Reuel? Now it's Jethro? We see Jethro later in Exodus 4, as well as in chapter 18.

Further complicating the matter is a passage in Numbers 10: "And Moses said to Hobab, son of Reuel the Midianite, *father-in-law* of Moses" (Numbers 10:29a). Furthermore, in Judges 4:11a, "Now Heber the Kenite had spread out from the Kenites, from the sons of Hobab, *the father-in-law of Moses*". Milgrom writes concerning Numbers 10:29, "The identification of Hobab is difficult. He is designated here as Moses' father-in-law (also in Judg. 1:16; 4:11), a role assigned to Reuel in Exodus 2:18 and to Jethro in Exodus 18".[34] In other words, we seem to have three individuals who are named in the Pentateuch as the father-in-law of Moses: Jethro, Reuel, and Hobab.

There are several different proposed solutions to this contradictory information (Propp lists seven different suggestions),[35] but this is no surprise, given what we have seen with the previously contradictory or inconsistent narrative problems. As with the earlier literary issues, we must ask ourselves if assuming that Reuel was really the *grandfather* of the daughters in Exodus 2, or that *hoten* ("father-in-law") should be understood as "brother-in-law", are really the most reasonable solutions, particularly in light of the larger literary issues that we have been identifying.

Can Israel Have Hebrew Slaves? It Depends.

For our final inconsistency, we will briefly look at the three legal sections of the Pentateuch that deal with the practice of slavery, particularly with respect to the taking of fellow Israelites as slaves. If these were the writings of a single author – particularly referring to the same set of laws given by God – we would expect to see consistency throughout the different sections. When we look at specific passages about the Hebrew slave, we see that they do not always align with one another.

The three primary legal sections concerning slavery are Exodus 21, Deuteronomy 15, and Leviticus 25.[36] In Exodus 21, we see the following regulations with respect to male Hebrew slaves: "If you buy a Hebrew slave, six years he will serve, and in the seventh he will go out free, without payment" (Exodus 21:2).

From this we learn several things. First, the Israelites can purchase slaves. Second, *fellow Israelites* can be purchased as slaves. Third, the term limit of service is set at six years for the Hebrew slave; he is to be released in the seventh year. Thus, an Israelite who owes a debt could find himself purchased by another Israelite. However, the law stated that he could only be kept as a slave for a maximum of six years.

When we turn to Deuteronomy 15, however, we see a slightly different set of laws:

> "If your brother – a male or female Hebrew – is sold to you, he will serve you six years, and in the seventh you will send him out free from you. And when you send him away from you, you will not send him away empty. You will surely supply him from your flock, and from your threshing floor,

and from your wine-vat; that which Yahweh your God has blessed you with, you will give to him" (Deuteronomy 15:12-14).

While there are certainly recognizable similarities, there are obvious differences between this passage and what is seen in Exodus 21. Both passages allow Israelites to be purchased as slaves by other Israelites. Both passages set the term of slave service to six years with release in the seventh. In Deuteronomy 15, however, the Israelite slave is not only to be released after six years, but the master is required to provide him with extensive provisions in order for him to be reestablished financially.

When we come to Leviticus 25, however, we see a vastly different legal scenario:

> "And if your brother with you becomes poor and sells himself to you, *you are not to make him serve the service of a slave*. As a hired worker or tenant farmer he will be with you; *until the year of Jubilee he will serve with you*. Then he will go out from you, he and his children with him, and he will return to his family, and to the landed property of his fathers he will return. *For they are my slaves*, whom I brought out of the land of Egypt; *they will not be sold in a slave sale*. You shall not rule over him with violence, but you will fear your God" (Leviticus 25:39-43, emphasis mine).

The differences in this section of the law are striking. While this is not the place to go through the various legal nuances, several things are clear. First, *the Israelite is not allowed to make a fellow Israelite serve as a slave.* Second, the 7th-year release does not appear in this section; rather, the Israelite is to serve as a hired worker or tenant farmer until the next year of Jubilee (which comes around every fiftieth year). At the year of Jubilee, the man and all of his family are to be released to return to their landed property. As the Israelites are *God's slaves*, they are not allowed to be sold as slaves to another.

While there are many other aspects to these three legal sections, my only point here is to highlight the different laws that appear within them concerning the Israelite slave. If you ask, "Can an Israelite keep another Israelite as a slave?" the answer will be, "It depends on where you look". The laws of Exodus 21 and Deuteronomy 15 explicitly allow for Israelite slavery that can last for up to six years, although the specifics of the laws differ in both passages. However, if you go to Leviticus 25, the law forbids an Israelite from keeping another Israelite as a slave. They are to serve as a hired worker and then be released – not after six years – but at the year of Jubilee.

Conclusion

The Mosaic authorship of the Pentateuch is highly contentious, and it generally hinges upon the unity of the narrative. If Moses had written the vast majority of the Pentateuch, it should show a unified and consistent story. If you open any number of biblical commentaries on the books of the Pentateuch (particularly Genesis), you will see that a significant percentage of scholars will go to (sometimes) great lengths to present evidence for the unity of the text. As we have seen, the obstacle to this unity is the presence of contradictions and inconsistencies in the narrative.

While there are at least two primary theories on how the Pentateuch came into its final or canonical form, explaining them was not the focus of this chapter. Instead, we examined the *reason that scholars form theories to account for what we see in the story*. Why have Pentateuchal specialists concluded that the text was not written by just one person? As we saw, the problems in the narrative – things like contradictions and inconsistencies – led scholars to engage in this investigation.

We briefly overviewed some of the history of research, but only to set the background for why scholars began to formulate theories for the multiple authorship of the Pentateuch. As we have seen, it was the problems in the narrative. In this chapter, we analyzed in some detail just a few of the *many* literary problems in the Torah. We examined the contradictions between the accounts of creation seen in Genesis 1 and 2, particularly with respect to the order in which the events took place. Our investigation then moved to the flood story, focusing on the curious differences between the commands to take animals on the ark, as well as the duration of the flood itself. The third story that showed narrative problems was Genesis 37 and the sale of Joseph into slavery. Who sold him? The text is not consistent on that issue.

We also looked at the way in which Bethel got its name. Did Jacob change it on his way *to* Laban's house or on his return trip *from* Laban's house? We looked at the conflicting information concerning the father-in-law of Moses. What was his name? Was it Jethro, Reuel, or Hobab? Finally, we turned our attention briefly to the legal sections of the

Pentateuch, examining the laws that were set forth concerning the keeping of Israelite slaves. We noted that there are inconsistencies between the three legal sections, including whether Israelites could even keep their fellow Israelites as slaves.

Although the chapter has generally avoided the discussion of the different theories on the authorship of the Pentateuch, it will be helpful to briefly address a challenge that is posed by Christian apologists with some regularity. You will often hear, "Biblical scholars can't even agree on *how they think* the Pentateuch was written!" as an argument against multiple authorship; if scholars can't agree on who *did* write the Pentateuch, why should we listen when they tell us that Moses *didn't*? While this criticism would in no way establish the validity of their own position, it is a gross oversimplification of the opinions of scholars in the field of Pentateuchal studies. This quote from Reinhard Kratz puts this "disagreement" into perspective:

> "The basic presupposition of all three hypotheses is that the Pentateuch is not a literary unity but instead developed over time and is comprised of different literary layers. This presupposition is not arbitrary but instead responds to problems presented by the text itself. In all of the hypotheses, scholars are in agreement that the Pentateuch (Genesis-Deuteronomy) or Hexateuch (Genesis-Joshua) is composed of at least three literary strata: Deuteronomy (D), the Priestly writing (P, including H, the Holiness Code), and the non-Priestly text in Genesis-Numbers (non-P). Everything else is open for discussion".[37]

In other words, scholars in the field of Pentateuchal studies may disagree on *the specific way in which the final form of the text came to be*, but they agree that *it was not written by one person*. It is clear to those in the field that the narrative problems in the text itself – not religious presuppositions – have led scholars to develop these hypotheses of composition.

In conclusion, ancient texts are rarely straightforward and easy to understand; this often applies to how they came into being and were transmitted through time. Many have taken for granted that the first five books of the Bible – the Pentateuch – were written by Moses, and underwent little to no redaction or editorial history during their transmission to us today. When Mosaic authorship is challenged, based on the data found in the Pentateuch itself, this can be seen as a direct attack on the God of the Bible, Christianity, or a person's faith in Jesus Christ. In addition, many proponents of Mosaic authorship view such critical analysis of the text as motivated by an anti-God or anti-Christian bias; in this view, critical scholars are out to prove the Bible "wrong" in any way that they can to advance their anti-God agenda. This is simply not the case.

As we have hopefully demonstrated, there are literary problems with adhering to a single Mosaic authorship, including contradictions and other such narrative and textual inconsistencies. This – and not some anti-Christian agenda – is what leads biblical scholars to critically examine the formation of the Pentateuch. The Bible is a complicated book; advancing our knowledge and understanding of its compositional history can only serve to move the field forward by seeking to honestly engage with the text in an unbiased and open-minded way.

[1] Hodge and Mortensen 2011. (https://answersingenesis.org/bible-characters/moses/did-moses-write-genesis/)

[2] I am greatly indebted to not only the research and publications of Joel Baden for much of the material presented in this chapter, but also his review of the material and invaluable critiques and suggestions. I cite his work liberally in this chapter.

[3] Dozeman 2017: 31-199 and Blenkinsopp 2000: 1-30.

[4] Collins 2018: 53-69.

[5] Collins 2018: 54-55.

[6] Collins 2018: 55.

[7] Collins 2018: 55.

[8] Collins 2018: 55.

[9] I would like to thank Joel Baden for his critique and suggestions in this particular section.

[10] Collins 2018: 79.

[11] Hamilton 1990: 176.

[12] Carr 2020: 142-143.

[13] Sarna 1989: 54.

[14] Hamilton 1990: 287.

[15] Waltke 2001: 137-138.

[16] Wenham 1987: 176.

[17] Hamilton 1990: 298.

[18] Hamilton 1990: 301.

[19] Collins 2018: 59.

[20] Collins 2018: 59 (combining the individual lines from the J source in this section).

[21] Dozeman 2017: 227.

[22] Dozeman 2017: 223.

[23] Grossman 2019: 251.

[24] I would like to thank Joel Baden for his valuable critiques of this section in particular. For his thorough analysis of the Joseph story – upon which this section depends – see Baden 2012: 3-12. There the reader can find the history of interpretation quite clearly laid out.

[25] I would like to thank Joel Baden for his insights into this section of the text as well. The NIV tends to smooth out difficulties in this way. For example, in Genesis 37:23a, the name "Joseph" appears twice: "And when *Joseph* came to his brothers, they stripped *Joseph* of his tunic". Repeating the name is odd in this context, so the NIV renders it, "So when Joseph came to his brothers, they stripped *him* of his robe".

[26] Ska 2006: 66.

[27] Baden 2012: 3-12. I will reference these pages in this brief overview of possible solutions that have been put forth.

[28] Translation from Vanderkam 2020: 122.

[29] Baden 2012: 6.

[30] Baden 2012: 4-6.

31 Ska 2006: 67-68.
32 Baden 2012: 44.
33 Baden 2012: 16-20.
34 Milgrom 1990: 78.
35 Propp 1999: 173.
36 For a more thorough treatment of slavery in the Old Testament, see chapter six in this volume, as well as my book *Did the Old Testament Endorse Slavery* (Bowen 2020a).
37 Kratz 2016: 531.

CHAPTER FIVE
Prophecy or History?
The Dating of the Book of Daniel

Introduction

Christian: "The Bible is OBVIOUSLY God's Word! Look at the book of Daniel; he prophesied so many events in history LONG before they happened!"

Atheist: "Wasn't the book of Daniel written *after* the events it describes?"

Growing up in a Christian household, we all knew the stories in the Bible. Without a doubt, some of my favorites were found in the book of Daniel. Reading about Daniel interpreting Nebuchadnezzar's scary dreams, or his three friends defying the king's command to worship his statue and being thrown into – and rescued from – a fiery furnace. And who could forget Daniel being tossed into a pit of hungry lions, only to have an angel deliver him from their jaws!

But the book is not all heroic stories; it is actually a very complex compilation. The first half consists of a group of folktales (chapters 1-6), which center on Daniel and his three friends who have gone into exile in the Babylonian captivity. Their fidelity toward the god of Israel results in god's power and presence being manifested in their lives. By trusting in god, these men are not only rescued from dire straits, but are also held up as examples of wisdom and righteous living (especially Daniel).

Chapters 7-12 shift from these tales of faithfulness and deliverance to a series of revelations given to Daniel concerning future events. The curtain to the spiritual, heavenly realm is pulled back for Daniel, and God reveals his divine plan for the future (at least in part). Events in Daniel's future – along with the future of God's chosen people – are laid out in order to encourage him (and the reader) to continue in the faith. Although times of great persecution would come, Daniel is given to know that all of these things are foreordained by god and will ultimately result in the salvation and blessing of the faithful.

What makes this book unique in the eyes of many is that Daniel is reported to have predicted many historical events *long before they ever took place*. In fact, it seems that the further in the future the event was from Daniel, the greater precision he was generally able to provide. The rise and fall of major world empires, the specific events as they transpired in battles between great powers... it is enough to make you stop and think.

The big question, however, is, "When was the book of Daniel written?" For better or for worse, this question continues to be a source of contention for many. The majority of scholars date chapters 7-12 (the chapters that contain most of the prophetic information) to the middle of the 2nd century, while dating the origins of the earlier fantastic tales in chapters 2-6 to a few centuries earlier.

If the book was written and compiled at such a late date, this would make Daniel's predictions a bit less impressive, as most of the events would have already transpired prior to the book being written. Some traditional conservative interpreters, however, argue that the book was indeed written during the time of Daniel, sometime in the late 6th c. B.C.E., although they often acknowledge the difficulties with their position.

We have eight manuscripts of the book of Daniel preserved from the group of texts known as the Dead Sea Scrolls. Of these eight, the earliest fragments date to the late 2nd or early 1st centuries B.C.E. Of course, the date of the earliest manuscripts is not conclusive evidence for the date of the original composition. The book could have been written centuries earlier, but the original autographs might not have been preserved. How, then, do we figure out when the book of Daniel was written? What evidence do scholars consider in order to make a determination as to the time of the book's composition?

This evidence primarily falls into two categories: linguistic and historic.

What do we mean by "linguistic" evidence? If you have ever seen the movie *Monty Python and the Holy Grail*, you are probably familiar with the "Holy Hand Grenade" scene (one of my favorites): "Then thou shalt count to three. No more, no less. Three shall be the number thou shalt count, and the number of the counting shall be three". If you are an English speaker, you immediately realize that people don't speak that way nowadays; this type of speech (using words like "thou", "shalt", etc.) represents an older form of the language (or a facsimile thereof). In the same way that we recognize older forms of English, it is possible to analyze the languages found in the book of Daniel and make determinations as to when, approximately (or relatively), the grammar, syntax, and vocabulary date to.

How about the "historical" evidence? Scholars that approach the book of Daniel (as with any other piece of ancient literature) can evaluate the historical details presented in the text to determine what the writer actually knew. For example, if the book of Daniel had been written in the 6th c. B.C.E., we would expect the writer to get historical details correct from the time and place in which he lived. While it might not be so problematic for him to get some of the contemporary details wrong, it would be very suspicious if he also got *many details right* about a time three centuries following his death! Yet this is precisely what we see in the book of Daniel.

A brief note about Daniel chapter nine: while it may seem strange that we will not concern ourselves with the prophecy of the "seventy weeks" (if you don't know what that means, don't worry about it), there are good reasons for bypassing this discussion here. First, although many Christian apologists "hang their hats" on Daniel 9:24-27 when it comes to dating the book to the sixth century (interpreting the passage as predicting either the coming of Jesus or of the destruction of the temple in 70 CE), there is little to no evidence to substantially support this position. The multitude of problems associated with pinpointing a specific chronological period for the beginning and end of the "seventy weeks" have been amply addressed in many publications.[1] Second, if it can be demonstrated (and we believe that it can) that the visions of the second half of the book of Daniel (including chapter nine) all culminate with the reign of Antiochus IV Epiphanes, then it renders discussions about chapter nine for dating purposes virtually moot. If you are interested in delving into the arguments concerning the "seventy weeks" of Daniel 9:24-27, please see the resources listed in footnote 1.

To sum up, this chapter will examine these two pieces of evidence: the linguistic data and the historical inaccuracies that appear in Daniel. In the end, we will be able to build a rather convincing case that the book of Daniel was not composed in the 6th century, but much later, in the 2nd c. B.C.E., during the Maccabean period.

Linguistic Evidence: Aramaic

One of the interesting features of the book of Daniel is the fact that it was composed using several languages. In the "canonical" version (the one that made it into the Hebrew Bible), chapters 1 and 8-12 were written in Hebrew, while 2:4-7:28 were composed in Aramaic. Some parts of the "non-canonical" version were even written in Greek.

Let's begin by analyzing the Aramaic used in the book of Daniel in order to place it within a certain period of time based on its vocabulary, grammar, syntax, etc. Evidence that comes from linguistic data can be quite complicated, so my goal here will be to summarize the data rather than delving into the details. My primary source for the structure of this section will be John J. Collins's commentary on the book of Daniel in the *Hermeneia* series.[2] There he provides a thorough analysis of this topic, along with an extensive list of bibliographic citations. To reiterate, while I am trained in Semitics and have studied the Aramaic language in a variety of dialects, I am not an Aramaic specialist, and I have yet to read through all of the Aramaic texts that would be necessary to firmly draw these conclusions on my own. Instead, this presentation will rely on the analysis of experts in the field, who will be cited accordingly.

Throughout the 18th century, scholars held varying opinions on the date of the Aramaic in Daniel. These early determinations were made based on the Aramaic writings that were available at the time. However, in the 19th and 20th centuries, many more Aramaic texts were discovered, providing a much larger corpus with which to make comparisons. But how are these types of comparisons and determinations made? What is it about the use of the Aramaic language itself that leads scholars to believe that the text is either early or late in date?

While this is obviously a complex issue with many factors involved, one significant diagnostic feature or indicator is the writer's use of words and grammar, and whether these appear to be earlier or later forms. As we saw above, if we picked up two English documents and tried to determine which was older, one of the things that we could look at is the writer's choice of words. If one document contained words like "thee", "thou", and "thine", we would likely consider that text to be older than one that used the pronouns "you" and "your". The same is true in Aramaic; there are certain words, grammatical forms, and particular usages that generally appear in either earlier or later periods of the language.

Without going into a great deal of detail, let's take a look at some of the more significant texts that are written in Aramaic and see how they compare to the book of Daniel. If we look at the Old Testament book of Ezra, it tends to use older forms of certain common grammatical structures, while Daniel uses forms that are later.[3] Unfortunately, there is not much material in the book of Ezra to use for comparison. However, when we turn to the group of Aramaic texts known as the Elephantine papyri of the 5th c. B.C.E., the situation changes. A key area of comparison is the use of the letter /z/; in later Aramaic, we see that the consonant /z/ was being replaced with the consonant /d/. In other words, generally speaking, *later Aramaic tends to use the letter /d/ instead of /z/.*[4]

A good analogy might be the old English word "shew" (no, it's not pronounced like "shoe"), which – over time – began to be spelled "show". If you pick up an old King James Bible, you might read something like, "Now the LORD had said unto Abram, Get thee out of thy country, and from thy kindred, and from thy father's house, unto a land that I will *shew* thee" (Genesis 12:1, emphasis mine). If we saw writing that contained the word "shew" in it, we would likely conclude that it is older than writing that spells this word "show".

With this analogy in mind, let's turn back to the Aramaic of Daniel. Remember, later Aramaic tended to replace the /z/ in certain words with the letter /d/. In the Elephantine papyri, we mostly see the /z/ consonant, while in Daniel, Ezra, and in the Dead Sea Scrolls, we see a consistent use of the /d/ consonant, suggesting that the Aramaic used in the latter texts is later.[5]

We move now to the Samaria papyri, which date to the early 4th c. B.C.E. In general, Daniel uses later forms, while the papyri *only* use older forms. Collins concludes, "It is remarkable that the papyri never use the later forms. The cumulative evidence suggests that *the Aramaic of Daniel is later than that of the Samaria papyri*" (emphasis mine).[6]

Finally, let's consider the famous Dead Sea Scrolls from Qumran, which are generally dated between 200 B.C.E. and 70 CE.[7] When the Qumran texts first began to be published, initial comparisons between the Aramaic of Daniel and what is preserved in *The Genesis Apocryphon* (an Aramaic text among the Dead Sea Scrolls) seemed to show that the

Aramaic used at Qumran represented a slightly later stage in the development of the language. However, as more Aramaic texts were published from the Dead Sea Scrolls, it became clear that there is not a unified "Qumran Aramaic" and that *The Genesis Apocryphon* did not represent all of the Aramaic in the corpus.[8]

Concerning the differences between the Aramaic of Daniel and *The Genesis Apocryphon*, Collins argues that this "shows the beginning of a transition in the language, but the usage of Daniel is still within the spectrum of what we find at Qumran".[9] He concludes:

> "It is doubtful whether a firm line can be drawn between the Aramaic of Daniel and that of Qumran. The Qumran library preserved a range of documents that illustrate a transitional phase in the language. Although individual documents such as *Genesis Apocryphon* may be somewhat later than Daniel, it would be hazardous to attempt a dating relative to *1 Enoch* or to the *Targum of Job* on linguistic grounds, especially in view of the variations between the Qumran fragments of Daniel and the MT. Even the language of the *Genesis Apocryphon* has many parallels with Daniel".[10]

To sum up, the Aramaic of Daniel can be compared with some of the other groups of Aramaic texts in the following ways. First, when Daniel differs from Ezra (5th c. B.C.E.), it generally uses *later* Aramaic forms (though the amount of data for comparison is limited). Compared to the Elephantine papyri (5th c. B.C.E.), again, Daniel prefers to use the *later* forms. Similarly, when compared to the Samaria papyri (4th c. B.C.E.),

Daniel favors *later* forms, while the papyri *never* do. Finally, when compared to the later Qumran texts (2nd c. B.C.E. and later), the Aramaic of Daniel appears *somewhat older*, but not significantly so. Based on this evidence, it is most probable that the Aramaic portions of Daniel were written "in the early Hellenistic period . . . although a precise dating on linguistic grounds is not possible".[11]

Similar conclusions have been made by other scholars in the field. The Aramaic material in chapters 2-6 is generally thought to originate sometime during the 3rd c. B.C.E., though giving a specific date for their original composition with any certainty is not possible with the evidence currently available.[12]

While there is obviously more that could be said about the Aramaic data, this amount of detail should suffice. We see that precisely dating the book of Daniel based on the Aramaic alone is not possible, given our current data set and knowledge. However, the evidence strongly suggests that *the Aramaic in the book dates to a period later than the Samaria papyri of the 4th century, but earlier than the 2nd century texts found at Qumran.*

Linguistic Evidence: Hebrew

In the previous section, we talked about the Aramaic language that is used in the book of Daniel and how scholars have determined the general period of time in which the texts were composed based on that linguistic data. Although we cannot come to a precise date by using only the Aramaic evidence, it appears that the earlier Aramaic tales should date sometime in the early Hellenistic period, as the features of the language seem to date generally later than the Aramaic used in the 6th and 5th centuries B.C.E., but slightly earlier than what we see in the Dead Sea Scrolls. In this section, we will turn our attention to the other major language that scholars use to date the book of Daniel: Hebrew.

Several features of the Hebrew in Daniel indicate that it doesn't align well with texts from the 6th and 5th centuries, but corresponds instead with later Hebrew. Collins notes that the Hebrew used in Daniel "has little in common with the exilic period", pointing out that it instead seems to be Second Temple Hebrew.[13]

Before we begin, however, we should take a moment and examine what is meant by "Second Temple" or "Late Biblical Hebrew". As we saw with Aramaic, the Hebrew language also went through different periods of development. Biblical Hebrew is conventionally divided into four stages, based on linguistic features:

1) Archaic/Old

2) Standard/Classical

3) Transitional

4) Late[14]

This final phase, known as "Late Biblical Hebrew", is described by Morgenstern as "a modern scholarly term applied to the language in the books of the Hebrew Bible that are regarded as composed during the Restoration and Second Temple periods".[15]

But where does the book of Daniel fit in? Well, between Ezekiel and Hosea... just kidding. The book of Daniel is identified as Late Biblical Hebrew. In fact, Morgenstern defines the corpus of Late Biblical Hebrew as "the books of Ezra-Nehemiah, Esther, Chronicles, Daniel, and Qohelet".[16] But how do scholars come to that conclusion? The features that were mentioned earlier are critical to this discussion.

Collins identifies several features of Second Temple Hebrew that show up in the Book of Daniel, including:

1) vocabulary preferences; and

2) diagnostic syntactical and grammatical features.[17]

Concerning *vocabulary preferences*, Collins notes that there are certain late words or phrases that Daniel prefers to use. For example, we see the first person pronoun ("I") appearing in the form *ani* instead of the older *anokhi*. He also notes *syntactical and grammatical forms* that are diagnostic of Late Biblical Hebrew, including the "periphrastic construction" (*hayah* + participle), used about fifty times at Qumran.[18] This late construction also occurs in Daniel in several chapters (1:16; 8:5; 10:2). Another interesting example is the development of certain infinitives. The older idiomatic "infinitive absolute" appears only once in Daniel 10:3. Morgenstern notes, "The use of the infinitive absolute in the so-called tautological construction (i.e., followed by a finite verb of the same root) *appears to be on the decline in LBH*" (emphasis mine).[19]

Let's briefly summarize this short section. There are several features of Second Temple Hebrew that show up in the book of Daniel. We have looked at two – *vocabulary preferences* and *syntactical and grammatical features*. Daniel tends to use *later* vocabulary and grammatical constructions, which leads scholars to place the book in the corpus of

Late Biblical Hebrew, along with books like Ecclesiastes, Chronicles, and Ezra-Nehemiah.

There are other languages that play a role in this discussion, including Greek, Persian, and Akkadian. There have been attempts to date the book based on the use of foreign words or influence in the text, although we need not spend a great deal of time here, as the evidence doesn't appear to be overtly suggestive.

Concerning the Persian loanwords, Collins notes:

> "Kitchen has claimed that 'the Persian words in Daniel are specifically *Old Persian* words,' that is, prior to 300 B.C.E. The Old Persian equivalent of many of these terms, however, are not extant, and several of these terms are reconstructed on the basis of later Persian forms".[20]

He concludes:

> "While a late sixth-century date is compatible with the Persian loanwords, a later date is more probable, because extensive linguistic borrowing does not occur instantaneously. Persian loanwords are well attested in the Aramaic papyri of the fifth century".[21]

There are three Greek words that are used in Daniel for musical instruments. Concerning these, Collins writes, "The crucial point here is that two of these terms are relatively late: ψαλτήριον is not attested before Aristotle; συμφωνία occurs in Plato", and ultimately concludes that there is too little Greek evidence to contribute meaningfully to the discussion, and that their relative lack shouldn't be used to argue for an early date "because 'Greek loans are conspicuous by their absence' also in the Dead Sea Scrolls".[22]

What can we conclude from all of this evidence? There are various features of the Hebrew language that can tell us generally when a particular text was likely written. Linguists have placed the book of Daniel into the group labeled Late Biblical Hebrew, along with other books like Ezra-Nehemiah, Ecclesiastes, and Chronicles. Some of the features that they use to identify Daniel as Late Biblical Hebrew are *vocabulary preferences* and *diagnostic syntactical and grammatical features*. We also briefly noted that, while other foreign words or influences are suggestive of a late date, we don't want to put a lot of weight on those data points, as they are not as secure as others.

Historical Evidence

In this section, we deal with the *historical* information found in the book of Daniel, particularly as it relates to the dating of its composition. We will begin by providing a general overview of some of the history of the period in which the book purports to have been written, followed by an examination of how that history is presented in the book of Daniel itself. We will then take a look at the problems that are encountered when attempting to align Daniel's history with what we know from our other sources.

While it is important to identify these historical inconsistencies, we don't want to stop there; understanding *why* the writer(s) might have gotten these details wrong is significant. We also want to note the important details that Daniel got *right* and how that information can help us identify when the book was likely written. Finally, we will deal with the idea that, if the book wasn't written in the 6th century by a guy named Daniel, then the writer(s) must have been simply lying. The truth is probably less flashy; Daniel is part of the apocalyptic genre, which explains much of why it was written the way it was.

History of the Period vs. Daniel's History

To begin, it's helpful to lay down a brief historical overview of the period in which many of these events are supposed to have taken place. We will then look at how the book of Daniel presents that same history, which will lead us into the specific historical issues that arise in the book. This will set us up to profitably discuss what the book is actually *doing*, specifically in light of its genre.

History of the Period

Let's begin by talking about the kings that ruled over what we call the Neo-Babylonian Empire from 626 until 539 B.C.E. Nabopolassar became king in 626 and was eventually able to defeat the weakened Assyrian Empire in 612 with the help of Cyaxares of Media. Nabopolassar's son, Nebuchadnezzar II, became king in 604, making many campaigns to the west in the beginning of his reign. Nebuchadnezzar took Jerusalem in 598/97 and deported Jehoiachin, the king of Judah, to Babylon. Nebuchadnezzar appointed Zedekiah over Judah, who nevertheless eventually rebelled and was also deported in 587/86, when the temple was destroyed.

Nebuchadnezzar II reigned until 561, when Amel-Marduk took the throne and reigned for two years. His brother-in-law, Neriglissar, assassinated Amel-Marduk and reigned from 559-556. Neriglissar's young son, Labashi-Marduk, reigned approximately one month before the throne was seized by Nabonidus, who reigned from 555 until the fall of Babylon in 539. During his reign, Nabonidus went to Teima for ten years, leaving his son, the crown prince, Belshazzar, in charge as co-regent. During the king's absence, the New Year's festival was not celebrated, and many in Babylon (particularly the priesthood of the god Marduk) were apparently rather disgruntled with his actions. Upon his return, he demoted Belshazzar and sent him away from Babylon to lead the army. In 539, Cyrus took Babylon, captured Nabonidus, and deported him. Finally, Cyrus's son, Cambyses, ruled over Babylonia for the year after its fall. Of course, there is much more that we could say about the history of the period, but this will suffice for the time being.

Daniel's History

Now that we know a little more about the history of the Neo-Babylonian and early Persian periods, let's take a look at how Daniel presents that history. We see in Daniel 1:1-2:

> "In the third year of the reign of Jehoiakim king of Judah, Nebuchadnezzar king of Babylon came to Jerusalem and besieged it. And the Lord delivered Jehoiakim king of Judah into his hand, along with a portion of the vessels of the house of God, and he brought them to the land of Shinar, to the house of his god, and the vessels he brought to the treasury of his god".

Since the first year of Jehoiakim is generally agreed to be 609 B.C.E., this would make Jehoiakim's third year 606. Thus, according to Daniel, in 606 B.C.E., Nebuchadnezzar came to Jerusalem, laid siege, took the city, and likely deported its king, Jehoiakim, some choice Israelites (including Daniel and his three friends), and vessels from the temple in Jerusalem. We then learn that Daniel revealed and explained the dream of Nebuchadnezzar in the second year of the king's reign. Because Nebuchadnezzar took the throne in 605, and his first official year was 604, the events of chapter two are likely to be dated to 603. We read in chapter five that Belshazzar held a feast on the night that Babylon fell; this fall is credited to one Darius the Mede. Since Babylon fell in 539, this event is dated to that year.

There are other dates that are given in Daniel. Chapter seven is dated to the first year of Belshazzar and chapter eight to his 3rd year. The chronology is complicated, but it seems like this should be roughly somewhere between 553 and 551 B.C.E. Two other dates are given in chapters nine and ten. Chapter nine is dated to the first year of Darius the Mede, which, according to the text, should be 539. Daniel 10:1 is dated to the 3rd year of Cyrus, which should be 536 B.C.E. Thus, Daniel is supposed to have come to Babylon in 606 and served through the reign of Cyrus, which ended in 530, a span of more than 70 years, when the book of Daniel speaks of the Babylonian Empire giving way to the Medes and then to the Persians.

Now that we know the purported setting of the book, we can investigate the prophetic historical layout that Daniel presents. There are three visions in Daniel 7, 8, and 10-12 that describe four kingdoms that will rule over the region (a "four-kingdom schema"), *ending with Greece.* Let's take a minute and read through some of the relevant sections of these prophecies.

In chapter seven, Daniel has a vision of four great beasts. The first looks like a lion, the second a bear, the third a leopard, and the fourth he described as simply terrifying to him. In verses 7 and 8 he writes:

> "It was different from all the former beasts, and it had ten horns. While I was thinking about the horns, there before me was another horn, a little one, which came up among them; and three of the first horns uprooted before it. This horn had eyes like the eyes of a human being and a mouth that spoke boastfully".

Here we have four beasts described; the fourth beast initially has ten horns, but a smaller horn comes up and displaces three of the original ten horns. Fortunately for us, the book provides interpretations for these visions, some more detailed or specific than others. In Daniel 7:17 we read, "These great beasts, which are four (in number), are four kings who will rise up from the earth". Specifically, beginning in verse 23:

> "Thus he said, 'The fourth beast will be the fourth kingdom on the earth, which will be different from all the kingdoms, and will consume all earth and tread it down and crush it. And the ten horns, from this kingdom ten kings will arise, and after them will arise another, and he will be different from the previous ones, and he will humiliate three kings. And he will speak against the most high and will wear out the holy ones of the most high, and will intend to change times and laws, and they will be given into his hand for a time, and times, and half a time'" (Daniel 7:23-25).

Scholars agree that the fourth beast in Daniel seven represents Greece. Newsom writes that while "the angel's initial interpretation of the beasts was as 'kings' (v. 17), here the fourth beast is identified as a 'kingdom,' that is, the Hellenistic kingdom of Alexander the Great".[23]

While some writers, starting with Porphyry, have argued that the ten horns represent ten contemporaneous kings of the Greek Empire, most scholars agree that they likely represent ten successive rulers of the Seleucid Empire.[24]

We see from the vision of chapter seven that the four beasts are four kingdoms that culminate with the rise of a leader who will speak boastfully against the Most High and persecute the people of God for "time, times, and half a time". The vision in chapter eight is very similar, but more specific in its identifications. Daniel sees a ram with two horns (one horn longer than the other), which is killed by a goat that comes from the west. The goat then becomes very powerful, but its horn is broken off, and four new horns grow up in its place. From one of the new horns *another* horn grows, and this one expands its power to the south and east. It stops the daily sacrifice from taking place and causes "desolation" for 2,300 evenings and mornings.

Daniel's vision is interpreted in this way:

> "The ram that you saw with two horns is the kings of Media and Persia. And the hairy goat is the king of Greece, and the big horn that was between his eyes, he is the first king. And the broken horn and the four that arose in its place are four kingdoms that will arise from that nation, but not with his strength. And in the latter part of their reign,

when the sinners have reached full measure, a king will arise, defiant and skilled in intrigue" (Daniel 8:20-23).

Newsom writes:

"In contrast to Dan 2 and 7, which generally use vague language ('another kingdom,' 'a fourth kingdom'), Dan 8 explicitly identifies the kingdoms of Media/Persia and Greece. Thus later Jewish and Christian interpreters, who often tried to contemporize the visions to include references to Rome, were not able to reassign these symbols. Josephus (*Ant.* 10.276) correctly identifies the events with the actions of Antiochus Ephiphanes, but he cannot resist adding 'in the same manner Daniel also wrote about the empire of the Romans.' Jerome skips over the passage altogether".[25]

The book of 2 Esdras, written around 100 C.E., states:

"He said to me, 'This is the interpretation of this vision which you have seen: The eagle which you saw coming up from the sea is the fourth kingdom which appeared in a vision to your brother Daniel. But it was not explained to him as I now explain or have explained it to you'" (2 Esdras 12:10-12).[26]

The text goes on to describe the Roman Empire. Thus, it was clear to the writer of 2 Esdras that the fourth kingdom spoken of in Daniel represented Greece.

This fact is also clearly seen in the final vision of Daniel 10-12. "In the third year of Cyrus king of Persia a word was revealed to Daniel" (Daniel 10:1a). The angelic messenger states in verse 20: "'And now I will return to fight with the prince of Persia; so I am going out, but the prince of Greece is about to come'".

Again in chapter 11, starting in verse 2:

> "'And now I will declare to you the truth: three more kings are about to arise in Persia, and the fourth will become much wealthier than everyone, and when he becomes strong by his wealth, he will arouse everyone against the kingdom of Greece. And a mighty king will arise and rule with great authority, and he will do whatever he wishes. But when he arises, his kingdom will be broken, and it will be divided up to the four winds of the heavens, but not to his descendants, and not according to his authority with which he ruled, because his kingdom will be uprooted and given to others besides these'" (Daniel 11:2-4).

The same figure that appeared in the visions of chapters 7, 8, and 9 also appears in this section of the book. Daniel asks the question in 12:6b, "How long until the end of these wonders?" The angel responds in verse 7b, "for a time, times, and a half". In verses 11 and 12 the angel states:

> "'And from the time that the daily sacrifice is taken away, and the abomination that desolates is set up: 1,290 days. Blessed is the one who waits and reaches the 1,335 days'" (Daniel 12:11-12).

In other words, the figure that rises up to persecute the people of God – who speaks boastfully, stops the daily sacrifice, and sets up the abomination – *is the same figure throughout the visions of the second portion of the book.* Goldingay writes:

> "*The small horn in ch. 8 is Antiochus.* The parallels just considered suggest that he is also the last king in ch. 7; within the OT period, he alone fits the portrait in v 8. Further, in 8:17 Daniel is told that his vision of the small horn relates to the time of the end; *the Greek Empire is the last empire.* A similar perspective emerges in Dan 10-12" (emphasis mine).[27]

This idea that successive kingdoms ruled in the 1st millennium B.C.E. is not unique to Daniel; it can be seen in Herodotus, Ctesias, Tobit, and the Sibylline Oracles.[28] The order is usually the Assyrians, followed by the Medes, then the Persians, and then the Greeks; later writers included the Romans. A clear example can be seen in Amelius Sura:

> "The Assyrians were the first of all races to hold power, then the Medes, after them the Persians, and then the Macedonians. Then, when the two kings, Philip and Antiochus, of Macedonian origin, had been completely conquered, soon after the overthrow of Carthage, the supreme command passed to the Romans".[29]

Concerning this Newsom writes:

> "Daniel also partially adapts the sequence of kingdoms to the Jewish experience of history. Instead of the sequence

'Assyria, Media, Persia,' which reflects the actual transition of power from the Persian perspective, Daniel substitutes Babylon for Assyria as the first kingdom ('Babylon, Media, Persia'), thus creating a historically incoherent sequence since Media did not rule after Babylon".[30]

Okay, let's take a second and sum up. First, we know an awful lot about the Neo-Babylonian Empire from a myriad of sources, particularly cuneiform texts from that period. We provided a brief overview of its history, as well as the beginning of the Achaemenid or Persian period. We then surveyed the way in which Daniel presents the history of the same two periods, and the "prophetic history" of the centuries that followed, *which culminated with the Grecian Empire.*

This last point is incredibly important. If:

1) each of the visions culminates with Greece as the ruling empire; and

2) the final ruler who speaks boastfully, stops the daily sacrifice, and sets up the abomination is the ruler of Greece (agreed to be Antiochus IV Epiphanes); then

3) the book of Daniel *describes Greece as the final empire to rule before the coming of the kingdom of God.*

As we saw above, this was clear to later writers in the 1st millennium C.E., who sought to amend or update what Daniel saw, describing the final kingdom as Rome, not Greece. In short, Daniel lays out a prophetic "timeline of history", in which four kingdoms would rule, culminating in the reign of Antiochus IV Epiphanes. Following his reign, the kingdom of God would be established on earth.

Comparing Known History to Daniel's History

When we compare Daniel's history to what we know from extra-biblical sources, we see that there is a wide variety of problems that are incredibly difficult to reconcile. In the remainder of this section, we will identify these problems, along with the most common arguments that are used to defend the historical claims in the book. Showing the problems with these apologetic arguments is not sufficient, though. It is incredibly important to identify – whenever possible – why the writer(s) got these details wrong. For example – and don't worry, we will deal with this issue in detail later in this section – take the problem of Belshazzar, the son of Nabonidus, being referred to as the son of Nebuchadnezzar. The immediate response from an apologist is that the words "father" and "son" in Hebrew and Aramaic *can* mean "father" and "son", but they can *also* mean "grandfather" and "grandson", "great-grandfather" and "great-grandson", etc. In the minds of many apologists, this is sufficient to solve the problem.

But it is not simply a question of "is it possible?" In other words, "Is it possible that Nebuchadnezzar was the grandfather of Belshazzar?" Sure, it's *possible*. The question is, however, given what we know about the text, *what is most likely the intent of the author*. In this example, it seems from the context that "father" and "son" are meant, although the semantic range of "father" can include "grandfather". But more importantly (as we will discuss later), there is a reason that Daniel refers to Nebuchadnezzar as Belshazzar's father: it is most likely because Daniel is following a historical tradition that has incorrectly attributed characteristics and actions of Nabonidus to Nebuchadnezzar. Thus, we need not stop at, "Should the Hebrew word *av* be translated 'father' or 'grandfather' contextually?" There are other factors at play that point to a very likely rationale behind these historical errors.

Here is how the rest of the chapter is going to break down. We will begin by talking about incorrect dates that appear in the book of Daniel, followed by the problems surrounding the "madness" of Nebuchadnezzar and the figure of Belshazzar. We will then discuss Darius the Mede. Because we are investigating the historical data to determine the date of writing, we not only want to look at what Daniel got wrong, but also what he got right. Thus, we will examine some of the details of chapter 11, looking at the events that are described and how these descriptions differ from those seen in the rest of Daniel. Finally, we will look at the genre of the book, which will help explain not only the reason for many of the errors, but also the purpose of the book in its original setting.

Before diving into these historical data, we need to consider how we are approaching the book of Daniel and its portrayal of history. Unfortunately, many Christian apologists are also fundamentalists (or have fundamentalist leanings or methodologies). Because of this, I think it is a good idea to quote Lester Grabbe concerning the fundamentalist defense of the biblical texts:

> *"Fundamentalism has already determined its conclusions*; it is not seeking because it already knows the answer. If it has good evidence on its side which supports the Bible, it uses it. If it has little data, it twists and interprets what it has to support the Bible. If it has no evidence, it

hypothesizes that such will eventually be found. And of course no amount of contrary evidence is sufficient. Fundamentalism can *never* conclude that the Bible is wrong" (emphasis mine).[31]

Grabbe's point here is that, *when one begins with a conclusion that they must reach*, the evidence can inevitably be twisted or construed in such a way as to render the desired conclusion at least *possible*.

Unfortunately, that is not how historiography is done. We must go where the evidence leads us and determine what is most likely to be the case, rather than defending what we want or need to be true *simply because it is possible*. If a detective were to identify a suspect in a murder investigation, run down that lead, but find that the suspect had a strong alibi, no motive, and no means to commit the crime, the detective should likely begin looking for another suspect. Let's say that another suspect is then identified. If our detective – in spite of positive evidence pointing to the second suspect as the killer – continued to develop possible scenarios in which the first suspect *could* have committed the crime – however remote or unlikely – this would likely get them removed from the case. That is not how good investigation is done as a detective, and the same is true for someone reconstructing historical events in the ancient past. This point will come up time and again in this section, beginning with the dates given in the book.

Problematic Dates

In Daniel 1:1-2, we run into our first series of problems with the historical data; some of these problems are easier to reconcile than others.

"In the third year of the reign of Jehoiakim king of Judah, Nebuchadnezzar king of Babylon came to Jerusalem and besieged it. And the Lord delivered Jehoiakim king of Judah into his hand, along with a portion of the vessels of the house of God, and he brought them to the land of Shinar, to the house of his god, and the vessels he brought to the treasury of his god".

There are several difficulties in these verses; some are potentially easier to reconcile than others. For example, the setting of Daniel chapter 1 is Jehoiakim's 3rd year, or 606 B.C.E. However, at this time, Nebuchadnezzar was not in the region, and Jehoiakim was a vassal of Pharaoh Neco II of Egypt. In fact, Nebuchadnezzar did not even become king until 605 B.C.E., after the death of his father Nabopolassar.

Now, some of these problems can potentially be reconciled. For instance, even though Nebuchadnezzar was not king at the time, this could be a proleptic use of the title. By way of comparison, if someone said, "President Obama voted for X when it came before the senate", this would be a proleptic use of the title "president". Clearly Barack Obama was not president when he was a senator, but because he is well known for his presidency, it would be quite common for someone to make such a statement.

We see a similar type of proleptic use in Jeremiah 46:2:

"To Egypt, concerning the army of Pharaoh Neco king of Egypt, which was on the river Euphrates in Carchemish, which Nebuchadnezzar *king of Babylon* struck in the fourth year of Jehoiakim son of Josiah king of Judah".

We know that Nebuchadnezzar was not yet king at the Battle of Carchemish; this is simply an example of the writer projecting the title back. Does that mean that this is definitely what is happening in Daniel? No, but it is easy to understand how this *could* be the case.

With some of these issues, it is easier to find possible reconciliations. However, we will focus here on one of the more difficult problems in this text: the supposed siege of Jerusalem. Daniel 1:1-2 states that Nebuchadnezzar besieged Jerusalem, and the Lord delivered the king of Judah, Jehoiakim, into Nebuchadnezzar's hand. Nebuchadnezzar then plundered the temple and took some of the vessels back to Babylon. Unfortunately, there is no evidence that this siege ever took place.

Two passages outside of Daniel are often cited in this discussion – 2 Kings 24 and 2 Chronicles 36. 2 Kings 24:1 states:

> "In his days Nebuchadnezzar king of Babylon went up and Jehoiakim became his slave for three years, but he turned and rebelled against him" (2 Kings 24:1).

In 605, Nebuchadnezzar defeated Pharaoh Necho II at the Battle of Carchemish and campaigned in the region of Hamath or Syria-Palestine. Cogan and Tadmor note:

> "The year 605, the third year of Jehoiakim, was the year of the battle of Carchemish. Nebuchadnezzar reached the land of Hamath, *but not Jerusalem*. He reached Judah, at

the earliest, in 604, Jehoiakim's fourth year" (emphasis mine).[32]

Thus, according to 2 Kings 24, Jehoiakim became Nebuchadnezzar's vassal most likely in 604, but at the earliest in 605.

It appears that Daniel 1:1-2 has other historical problems, which might lead us to conclude that it is likely also incorrect about the siege of Jerusalem in 605. In 2 Chronicles 36:5-7, we see that Jehoiakim was taken in shackles to Babylon by Nebuchadnezzar:

> "Jehoiakim was 25 years old when he began to rule and he ruled 11 years in Jerusalem. And he did evil in the eyes of Yahweh his God. Nebuchadnezzar king of Babylon came up against him and he bound him with bronze shackles in order to bring him to Babylon. And Nebuchadnezzar brought some of the vessels from the house of Yahweh to Babylon and he set them in his temple in Babylon" (2 Chronicles 36:5-7).

This is what we see described in Daniel 1:1-2 (Jehoiakim and the temple vessels being taken to Babylon). However, 2 Kings 24:6 reads, "And Jehoiakim rested with his fathers, and Jehoiachin, his son, ruled in his place". In other words, Jehoiakim died and was buried with his ancestors in 2 Kings 24, but in 2 Chronicles 36 and Daniel 1, he is taken captive to Babylon. Which is correct? Concerning this discrepancy, Japhet writes:

> "The specific phrasing of Chronicles, 'to take him', should be explained as denoting actual deportation . . . It is

difficult to see how the passage in Chronicles can be separated from the parallel tradition of Daniel 1:2, which states clearly that Nebuchadnezzar brought Jehoiakim to Babylon".[33]

Thus, one historical tradition is seen in 2 Kings 24, while another appears in 2 Chronicles 36 and Daniel 1:1-2. Japhet concludes:

> "The unavoidable conclusion seems to be that II Kings 24.1-6 and the Chronicler's view are not complementary but deliberately exclusive, expressing alternative views of the fortunes of king and land at the time".[34]

Similarly, Cogan and Tadmor write:

> "The item in Dan 1:1-2, that in Jehoiakim's third year Nebuchadnezzar despoiled the Temple and exiled some Judeans, often cited in this connection, cannot be used for historical purposes; the book of Daniel is not on par with 2 Kings and the Babylonian Chronicle. 'The third year' is a literary topos, like 'the third day' (e.g. Gen 22:4), 'the third month' (e.g. Exod 19:1), 'the third year' (e.g. 1 Kgs 22:2) . . . One should consider the possibility that the tradition in Dan 1:1-2 derives ultimately from the text of 2 Chr 36:6".[35]

Thus, it appears that Daniel 1:1-2 is utilizing a historical tradition from Chronicles that is unreliable, when compared to 2 Kings. When we turn to the siege spoken of in Daniel 1:1-2, we see that it appears to follow the same pattern. The siege is not mentioned in the Babylonian

Chronicle. However, the Babylonian Chronicle DOES describe a siege against Judah in Nebuchadnezzar's *seventh* year:

> "In the month of Kislev the king of Akkad mustered his army and marched to Hattu. He encamped against the city of Judah and on the second day of the month Adar he captured the city and seized its king. A king of his own choice he appointed in the city and taking the vast tribute he brought it into Babylon".[36]

Furthermore, the narrative describes Jehoiakim's son, Jehoiachin, being besieged in 2 Kings 24:10-15:

> "At that time the slaves of Nebuchadnezzar king of Babylon went up to Jerusalem and the city came under siege. And Nebuchadnezzar king of Babylon came to the city, and his slaves were laying siege to it. And Jehoiachin king of Judah went out to the king of Babylon – he and his slaves and princes and eunuchs with him – and the king of Babylon took him captive in the eighth year of his reign. And he brought out from there all the treasures of the house of Yahweh, and the treasures of the house of the king, and he cut up all the vessels of gold that Solomon king of Israel had made in the temple of Yahweh, just as Yahweh has spoken. And he took into exile all Jerusalem and all the princes and all the mighty men of the army, 10,000 captives, and all the craftsmen and the smiths; only the poorest people of the land remained. And he took Jehoiachin to Babylon into exile, and the mother of the

king, and the wives of the king, and his princes and the leaders of the land he brought into exile from Jerusalem to Babylon" (2 Kings 24:10-15).

In light of the more serious or seemingly irreconcilable discrepancies, there may be a more appropriate solution. Goldingay summarizes concerning many of these historical issues in Daniel 1:1-2:

> "Danielic dates cluster in the first three years of a king's reign and perhaps affirm God's lordship at key transition points in history, with 'first' or 'third' being simply concrete ways of saying 'at the beginning' or 'not long after the beginning.' A date can make a more than merely historical point".[37]

Seow comes to a similar conclusion:

> "The stories in the book of Daniel are set in the context of Israel's defeat and consequent exile. The details of that historical setting are, however, difficult to coordinate with other biblical passages (2 Kgs. 24:1-25:20; 2 Chr. 36:5-21; Jer. 39:1-40:6; 52:1-34) and extrabiblical sources for a number of reasons . . . Such discrepancies prompted the third-century philosopher Porphyry and his intellectual successors to question the historical veracity of the book altogether, while apologists (both ancient and modern) have proffered various ways to harmonize the data. The notice in verses 1-2 appears, however, to be merely a telescoping of various events that led up to the eventual dispersion of the Israelites in the sixth century. In any

case, the notice serves its purpose well by providing a narrative setting to tell the stories of individuals who are trying to live out their convictions in a world dominated by those who do not share their faith".[38]

However one makes sense of the discrepancies, it seems quite clear that it is not possible to reconstruct reliable history simply by presenting the details that are found in this section of Daniel.

Madness of Nebuchadnezzar

The madness of Nebuchadnezzar is another difficult event to reconcile with what we know of the historical period. In Daniel 4, Nebuchadnezzar is apparently writing in the first person, declaring what God had done to him and his resultant conversion to the worship of the Most High God. Because of the king's hubris, he was "driven away from men" to "live with the wild animals" (Daniel 4:32). This situation continued for seven years "until you [Nebuchadnezzar] know that the Most High rules over all kingdoms of men and gives them to anyone he pleases" (v. 32).

Several things stand out about this passage that lead us to believe that this story not only lacks historical reliability, but *it is not even about Nebuchadnezzar*. Rather, it is about Nabonidus, the final king of the Neo-Babylonian Empire. First, one would expect to find something in the historical record concerning a seven-year absence of the king, as we do with Nabonidus. With the king gone, for example, the Akitu festival would not have been able to be carried out, as was the case with Nabonidus.

Of course, there is a common apologetic argument to explain this lack of historical data for such a hiatus; it simply wasn't something that the king wanted recorded in his official inscriptions, and so was left out.[39] It is true that Nebuchadnezzar's reign is not thoroughly documented in a detailed historical fashion. But is it reasonable to conclude that this would not be found somewhere in the textual evidence (perhaps administrative texts)?

Furthermore, if we keep with the narrative, would not Nebuchadnezzar have wanted such a thing documented in his inscriptions (or in royal proclamations of any kind)? Look at how the story begins:

> "Nebuchadnezzar the king, to all the peoples, nations, and those of every language who dwell in all the earth – may your peace increase greatly! *The signs and wonders that the most high God performed for me, it seemed good for me to make known*" (Daniel 4:1-2, emphasis mine).

Or consider Daniel 4:34-37:

> "And at the end of those days, I, Nebuchadnezzar, lifted my eyes to heaven, and my reason returned to me, and I blessed the most high and the one who lives forever I praised and honored, for his rule is an everlasting rule, and his kingdom is from generation to generation. And all those dwelling on the earth are regarded as nothing, but he does as he pleases with the host of heaven and those who dwell on the earth, and there is no one who can hinder his hand, or can say to him, 'What have you done?' At that time my reason returned to me, along with the honor of my kingdom

and majesty and splendor were returned to me, and my ministers and nobles were seeking me, and I was re-established over my kingdom and surpassing greatness was added to me. Now I, Nebuchadnezzar, praise and exult and glorify the king of heaven, for all his works are true and his ways are just and those walking in pride he is able to humble" (Daniel 4:34-37).

We would have to conclude that, following such a drastic turn of events in the king's life – and the immense change that resulted from his punishment and subsequent restoration – that Nebuchadnezzar *immediately changed his mind about the God of Heaven* and worked to remove any evidence for his seven-year absence, conversion, and proclamations. Not only does this seem highly improbable, but it also goes directly against the nature of the text. *The point of the passage is that God, through his power, changed the heart of even the most powerful and arrogant of kings.* It would be counter to the text to conclude that God's efforts were so completely ephemeral as to be forgotten as soon as they had taken effect.

It is also incredibly suspicious that the prayer of Nebuchadnezzar seems to contain characteristics similar to those found in the text of the Hebrew Bible. Hartman and Di Lella write:

> "The Nebuchadnezzar of this narrative speaks and acts like a pious Jew who is quite familiar with the Old Testament rubrics and forms of prayer".[40]

There are many similarities between the prayer of Nebuchadnezzar in Daniel four and parallel phrases in the Psalms and Isaiah as presented in Hartman and Di Lella's commentary on Daniel.[41] Thus, there is strong evidence against the historicity of this account with respect to Nebuchadnezzar.

While scholars would not argue that the events are accurate, it has become clear that the book of Daniel has followed an erroneous tradition in several places, attributing characteristics of one historical figure to another. Here, Nebuchadnezzar has been confused with Nabonidus. The account of Nebuchadnezzar's madness is generally agreed by scholars to be a garbled memory of Nabonidus' religious oddities and self-imposed exile to the north Arabian oasis of Teima.[42]

As we will see later in this section, Daniel presents Belshazzar as the son of Nebuchadnezzar, although we know that he was the son of Nabonidus. While apologetic arguments are made to show how this could possibly be so (although they admit it is simply speculation), there is a far easier solution that fits well with the data that we have: *traditions and facts about Nabonidus were incorrectly attributed to Nebuchadnezzar*. One of the texts that solidified this interpretation came to light in the discovery of the Qumran text *The Prayer of Nabonidus*. Although somewhat fragmentary, it clearly demonstrates that the tradition was not to be attributed to Nebuchadnezzar but to Nabonidus.

> "The words of the prayer uttered by Nabunai king of the l[and of Ba]bylon, [the great] king, [when he was afflicted] with an evil ulcer in Teiman by decree of the [Most High God]. I was afflicted [with an evil ulcer] for seven years . . . and an exorcist pardoned my sins. He was a Jew from

[among the children of the exile of Judah, and he said], 'Recount this in writing to [glorify and exalt] the name of the [Most High God'. And I wrote this]: 'I was afflicted with an [evil] ulcer in Teiman [by decree of the Most High God]. For seven years [I] prayed to the gods of silver and gold, [bronze and iron], wood and stone and clay, because [I believed] that they were gods . . . ."[43]

Carol Newsom summarizes this discussion well in her 2014 commentary on Daniel:

"Already in the twentieth century, on the basis of new cuneiform documents from Mesopotamia, scholars had proposed that behind Dan 4 was a story originally told about Nabonidus and only subsequently reconfigured as a narrative about Nebuchadnezzar (Riessler 43; Hommel; Soden 1935, 81-89). It was recognized that Belshazzar was the son, not of Nebuchadnezzar, but of Nabonidus. Moreover, Nabonidus was absent from Babylon for a period of ten years, in the Arabian desert oasis of Teima, and he was the object of harsh polemics from the priests of Marduk in Babylon because of his advocacy of the supremacy of the moon-god Sin . . . That there was a tradition of Jewish storytelling about Nabonidus was confirmed by the discovery of the *Prayer of Nabonidus* (4Q242) among the Dead Sea Scrolls".[44]

Beaulieu concurs:

> "The discovery of the *Prayer of Nabonidus* among the Qumran manuscripts (4Q242) shows that even after the compilation of Daniel in the first decades of the second century, there continued a parallel tradition that correctly ascribed to the historical Nabonidus the episodes of the royal disease and the residence in the oasis of Teima".[45]

In other words, Daniel 4 contains a narrative that, when applied to Nebuchadnezzar, presents numerous historical problems. However, when we recognize that *the story goes back to a common tradition associated with Nabonidus* (and need not be historically inerrant, as this was not the purpose of the text), these issues are no longer problematic.

It is very interesting to note that, in the Prayer of Nabonidus, the king references making prayers to the "gods of silver and gold, bronze and iron, wood and stone and clay", while in Daniel 5:4, 23, Belshazzar praises "the gods of silver and gold, of bronze, iron, wood and stone". This appears to further connect these two narratives to a common tradition. Thus, it is almost certain that stories about Nabonidus were incorrectly attributed to Nebuchadnezzar.

Belshazzar

The correct understanding of Nebuchadnezzar's "madness" also helps us with our next issue: Belshazzar. If you have looked into the dating of the book of Daniel, you have probably run into this argument. It goes something like this:

Atheist: "Daniel got it wrong. Look, it says that Belshazzar was the king and the son of Nebuchadnezzar, but he wasn't. He was just a co-regent, and he was the son of Nabonidus".

Christian Apologist: "Yeah, well you guys didn't even think that Belshazzar existed before we proved you wrong!"

Atheist: "So? Who cares? It still doesn't make Belshazzar the king or Nebuchadnezzar's son!"

Christian Apologist: "Duh. They could have just been using the word 'king' loosely, since he was mostly acting as the king. And don't you know Hebrew? The word 'father' can mean 'grandfather' or even 'great-grandfather'".

Atheist: "How does that help you? You're saying that Daniel used an incorrect term to refer to Belshazzar. And Nebuchadnezzar wasn't Belshazzar's grandfather either. Nabonidus was a usurper; he wasn't part of Nebuchadnezzar's dynasty".

Christian Apologist: "Shows how much you know! One of the other kings married one of Nebuchadnezzar's daughters, and Nabonidus might have married one too. So Nebuchadnezzar *was* Belshazzar's grandfather! Booya!"

Okay, so, that's a little contrived (or not?). The point is that Belshazzar is a common point of contention in this debate. What we want to do here is dig down and get to the bottom of this debate. What evidence do we actually have?

First, it is true that the words "father" and "son" can be used in Hebrew and Aramaic to indicate "father" and "son" (as in English), or as a more distant descendant or progenitor. Seow writes:

> "Perhaps to the narrator, Nebuchadnezzar and Belshazzar *both belonged to the same family of arrogant Chaldean oppressors.* The father-son language serves to link the two kings: *the one who took the vessels from the temple in Jerusalem with the one who desacralized them*" (emphasis mine).[46]

Thus, if one is going to argue that the writer got it right, it is possible that this sort of group association is what is intended.

Some have instead argued that Nebuchadnezzar was in fact the biological grandfather of Belshazzar, including Alan Millard in a 1977 article, in which he suggests that:

> "Nabonidus, too, was a son-in-law of Nebuchadnezzar, putting him in as good a place to take the throne as Neriglissar. Then the mother of Belshazzar would have been a daughter of Nebuchadnezzar. But this remains speculation until more evidence is available".[47]

A similar argument is made by Wiseman, who argues based on what is possible, rather than what is most likely:

> "Nothing is yet known of Nabonidus' wife, *so that it is not impossible* that she was another daughter of Nebuchadrezzar who married Nabonidus who was already

of high rank (lú.lugal) in Nebuchadrezzar's eighth year" (emphasis mine).[48]

Both Millard's and Wiseman's suggestions are based on the speculation that, because Neriglissar married one of Nebuchadnezzar's daughters and because Nabonidus was likely a courtier at the palace of Babylon, Nabonidus *may* also have married one of Nebuchadnezzar's daughters. Therefore, if we assume that the meaning of "father" and "son" is "grandfather" and "grandson", *and* that Nabonidus married one of Nebuchadnezzar's daughters (something for which we lack any evidence), *then* this passage could make more sense historically. To be clear, these are things that are only in the realm of possibility and speculation.

In contrast to this, there is *strong* evidence that the traditions concerning Nabonidus were incorrectly transferred to Nebuchadnezzar. As Nebuchadnezzar took the vessels from the temple in Jerusalem he is seen as connected to Belshazzar, who used the temple vessels in a profane way. As we will see in our discussion of Darius the Mede, the writer of Daniel has a tendency to make these kinds of incorrect transfers of traditions to characters in the book. With this understanding, the terms "son" and "father" would be read in their standard fashion, as Nabonidus (confused with Nebuchadnezzar in Daniel) was actually Belshazzar's father. However, if we wish to interpret the claim of lineage to be historically accurate, we likely have to understand the "father" and "son" terms to indicate something akin to "inclusion in a group". It would also be possible that "grandfather/grandson" is meant, and that Nabonidus (who is oddly not mentioned in the text... more on this below) married one of

Nebuchadnezzar's daughters. Again, these possibilities are merely speculative.

It is also very problematic that, according to Daniel, Belshazzar is on the throne when the Neo-Babylonian Empire falls. In fact, we know for certain that Nabonidus had returned from Teima in his 13th regnal year and very likely took back all activities of kingship following his return. [49] Furthermore, Beaulieu surmises – based on the textual evidence from the end of Nabonidus's reign – that Belshazzar was most likely stationed outside of Babylonia after Nabonidus's return. He comments on three archival texts that come from Nabonidus's fourteenth year and refer to Belshazzar:

> "Two of the three archival texts yield more information as to the role of Belshazzar after Nabonidus' return . . . Both are lists of travel equipment such as garments, shoes, and foodstuffs allotted to various individuals *who are dispatched to the son of the king*" (emphasis mine). [50]

Not only had Nabonidus returned several years before the fall of Babylon, but Belshazzar – whom Daniel presents as the king ruling in Babylon at the time of its defeat – *was most likely not even in Babylonia at the time of its fall to Cyrus*. Unfortunately, cuneiform texts don't record *where* Belshazzar was when he received the goods mentioned above. Beaulieu suggests that he may have been at the city of Dūr-karāšu, or perhaps stationed outside Babylonia entirely, overseeing the kingdom's defenses. [51]

These details make Daniel 5:30-31 incredibly difficult to reconcile with the textual evidence:

"In that same night Belshazzar, the Chaldean king, was killed, and Darius the Mede received the kingdom at the age of 62" (Daniel 5:30-31).

If Belshazzar was not even in Babylonia (and most likely quite far away), *how could he be present to have a feast and to be killed as the ruling king*? Lester Grabbe points out another very problematic aspect of this passage:

> "Dan. 5:30 says, 'That very night, Belshazzar, the Chaldean king, was killed.' It is now known that Babylon was taken by the Persian army without a fight. One might still argue that perhaps Belshazzar alone resisted or that he was assassinated, unlikely but perhaps possible [Beaulieu's study came out two years after Grabbe's article was published]. But there is clear evidence that Belshazzar almost certainly *did not die at this time*".[52]

The Nabonidus Chronicle, a fairly reliable source from this period, lists all Babylonian kings who ruled at this time, and most likely includes all important events that impacted Babylonia during their rules.[53]

Not only do we know that Belshazzar was very likely not in Babylonia, and that Babylon fell without a fight, but the chronicle notes that Nabonidus retreated as Cyrus approached, following the fall of Sippar. Cyrus entered Babylon without a fight and Nabonidus was subsequently captured there:

> "In the month of Tishri when Cyrus (II) did battle at Opis on the [*bank of*] the Tigris against the army of Akkad, the

people of Akkad retreated. He carried off the plunder (and) slaughtered the people. On the fourteenth day Sippar was captured without a battle. Nabonidus fled. On the sixteenth day Ugbaru, governor of the Guti, and the army of Cyrus (II) entered Babylon without a battle".[54]

Therefore, if:

1) the chronicle describes the events surrounding these kings without omitting "any important events which have a bearing on Babylonia during their reigns";

2) Belshazzar, the crown prince, is not mentioned (much less described as being killed); and

3) Cyrus – while taking the city of Babylon without a fight – captured Nabonidus as prisoner;

then it seems highly improbable that the chronicle would *leave out the significant detail of the death of the crown prince.* And while we must be cautious in using sources like Berossus, confirmation from additional sources, such as the Nabonidus Chronicle, can provide more confidence in the veracity of the account. Grabbe notes confirmation of Berossus's narrative described in the Nabonidus Chronicle:

"Berossus, whose account of the fall of Babylon is extant, says nothing about the death of the king's son. On the other hand, he does state that Nabonidus, after first fleeing, decided to surrender to Cyrus, who treated him well and let him settle in Carmania. The gracious treatment of conquered rulers was a general characteristic of Persian rulers, Nabonidus being no exception".[55]

He concludes:

"But if Nabonidus was treated well, why should Belshazzar have been killed? And if he had been killed, a particularly notable event for the reasons already indicated, *why would both Berossus and the Chronicle be silent on the matter*. In sum, the current state of our information *is overwhelmingly against the historicity of Dan 5:30 as it stands*" (emphasis mine).[56]

Okay, that was a lot of information about Belshazzar: let's sum it up.

1) Whether "father" and "son" can mean "grandfather" or "grandson" in this context is somewhat irrelevant.

2) Daniel tends to transfer characteristics or events of historical figures to other characters in the text, and the evidence strongly suggests that the stories about Nebuchadnezzar are actually part of the Nabonidus tradition.

3) Thus, the reference to Nebuchadnezzar as Belshazzar's father is simply explained by understanding the tradition to be about Nabonidus, who was in fact Belshazzar's father.

4) Nabonidus returned to Babylon in his 13th regnal year, after which time Belshazzar was not present in Babylon, but was likely sent off some distance from Babylon, no longer functioning as co-regent.

5) Babylon fell in Nabonidus's seventeenth year to Cyrus, who took the city without a fight; Nabonidus fled, but was captured/surrendered in Babylon, and was likely treated well by Cyrus.

6) Because no source – particularly the Nabonidus Chronicle – mentions Belshazzar's death (and he was probably not even in Babylonia at the time), *the events described in Daniel 5 are almost certainly not historical.*

Darius the Mede

This leads us to our next significant historical problem in the book: Darius the Mede. Since we dealt with the history of the Neo-Babylonian and early Achaemenid periods at the beginning of this chapter, we should probably talk a bit about the history of the Medes before we continue.

The Medes are spoken of by Herodotus; their last two kings were Cyaxares and Astyages (pronounced "Cy-axe-er-ees" and "Ass-tie-ya-geez"), who are mentioned in the Babylonian Chronicles. Kuhrt explains:

> "If we take all the evidence together (Babylonian chronicles and Herodotus), we see that, by the time of the last Median ruler, Ecbatana had become a royal centre with substantial amounts of goods stored there. The Medes appear to exercise some sort of hegemony, or claim to do so, from the Halys to the Iranian plateau, but its precise nature and extent is nebulous. The Medes are able to mobilize sizeable

forces, to mount attacks on neighbors (Assyria, Persia, Lydia), although the success of their ventures is limited".[57]

In 550, Cyrus defeats Astyages of Media, according to the Babylonian Chronicle:

> "[The sixth year, . . . Astyages] mustered [his troops] and, with con[quest] in view, [m]arched on King Cyrus of Anšan in order to seize him, and deliv[ered] him to Cyrus. Cyrus <marched> on Agamtanu (= Ecbatana), the royal residence, and took to Anšan the silver, gold, goods, valuables, [and . . .] that he had taken as plunder (in) Agamtanu".[58]

Here, the Chronicle states that Astyages attacked Cyrus, but Herodotus says that Cyrus was rebelling against his Median overlord. In other words, the chronicle has the Medes subjected to the Persians, while Herodotus has the Persians subjected to the Medes. Concerning this, Kuhrt notes that "we have no clear evidence outside of this that the Persians were ever subjects of the Medes".[59] In the mid-540's Cyrus defeats the Lydians and ultimately makes his way to Babylonia in 539 B.C.E.

But who was *Darius the Mede*? In Daniel 5:30, the text reads, "That very night Belshazzar, king of the Babylonians, was slain, and Darius the Mede took over the kingdom at the age of sixty-two". In spite of Daniel's description of these events, we have no historical evidence for this Darius the Mede, in spite of knowing a great deal about who was involved in taking over Babylon. It would be a bit like saying, "And in the 2020 election, Frankie won the presidency". Not only do we have no evidence of any "Frankie" becoming president, but we also know who the candidates were and who won the election.

Newsom describes the situation in this way:

> "The figure of Darius the Mede has posed an interpretive puzzle since antiquity because his existence cannot be reconciled with other historical sources. Josephus struggles to make sense of the contradictions, maintaining that he was a son of Astyages, which would make him Cyrus's cousin (*Ant.* 10.248-49). Jerome, who follows Josephus, adds that Darius must have heard of the portent disclosed to Belshazzar and Daniel's interpretation of it and so joined with Cyrus to attack Babylon . . . Josephus's and Jerome's attempts at harmonizing the sources, however, cannot stand up to historical scrutiny".[60]

Conservative scholars have attempted to identify Darius the Mede with known or theorized figures from the time, including the military leader Ug/Gubaru, Cyaxares II, and even Cyrus himself. Newsom observes that conservative biblical scholars who argue for the historical accuracy of Daniel 5 fundamentally misunderstand the details of the story.[61] The following discussion draws on Lester Grabbe's analysis of the work of several such scholars, who sought to defend the historicity of Darius the Mede: Shea, Whitcomb, and Wiseman..[62]

Shea, in his earlier articles, argued that Darius the Mede should be identified with Ug/Gubaru, the governor of the Guti who took Babylon in the Nabonidus Chronicle. Without going into a great deal of detail, there are two names that appear in the Nabonidus Chronicle: Ugbaru and Gubaru. These two are certainly to be identified as the same person.

Shea's argument is that Ug/Gubaru was placed over Babylon for a brief period of time, only to die shortly after his appointment. Grabbe demonstrated, however, that it was *Cambyses* – the crown prince and son of Cyrus – who was placed over Babylon during the year after its fall to Cyrus. In his 2001 article, Shea modified his position and created an almost fanciful timeline in which the events depicted in Daniel 6, 9, and 11 all took place within an incredibly short period of time. This position has not been widely accepted, even within conservative circles.[63]

Whitcomb also argued that Darius the Mede should be identified as Ug/Gubaru, but made a far less convincing case. Grabbe writes:

> "The vital point, however, is the time of office of the Gubaru with whom Whitcomb identifies as Darius the Mede. In pointing to the governor of Babylon and Ebir-nari in various texts down to (possibly) the beginning of Darius' reign, he is evidently unaware that this Gubaru did not take office until Cyrus' *4th year*, long after the alleged activities of the Darius the Mede of Daniel".[64]

Finally, Grabbe examines the suggestions of D.J. Wiseman, who sought to identify Darius the Mede with Cyrus himself.[65] Essentially, Wiseman was not making a case to *demonstrate* this connection, but only to show that *it is not outside of the realm of possibility*. Grabbe writes:

> "It is difficult to falsify such a theory because the argumentation is consistently about what 'could have

been,' not what can now be demonstrated. Ultimately, such a theory has plausibility only for one who is determined to accept the historicity of the biblical data at all costs without worrying that it also makes the writer of Daniel appear either ignorant or deceptive. Contrary to Wiseman's statement, it is not really a 'working hypothesis,' but only an exercise in apologetics".[66]

This type of apologetic approach can also be seen in the recent publication of Steven Anderson, *Darius the Mede: A Reappraisal*.[67] Anderson graduated with his PhD from Dallas Theological Seminary, and this is the publication of his dissertation. He argues that Darius the Mede should be identified with Cyaxares II, the unknown final ruler of the Median Empire. His arguments are largely based on the reliability of Xenophon, whose writings are problematic from a historical standpoint. But Anderson's methodology is far from objective, as can be seen in the following quote from his book:

> "Most importantly, Daniel was a prophet who wrote infallibly under the inspiration of the Holy Spirit, whereas extrabiblical sources for the life of Cyrus are ordinary human writings. Since God was speaking through Daniel as he wrote, the book of Daniel is not to be viewed as an account of uncertain trustworthiness, whose veracity is to be judged by other data, *but rather must be the standard by which all other accounts are measured*" (emphasis mine).[68]

What is a reasonable conclusion here? Is there anything that explains why Daniel might make such an error? There is some indication that the writer had in mind Darius the Great, son of Hystaspes (522-486 B.C.E.). Grabbe notes some of the similarities between Darius I and Darius the Mede; "The statement of Dan 9:1 that Darius the Mede was son of Ahasuerus (Xerxes) could be a case of confusion since it was the other way around: Xerxes was son of Darius", and

> "Darius the Mede appointed 120 satraps over the entire kingdom. It is generally argued that Darius I was the first to give formal organization to the Persian empire into 20 satrapies, though some sort of organization was already in effect in Assyrian times".[69]

Newsom notes that Darius I was "a very important figure in the cultural memory of the Jews since it was during his reign that the temple was rebuilt (Hag 1:1; 2:1)".[70] She also observes:

> "Darius was remembered in classical sources for his administrative reforms, including the organization of the kingdom into a number of satrapies (Herodotus 3.89), a detail that leaves its trace in the claim of Dan 6:1 (2) that Darius appointed 120 satraps over his whole kingdom".[71]

If we remember the four-kingdom tradition from earlier in this chapter, it portrays the Medes and Persians ruling in succession. This may explain – at least in part – the shift or association between the two Dariuses. Newsom states:

> "This change was perhaps facilitated by the prophetic tradition that the Medes would be the ones to attack and destroy Babylon (Isa 13:17; Jer 51:11, 28). Furthermore,

the schema of the four kingdoms in Nebuchadnezzar's dream (Babylon, Media, Persia, Greece) created the need for the story cycle to represent a Median dominion succeeding that of the Babylonians and preceding that of Cyrus".[72]

Because the writer of Daniel almost certainly utilized earlier sources in his composition (Jeremiah 25, 2 Chronicles 36, etc.), it would make sense that they would attempt to utilize and interpret the prophetic tradition.

Historical Details of Daniel 11

We will now take a look at the specific historical details in chapter eleven and why these details suggest a late date of writing. We have seen that there are many historical details that are either incorrect or vague leading up to the end of the book, but when you get to chapter eleven, things get *relatively detailed and accurate*, historically speaking. Many biblical scholars have written about this chapter, and the reader can refer to the bibliography at the end of the book for further discussion on this passage. Our goal here is to provide an overview the layout of Daniel 11, the nature of the historical events it describes, and what this analysis might mean for attempting to date the book. We will begin with a VERY brief overview of the general history that followed the conquest of Alexander the Great, as this chapter deals with that time period.

The time following the death of Alexander the Great was tumultuous. Seeman and Marshak write:

"Alexander died in 323 without a viable heir and apparently without any clear instructions for choosing one.

The result was a series of ultimately unsuccessful attempts by his former companions to prevent the fragmentation of Alexander's realm".[73]

Alexander's generals took control under the guise of protecting Alexander's heirs. Years of fighting and power shifts culminated in the Battle of Ipsus in 301 B.C.E., which resulted in Egypt being under the control of the Ptolemies, while the areas to the east (modern Syria, Iraq, Iran, etc.) were controlled by the Seleucids. The area of Palestine and its environs became a source of great contention between the Ptolemies and Seleucids.

Daniel 11 deals, in some detail, with this period of time. Following a description of Alexander the great and the Diadochi, we see in verses 5-8:

> "And the king of the South will become strong, as well as one of his princes, and he will overpower him and gain dominion; his dominion will be great. And at the end of some years they will join forces, and the daughter of the king of the South will come to the king of the North to make an agreement, but she will not retain the power of her position, nor will he remain with his power, but she will be given over, along with the ones who brought her, and the ones who bore her, and the one who strengthened her in those times. And one from her family will arise in his place, and he will come against the army and come into the fortress of the king of the North, and he will deal with them and have victory. And even their gods, along with their

metal images and their precious vessels of silver and gold he will bring to Egypt into captivity, and he will refrain from the king of the North for some years".

The events described are those concerning Ptolemy I and Seleucus I; the latter joined the former as a general to fight off Antigonus. However, after Antigonus died in 301, Seleucus I became more powerful than Ptolemy I. About 50 years later, Ptolemy II attempted to reconcile with the Seleucids by marrying off Berenice to Antiochus II. However, this ultimately backfired, and Berenice, her son, her Egyptian servants, and her father all died. Berenice's brother, Ptolemy III, attacked Antiochus II and carried off plunder; there were then two years without conflict between the Ptolemies and Seleucids. From these verses alone, you can see that the events describing the 3rd and 2nd centuries (just before the book is agreed to have been compiled) are far more detailed and accurate.[74]

There can be little doubt that these detailed sections of Daniel 11 concern the period following Alexander's death until the time of Antiochus IV. Tremper Longman III, for example, says this:

> "Daniel 11 covers a period from the Persian period to the time of Antiochus Epiphanes. From what we know about the period we can affirm that the prophet writes with the accuracy of a historian. As a matter of fact, that is what many scholars feel is going on in this passage. That is, Daniel 11 is not a forward-looking prophecy from the standpoint of the sixth century B.C., but rather a backward-looking history cast in the literary form of

prophecy. *The arguments in favor of the latter view are strong*" (emphasis mine).[75]

So how does this help us in determining the date of Daniel's composition? Notice Longman cites the specificity and accuracy of Daniel 11 as evidence that many (I would say most) scholars think points to this being "prophecy after the fact" or "backward-looking history cast in the literary form of prophecy", as Longman puts it. By the way, Longman holds to an early date for the composition of Daniel.

Collins writes:

> "The 'prophecy' of Hellenistic history mentions no names, but the people and events can be readily identified. The struggles of the kings of the south (Ptolemies) with the kings of the north (Seleucids) are swiftly reviewed, reaching a preliminary crescendo with the career of Antiochus III (the Great). The main focus of attention is Antiochus IV Epiphanes, to whose reign more than half the chapter is devoted".[76]

The significance of this historical detail becomes very important toward the end of the chapter. As early as the 3rd c. C.E., the argument that Daniel wrote during the time of Antiochus IV rather than during the Babylonian exile had already been made; Porphyry noted that the accuracy of the prophecy only lasts until the time of Antiochus Epiphanies.[77] As Collins succinctly states, "This argument has stood the test of time". [78]

Beginning at Daniel 11:40, however, the text switches from an accurate to an inaccurate presentation of history. This section is summarized well by Hartman and Di Lella, who note that the section is supposed to be a "genuine prediction of events", though the information contained within the verses doesn't at all match actual historical events that we know from other sources.[79] They observe that:

> "This untoward situation has caused believers through the centuries great difficulty. And unusual interpretations, however well intentioned and prompted as they were by deep faith in the Sacred Scripture, were put forward in a misguided attempt to salvage the inerrancy of the biblical text".[80]

In short, when the historical *inaccuracies*, *imprecision*, and *vagueness* that was frequently used to describe earlier events in the book of Daniel are juxtaposed with the *accuracy* and *detail* seen in chapter eleven, it strongly indicates that the compiler of Daniel did his work in the 2nd century, when these events were taking (or had recently taken) place. Further evidence for this position can be seen in the *imprecision* that appears at the end of chapter eleven. The author ostensibly engaged in an attempt at actual prophecy, only for his prophecy to prove incorrect.

By way of example, suppose we found a document that contained a "prophecy" by Thomas Jefferson that predicted the events of American history. The prophecy read, "In the future, the nation will be at war. First, brother will be divided against brother, and the North will fight against the South. After this, the nation will declare its independence and fight an enemy from the east". Upon reading this, we might wonder why the author (purported to be Thomas Jefferson) would get the Civil War and the Revolutionary War in the wrong chronological order.

The prophecy then read, "There will arise two contestants, one who will seek the presidency as her husband had done before her. She will be opposed by the man of the tower, who will polarize the nation. This man, with no political background, will rise to prominence against all expectations, to the chagrin of many". After describing many specific details (in couched language) concerning the political race between these two figures, the prophecy concluded, "Yet fear not, O nation! For God will not allow such a man to come to power! She who opposes him will be strengthened by our God and will rise above him in the final hour".

We could posit a number of things with relative certainty from this information. First, the tremendous detail that is accurately represented concerning the presidential race between Senator Hillary Clinton and Mr. Donald Trump, contrasted with the general and sometimes incorrect information presented concerning early American history, would lead the reader to believe that the writer actually lived through the events described in 2016. Furthermore, we would likely conclude that the prophecy was written before the election took place, as the prophecy reassured the people that Mr. Trump would *not* become president. Thus, we could safely date this portion of the prophecy at least to around the middle of 2016.

This situation is similar to what we have discussed above in the book of Daniel. As we have seen, the historical information concerning the Neo-Babylonian and Persian periods is often confused, out of order, or simply inaccurate. However, prophecies concerning events during the end of the third and second centuries, particularly in chapter eleven, are much more detailed and refer to certain portions of the reign of Antiochus IV Epiphanes. This has led scholars to conclude that the book was composed at a relatively late date and that certain sections can be dated with some precision based on the specific events that are described in the text.

Seow compares the book of Daniel to Shakespeare's *Julius Caesar*, which was set in the early Roman period, though written centuries later and containing a variety of historical inaccuracies.[81] Concerning Daniel, he concludes, "In contrast to the discrepancies in details from the period of its historical setting in the sixth and fifth centuries, the book is remarkably precise in its allusions to certain events in the Ptolemaic and Seleucid periods down to the time just before the death of Antiochus IV Epiphanes, at the end of 164 B.C.E".[82] These historical details found in the book strongly suggest (among other things) that the book was written in the second century.

"Liar, Lunatic... or Skilled Writer": The Genre of Daniel

But why should we believe that a writer from the Hellenistic period would write in this way? Why would he falsely present the prophecies as stemming from the 6th c.? The answer may lie in the *genre* of the book of Daniel – pseudepigraphy. This is the practice of using the name of a well-known historical figure to give new compositions a veneer of historicity. Pseudepigraphic compositions from Qumran in particular use this method to present texts as prophetic, when they were in fact written long after the events they describe.[83] Collins notes that this kind of "prophecy after the fact, authorized by a venerable pseudonym, is well known throughout the Hellenistic world from Persia to Rome".[84]

For example, the Apocalypse of Weeks, found in the book of 1 Enoch, gives a historical overview that is divided up into periods of "weeks", similar to Daniel 9.

> "And Enoch took up his discourse and said, 'I was born the seventh in the first week, and until my time righteousness endured. After me there will arise a second week, in which deceit and violence will spring up, and in it will be the first end, and in it a man will be saved. And after <that, at its conclusion>, iniquity will increase, and a law will be made for sinners" (1 Enoch 93:3-4).[85]

The sixth week appears:

> "After this <three will arise a sixth week, and> all who live in it will become blind, and the hearts of all will stray from wisdom; and in it a man will ascend. And at its conclusion, the temple of the kingdom will be burned with fire, and in it the whole race of the chosen root will be dispersed" (1 Enoch 93:7-8).

Finally, the 10th and final week culminates in the ultimate salvation of the righteous and the punishment of the wicked, where the "first heaven will pass away in it, and the new heaven will appear" (1 Enoch 93:16). Concerning this historical periodization, Collins writes,

> "The division of history into a set number of periods is a common feature of the 'historical' type of apocalypse. One

effect of this periodization is the impression of an ordered universe where everything proceeds in a predetermined manner . . . The use of an ancient pseudonym like Enoch permits a *vaticinium ex eventu*, a review of past history as if it were future, and so adds to the impression that all is determined in advance, and under divine control".[86]

It seems that Daniel, in this respect, is not unique; there were several pseudepigraphal works written during this period. In fact, few (if any) scholars that would argue for the authenticity and early dating of Daniel would *also* argue for the authenticity of these other works. This type of selective acceptance was noted by Grabbe concerning other texts that contain clear historical inaccuracies but are rarely defended by those that advocate for Daniel. He writes, "This is all stark testimony to how the fundamentalist approach to scholarship is determined not by objective study but by preconceptions about what is inspired".[87]

So what *was* Daniel doing? What was the purpose of compiling this book in the 2nd century? Daniel is an *apocalypse* – a genre of text that gives the reader a glimpse into the heavenly realm to see that, despite the atrocities taking place on earth, God is *still* in control. Steven Cook summarizes this well:

"The visions of Dan 7-12 expect a steady increase of worldwide evil, followed by an end-time triumph of God over its forces. God is about to intervene in history, according to Daniel's visions, destroying the evil embedded within the world's empires. When that happens, God will overthrow all imperial systems of control, establish an everlasting dominion on earth, and reward those who have remained faithful".[88]

Specifically he writes,

"The writings of the Daniel group became less lighthearted and comedic as the new Seleucid rulers of Judea revealed their true colors. As Antiochus moved to Hellenize the Judeans, the Daniel writings took on a deadly seriousness and an even more cosmological perspective. They become progressively more concerned with honestly revealing that God's reign will not come without horrible birth pangs. But it will come. A terrifying state of chaos preceded God's original creation of the cosmos. This chaos would reassert itself in the end times, but only to pave the way for God's new, re-creative work".[89]

Josephus and Alexander the Great

I would like to conclude this chapter with an interesting story that has been used to argue for an early date of the book of Daniel. The story is told by Josephus, a Roman-Jewish historian who lived during the 1st c. C.E., and concerns a visit to Jerusalem by Alexander the Great and his encounter with the book of Daniel. If Alexander was able to read the book of Daniel in a trip to Jerusalem in the late 4th c. B.C.E., this would mean that the book (and a prophetic portion about Alexander in particular) *had to be written by the time of his arrival.* Thus, if Josephus's account is true, it seems that Daniel must date much earlier than the time of Antiochus IV Epiphanes.

Before we examine Josephus's account and see what scholars have to say about it, let's briefly consider how the works of Josephus (and those of any ancient historian) must be treated. Simply because a story is included in the works of an ancient author does *not* necessarily mean that that story is historically accurate. Ancient sources should not merely be taken at face value; people write things down for a purpose, and sometimes that purpose is best served by embellishing, or even completely fabricating, an event. Maier phrases it this way:

> "[A]ll these defects – conceit, inconsistencies, embellishment, exaggeration, credulity, and desultory digressions were widely shared by ancient historians, few of whom brought critical tools to their craft in any modern sense".[90]

The works of Josephus are no exception. Again, Maier explains:

> "Josephus's accuracy and reliability as a historian have been challenged repeatedly. His free interpretation of his sources and his embellishments of the biblical record have already been cited. That he had a habit of overstating for dramatic purposes is also clear".[91]

The story can be found in Josephus, *Antiquities* 11, chapters 7-8. To summarize: as Alexander conquered his way down the Levantine coast, he sent word to Yaddua, high priest of the temple at Jerusalem, commanding him to provide assistance and tribute. Yaddua, however, had already sworn an oath to Darius III and responded that he could not go back on his oath. Alexander then determined to attack Yaddua after taking Tyre. After Tyre, Alexander went to Gaza and besieged it.

When Alexander finally began to move toward Jerusalem, Yaddua sought God's help and protection. God came to him in a dream and told him not to fear, but to welcome Alexander. When Alexander came, Yaddua and the priests met him on the way, outside of the city. Those with Alexander thought that he would destroy and plunder Jerusalem and kill Yaddua, but instead Alexander showed them favor, and ultimately entered Jerusalem, sacrificed to God, *and was shown the book of Daniel, which he interpreted as referring to himself.* Thus, if the book existed to be shown to Alexander at the time of his arrival, it must have been written much earlier than the 2nd century.

As a general note, we need to remember that Josephus is not simply an unbiased historian (should such a thing even exist), but had his own agenda in writing his accounts. Concerning Josephus's representation of the book of Daniel in *Antiquities*, Collins writes,

> "Josephus follows the biblical account fairly closely, but with some interesting embellishments. Thus he reports that some of the Jewish youths were made eunuchs (§186) and that Daniel and his companions 'resolved to live austerely' (§190). He also attempts to resolve some historical problems. Thus Nebuchadnezzar's dream (Daniel 2) is dated to the second year after the sacking of Egypt rather than to the second year of his reign (§195); Belshazzar (Baltasares) is 'also called Naboandelos' (Nabonidus; §231); and Darius the Mede is a son of Astyages and known by another name among the Greeks (§248)".[92]

In other words, Josephus is *doing* something with his writing, and it would be unwise to simply take what he says at face value.

It seems as though scholars take this approach when it comes to the story of Alexander and Jerusalem. Three such scholars are Peter Green, Celicia Peck, and Jonathan Goldstein. All three appear to argue that, while it is possible that Alexander may have come to Jerusalem, it seems very unlikely. Instead, this fictional or legendary story may have served as an explanation and encouragement, showing how God remains in control, despite the ruler in power, and obeying such earthly powers is not necessarily in conflict with serving God.

Green clearly considers Alexander's visit to Jerusalem to be a later legend that was used to show the special character of the city of Jerusalem. He writes that Alexander "spent little time on Palestine, having other goals in mind", arguing that later records (including Josephus's account), which show him making a special journey to Jerusalem, are simply stories trying to emphasize the special status of the holy city.[93]

Peek holds a similar position, noting that "no surviving non-Jewish source mentions any connection between Alexander and the Jews . . . It is possible that Alexander visited Jerusalem, but the preserved descriptions of his visit are almost certainly fictional".[94] Peek goes on say that this doesn't diminish the historical importance of Josephus's work, as "it does offer valuable insight into at least one Jewish view of the appropriate relationship between the Jews and a Greek ruler".[95]

Finally, Goldstein shows great incredulity concerning the idea that the king's historians would have failed to record such a visit to Jerusalem by Alexander:

> "None of these legends can be true. Pagan eye-witnesses chronicled Alexander's career, and though their works have perished, later writers were able to draw upon them, particularly Arrian. The pagan authors took pains to record the king's visits to the shrines of non-Greek deities and his participation in their rituals, especially during the years 333-331 B.C.E. when he was in the vicinity of Judaea. Throughout, the pagan Alexander historians tell how the king showed respect to deities, and there is no reason to assume that they would have suppressed a report that Alexander made obeisance to the God of the Jews or even to His high priest. On the other hand, if Alexander had made obeisance to any human being, as related in Josephus and in the rabbinic tale, the fact would have been so astounding that no biographer of the king would have passed over it in silence".[96]

If it doesn't preserve historical fact, what, then, is the point of this story? Peek argues that legend explains the situation of the Jewish people as under the care and protection of God, yet still subject for a time to the earthly powers:

> "The story as a whole represents an effort to clarify and relieve that tension by defining the Jewish place in a world dominated by the Hellenistic world-conqueror. The hard

fact is that the Jews must acknowledge the *temporal* overlordship of the victorious Alexander and, by extension, whichever of his successors should control Palestine. But their lives are also governed by their God and the laws established by him, and He takes precedence".[97]

Finally, she writes, "Fanciful though Josephus's account of Alexander the Great's visit to Jerusalem may be, it is powerful metaphor. It commemorates and contemplates the introduction of Hellenism to Judea".[98]

Goldstein draws a similar conclusion, arguing that Josephus's account shows that Jews should be loyal to whatever pagan ruler God places over them, and that regardless of who is ruling in the earthly realm, ultimately, God is in control and will protect the Jewish people.[99]

In short, the story told by Josephus does not appear to be historically reliable, but can be understood as explaining the position of the Jewish people in a world under God's control. This account of Josephus should not be used to argue for an early date of Daniel.

Conclusion

Okay, let's try to summarize what we have presented here... because it was *a lot*. We began with the linguistic data that exists, particularly from the Aramaic and Hebrew languages. After some tedious analysis, we saw that it is not possible to date the book of Daniel precisely based on the Aramaic evidence alone, as our current data set and knowledge do not allow it. However, what we can deduce strongly suggests that *the*

Aramaic in the book dates to a period later than the 4th century but earlier than the texts found at Qumran dating from the 2nd c. B.C.E.

When we examined the Hebrew language, we saw that linguists label Daniel as part of the group belonging to the category Late Biblical Hebrew, along with other books like Ezra-Nehemiah, Ecclesiastes, and Chronicles. Certain features found in Daniel are indicative of Late Biblical Hebrew (539/538-165 B.C.E.), including *vocabulary preferences* and *diagnostic syntactical and grammatical features*. Finally, while other foreign words or influences do suggest a late date for Daniel, the evidence is not as conclusive and should be weighted accordingly.

We then provided a brief overview of the history of the Neo-Babylonian and early Persian Empires, followed by a description of how Daniel presents the history of these periods. We saw that Daniel follows the known four-kingdom schema, ending his history with the kingdom of Greece.

But there are many problems with the history as presented in the book, and it will not suffice for a historian or biblical scholar to say, "Well, it is *possible* that Daniel was right", particularly when there are explanations that are far more likely and better account for the data. We began by looking at some of the dates provided in the book, how they do not fit well with what we know from extrabiblical sources, and how they are problematic when compared to other biblical passages. However, we demonstrated that the dates in the book do fit well if we understand that the compiler was likely attempting to make sense of other passages in the biblical texts, as he did at other times in the book.

We then looked at the "madness" of Nebuchadnezzar and demonstrated that this story was almost certainly part of a tradition about Nabonidus. This explains several problems in the text, including who Belshazzar's father was. This understanding renders arguments about Nabonidus marrying an unknown daughter of Nebuchadnezzar or how Belshazzar could have been understood as king unnecessary, as the common tradition was not about him, but about Nabonidus.

We looked at the problem of Belshazzar and his reign and death as presented in Daniel 5. Although Belshazzar had been co-regent with his father, Nabonidus, during the latter's stay in Teima, we know that Nabonidus returned and took back his reign long before the fall of Babylon to Cyrus. It is also quite likely that Belshazzar was far from Babylon or Sippar leading up to the fall. Even if we conclude that Belshazzar died in the attack on Sippar (something for which we have no evidence), it still flatly contradicts the narrative in Daniel 5.

This led us to our discussion of Darius the Mede, a figure for whom we have no evidence outside of the biblical text. Conservative scholars have attempted to identify Darius with other figures from the period, including Ug/Gubaru, Cyaxares II, or Cyrus. However, none of these appear to solve the problem of Darius. What does make sense, though, is that Darius I had characteristics transferred to this Darius the Mede, which is the type of thing that the compiler(s) of Daniel frequently did.

We then looked at Daniel 11 and the history that it presents. The detail and accuracy that it contains is striking, as is the inaccuracy of the prophecies given at the end of the chapter. This is strong evidence for the writer having utilized the literary technique "prophecy after the fact", as was common and useful during the Hellenistic period.

Finally, we briefly looked at a story that appears in Josephus's writings concerning a trip to Jerusalem by Alexander the Great. It has been argued that, if Alexander was shown the book of Daniel by the high priest, then the book must have been written before that time (the late 4th c. B.C.E.). However, we saw that scholars do not view Josephus's account as historically reliable, but instead have determined that the story serves a separate ideological purpose altogether.

In short, when we consider the linguistic and historical data, it seems highly likely that the book of Daniel is an apocalyptic text whose composition should be dated to the 2nd c. B.C.E. Of course, this in no way negates its usefulness or meaning as a theological text; quite to the contrary, when we understand the original context and purpose of writing for the book, it allows us to appreciate its theological significance all the more.

---

[1] For recent overviews of the issues involved (including bibliographic citations), see Goldingay 2019: 495-499 and Lucas 2002: 241-248.
[2] Collins 1993: 2-24.
[3] Collins 1993: 15.
[4] /z/ reappears in Murabba'at (1st c. C.E.); thus, matter of orthography, not phonology. See Collins 1993: 15-16.
[5] Collins 1993: 15-16.
[6] Collins 1993: 16.
[7] For an introduction and translation of the Dead Sea Scrolls, see Vermes 2012.
[8] Collins 1993: 16-17.
[9] Collins 1993: 17.
[10] Collins 1993: 17.
[11] Collins 1993: 17.
[12] Hartman and Di Lella 1978: 13; Seow 2003: 7-8.
[13] Collins 1993: 20.

¹⁴ Lam and Pardee 2016: 1.
¹⁵ Morgenstern 2016: 43.
¹⁶ Morgenstern 2016: 44.
¹⁷ Collins 1993: 20-23.
¹⁸ Collins 1993: 21.
¹⁹ Morgenstern 2016: 48.
²⁰ Collins 1993: 18.
²¹ Collins 1993: 19.
²² Collins 1993: 20.
²³ Newsom 2014: 240.
²⁴ Collins 1993: 320.
²⁵ Newsom 2014: 270.
²⁶ Translation from Charlesworth 1983: 550.
²⁷ Goldingay 2019: 373.
²⁸ Newsom 2014: 80-81.
²⁹ See Newsom 2014: 80 with references.
³⁰ Newsom 2014: 81.
³¹ Grabbe 1987: 148-149.
³² Cogan and Tadmor 1988: 308.
³³ Japhet 1993: 1066.
³⁴ Japhet 1993: 1066.
³⁵ Cogan and Tadmor 1988: 308.
³⁶ Grayson 1975: 102; Chronicle 5 (BM 21946, rev. 11-13).
³⁷ Goldingay 2019: 153.
³⁸ Seow 2003: 21.
³⁹ Longman III 1999: 116 Kindle version.
⁴⁰ Hartman and Di Lella 1978: 51.
⁴¹ Hartman and Di Lella 1978: 51.
⁴² Beaulieu 2009: 275.
⁴³ Vermes 2012: 614.
⁴⁴ Newsom 2014: 128.
⁴⁵ Beaulieu 2009: 288.
⁴⁶ Seow 2003: 77.
⁴⁷ Millard 1977: 72.
⁴⁸ Wiseman 1995: 11.
⁴⁹ Beaulieu 1989: 203.
⁵⁰ Beaulieu 1989: 204.
⁵¹ Beaulieu 1989: 205.
⁵² Grabbe 1988b 141.
⁵³ Grayson 1975: 10-11.
⁵⁴ Grayson 1975: 109-110; Chronicle 7 (BM 35382, iii 12b-15).
⁵⁵ Grabbe 1988b: 61-62.
⁵⁶ Grabbe 1988b: 62.
⁵⁷ Kuhrt 1997: 655.
⁵⁸ Glassner 2004: 235.
⁵⁹ Kuhrt 2007: 657.

[60] Newsom 2014: 191-192.

[61] Newsom 2014: 163.

[62] Grabbe 1988a. Grabbe's analysis, though a bit dated, represents a thorough and effective critique of several apologetic attempts to validate the historicity of Daniel's Darius the Mede, particularly those of William Shea, who wrote several influential articles on the topic.

[63] Shea 2001: 97-105.

[64] Grabbe 1988a: 206.

[65] Wiseman 1965: 9-18.

[66] Grabbe 1988a: 207.

[67] Anderson 2014.

[68] Anderson 2014: 38.

[69] Grabbe 1988a: 209.

[70] Newsom 2014: 192.

[71] Newsom 2014: 192.

[72] Newsom 2014: 192.

[73] Seeman and Marshak 2012: 33.

[74] For recent explanations of the historical events depicted in chapter 11, see Goldingay 2019: 528-542 and Newsom 2014: 338-339.

[75] Longman III 1999: 270-271 Kindle version.

[76] Collins 2016: 137.

[77] Collins 2016: 110.

[78] Collins 2016: 110.

[79] Hartman and Di Lella 1978: 303.

[80] Hartman and Di Lella 1978: 303.

[81] Seow 2003: 5.

[82] Seow 2003: 6.

[83] Examples include the *Apocalypse of Weeks* and the *Animal Apocalypse* of *1 Enoch*; in Daniel 10-12; in *Jubilees* 23; in 4Q390 (Pseudo-Moses); and in the Pseudo-Daniel fragments. See Collins 2015: 219.

[84] Collins 2015: 219.

[85] For quotes from 1 Enoch, see Nickelsburg 2001.

[86] Collins 2016: 81.

[87] Grabbe 1987: 148.

[88] Cook 2003: 27.

[89] Cook 2003: 147.

[90] Whiston and Maier 1999: 14.

[91] Whiston and Maier 1999: 14.

[92] Collins 1993: 85.

[93] Green 1990: 499.

[94] Peek 1996: 104-105.

[95] Peek 1996: 104-105.

[96] Goldstein 1993: 70-71.

[97] Peek 1996: 106-107.

[98] Peek 1996: 107.

[99] Goldstein 1993: 90.

CHAPTER SIX
Did the Bible Endorse Slavery?

Introduction

The problem of slavery is a perennial one, and much of humanity has gone to great lengths to one day see its abolition. Article 4 of the *Universal Declaration of Human Rights* reads, "No one shall be held in slavery or servitude; slavery and the slave trade shall be prohibited in all their forms".[1] Given our nation's relatively recent history, slavery and its devastating consequences remain fresh in the minds of many – as well it should. Maybe because of our modern outlook on slavery, many people are surprised to find that the practice of slavery appears within the pages of the Bible in both the Old and New Testaments. Not only is it described in the narrative portions, but – particularly in the Hebrew Bible – it also appears in the legal sections, where its appropriate practice is set forth.

The presence of laws relating to slavery is often quite jarring to believer and unbeliever alike. How could a text – either divinely inspired by God or standing at the heart of an all-pervasive religion – contain laws that regulate the appropriate practice of slavery, endorsing it through such regulation? For some believers, these laws are part of an outdated system that has been superseded by the teachings of the New Testament. For others, these laws are studied in their ancient Near Eastern context in the hopes that this comparative data will show the Old Testament laws to be superior to those obtained in the ANE. Still others seek to demonstrate that the word "slavery" should not be applied at all to these laws in the Hebrew Bible; furthermore, this type of "servitude" cannot (and should not) be compared to slavery in the antebellum South. This, it would seem, casts the Old Testament "slavery" laws in a better light, making them appear less severe and atrocious than what we might imagine.

What are we to make of all of this? What was slavery like as described in the Hebrew Bible? Were there laws concerning the appropriate practice of debt- and chattel-slavery? How did these laws compare to those from other ancient Near Eastern nations? If there was genuine slavery in the laws of the Old Testament, did the New Testament do away with this practice?

Before we look at specific biblical passages, it is important to define our terms. While the definition of slavery can be nuanced depending on the context in which the term is used, there are essential aspects that can been seen in each of these contexts. For example, Gene Haas defines slavery as it appears in the Pentateuch as "a condition . . . in which a person is deprived of freedom, at least for a period of time, by being in subjugation to a master in order that the master may benefit from the labor of the slave".[2] Dandamayev defines slavery as "the institution whereby one person can hold ownership rights over another".[3] In what follows, we will essentially define slavery as "A condition in which an individual – or rights to their labor – is owned by another, either temporarily or permanently. The owner controls and benefits from the actions and activities of the owned individual".

With that being said, slavery remains a difficult condition to define, even in the ancient world. Westbrook explains:

"A better criterion for a legal definition of slavery is its property aspect, since persons were recognized as a category of property that might be owned by private individuals. A slave was therefore a person to whom the law of property applied rather than family or contract law. Even this definition is not wholly exclusive, since family and contract law occasionally intruded upon the rules of ownership. Furthermore, the relationship between master and slave was subject to legal restrictions based on the humanity of the slave and concerns of social justice".[4]

My goal in this chapter will be to provide the reader with a broad overview of slavery in the Hebrew Bible, starting with an examination of the three primary legal sections in the Old Testament that deal with the issue of slavery: Exodus 21 (part of the so-called Covenant Code), Deuteronomy 15, and Leviticus 25 (part of the Holiness Code). Exodus 21 contains laws that govern debt-slavery (Exodus 21:2-6), the sale of girls by their fathers (Exodus 21:7-11), and the legal consequences if a slave were to come to physical harm (Exodus 21:20-21, 26-27, 28-32). Deuteronomy 15:12-18 develops at least some aspects of the laws in the Covenant Code, most notably the requirement to provide the slave with material provisions following his six-year term of service, in order that he might not so easily fall back into debt-slavery. Finally, Leviticus 25 – the latest of the three legal sections – develops the laws concerning the Israelite slave even further. The text outlaws the possession of one Israelite by another, and instead restricts the ownership of slaves to foreigners, who can be taken from the nations that surround them and from tenant farmers residing in the land of Israel. These foreign slaves can be treated as inheritable property as described in the passage (verses 44-46).

We will also consider biblical slavery in light of the slavery that was legislated in the antebellum South, looking at the laws and legal discussions from the period in order to determine how similar or distinct they were from the laws in the Old Testament. Finally, we will wade into several New Testament texts (although that is obviously not my field of expertise) in order to engage with a common apologetic. Specifically, it is often argued that God *did* allow slavery (of some sort) in the Old Testament, but this was due to man's wickedness. Instead of overtly condemning it, God "worked with" mankind until the time of Jesus and the New Testament, when He was ready to condemn the practice.

Where relevant, other passages, including legal texts from the wider ancient Near East, will be included in the chapter.

Since our discussion on slavery is limited to a single chapter, it will be impossible to develop all aspects of the topic. However, if the reader is interested in pursuing the issue of Old Testament slavery in greater detail, we have published a separate resource on the topic that is also written for a general audience: *Did the Old Testament Endorse Slavery?*[5] Most of the primary topics discussed in this chapter are covered in greater detail in the book, along with their setting in the wider ancient Near Eastern context.

As with most everything in this book, the general overview of slavery in the Hebrew Bible that is presented below *is the consensus view among scholars in the field*, and accords well – as we will see – with what these texts say and what they are doing in their respective contexts.

Exodus 21: Slavery in the "Covenant Code"

There is no question that Exodus 21 is the central passage under discussion in scores of debates concerning slavery. Given the variety of issues related to slavery in Exodus 21, it is unsurprising that so much time is spent dealing with this section of the Mosaic law. Included in Exodus 21 are laws concerning a male debt-slave and his release (or permanent voluntary servitude), the female slave-wife/concubine, the abuse of a slave, and required compensation if a slave is gored to death.

The Male Debt-Slave (Exodus 21:2-6)

"If you buy a Hebrew slave, six years he will serve, and in the seventh he will go out free, without payment. If he comes in alone, he will go out alone. If he is the husband of a wife, then his wife will go out with him. If his master gives him a wife and she bears him sons or daughters, the woman and her children belong to the master, but he will go out alone. But if the slave in fact says, 'I love my master and my wife and my children, I will not go out free', then his master will bring him to God, even to the door or the doorpost, and his master will pierce his ear with an awl, and he will serve him forever" (Exodus 21:2-6).

Exodus 21 begins with laws for the Hebrew slave. An initial difficulty with this passage is identifying what people group is being referred to – who are the "Hebrews" (the Hebrew word is *ivri*) that are being referenced here? There is a group of people known from the ancient Near East that are sometimes found in the context of slavery: they are called the *ḥabiru* in the Akkadian language. While it might not be apparent to the reader, there are several similarities between the words *ḥabiru* and *ivri*, so much so that scholars have debated whether the *ivri* spoken of here in Exodus 21 are actually referring to the *ḥabiru*.

But who were the *ḥabiru*? The term often refers to a social class, what Dozeman describes as "a reference to fugitives and outlaws in the ancient Near East". [6] While the *ḥabiru* appear throughout the 2nd millennium B.C.E., we take special interest in their appearance in the written records that were found at the city of Nuzi in Mesopotamia. Lemche observes that private contracts from Nuzi show *ḥabiru*/*ḥapiru* as non-citizens, without any legal rights, who voluntarily enter into contracts with citizens to gain a kind of "social security" for the course of that contract. [7]

If we understand these *ḥabiru* to be foreigners who make contracts with residents of the city to serve them, and there is a possible connection between the word *ḥabiru* and *ivri*, then (it is sometimes argued) the slaves who are selling themselves in Exodus 21:2-6 are not fellow Israelites, but actually *foreigners*.

Suffice it to say that a closer examination shows that these *ivri* are indeed fellow Israelites. [8] When we look at how the word *ivri* is used in the Old Testament, we see that it almost (if not) exclusively functions as a "gentilic" (that is, a word that refers to an ethnicity or nationality). For example, in Exodus 1:19, a contrast is made between the "Hebrew" women and the Egyptian women: "The midwives answered Pharaoh,

'Hebrew women are not like Egyptian women; they are vigorous and give birth before the midwives arrive'". We see a later parallel to this particular type of slavery in Deuteronomy 15:12: "If any of your people – *Hebrew men or women* – sell themselves to you and serve you six years, in the seventh year you must let them go free" (emphasis mine). In short, Exodus 21:2-6 is dealing with an Israelite purchasing a fellow Israelite as a slave.

So what is the law describing here? An Israelite buys a fellow Israelite – likely due to impoverishment, or defaulting on a loan – and the law sets the limit of debt service to six years. First, how are we to understand this language of "buying"? Many apologists are quick to point out that one of the ways in which the Hebrew word *qanah* "to buy" can be translated is "to acquire". Softening the phrase from "If you buy..." to "If you acquire..." can make the idea of "procuring" a slave a bit more palatable. The reality, however, is that the verb should certainly be translated "to buy", as this is not only expected in the context, but is the typical way in which the verb *qanah* is used in similar passages.

In fact, there are many verses in the Hebrew Bible that refer specifically to slaves being purchased. Abraham, for example, owned different types of slaves. In Genesis 17:12-13 we read:

> "'And every male among you who is eight days old will be circumcised throughout your generations; a home-born slave and one purchased with silver from every foreigner who is not from among your descendants. Your home-born slave and your slave purchased with silver will surely be

circumcised, and my covenant will be in your flesh as an everlasting covenant'" (Genesis 17:12-13).

Abraham carries out God's command in verse 27: "And all the men of his house – the home-born slave and the one purchased with silver from a foreigner – were circumcised with him". Hamilton comments on this passage: "Circumcision is to extend even beyond the family circle. It is to be done for the *houseborn slave or for one bought with money from any foreigner*" (emphasis mine).[9]

The verb *qanah* is, in fact, used quite commonly to describe the process of purchasing goods and property. In Genesis 49:30, we see Abraham buying a field using this same verb: "in the cave, which is in the field of Machpelah, which is in front of Mamre, in the land of Canaan, which Abraham **purchased** (Hebrew *qanah*), with the field, from Ephron the Hittite as a burial site". Similar transactions can be seen in Jeremiah 13:2 (purchasing a belt) and 19:1 (purchasing a clay jar). Kitchen observes, "Slaves could readily be bought from other owners and general merchants (*cf.* Gn. xvii. 12, 13, 27; Ec. ii. 7)".[10] In short, slaves were purchased regularly in the Old Testament, along with other goods and property, utilizing the Hebrew verb *qanah*; this is the same word that appears in Exodus 21:2.

So, we have an Israelite who is purchasing another Israelite as a slave; what are the rules that govern this debt-slave's service? The male debt-slave is to serve for six years and to be released free of debt in the seventh. Thus, the principal, any interest, and/or additional charges would be satisfied by the six years of service. This is the basic rule concerning the male Hebrew slave.

However, there are other circumstances to be considered in this transaction. "If he comes in alone, he will go out alone. If he is the husband of a wife, then his wife will go out with him" (Exodus 21:3). This seems fairly straightforward; if the debt-slave is purchased as a single man, he is to be released a single man. If he was enslaved as a married man, both he and his wife go free upon his release in the seventh year. So far, so good.

However, the situation is complicated in verse 4: "If his master gives him a wife and she bears him sons or daughters, the woman and her children belong to the master, but he will go out alone". The text has set forth the general principle that a Hebrew slave can only be made to serve for six years in order to pay off his debt. Now we are dealing with the different scenarios that can occur within that general principle. If he is single when he comes in, he goes out single. Married? He goes out married. In other words, as you came in, that's how you go out.

This would also apply, therefore, to a Hebrew slave who is given a wife by his master during his term of service. Because she was the property of the master, the law required that she *remain* his property, along with any children that she would produce. Durham notes:

> "If, however, his wife has married him during his servitude, obviously by the permission and through the provision of his owner, both the wife and any children born to such a union must remain with the owner when the 'temporary' slave claims his freedom of the seventh year. They are obviously the owner's property".[11]

In other words, although the male debt-slave has a set term of service, the female slave and her children are chattel slaves and remain the property of their owner.

This stipulation in the law explains what follows in Exodus 21:5-6:

> "But if the slave in fact says, 'I love my master and my wife and my children, I will not go out free', then his master will bring him to God, even to the door or the doorpost, and his master will pierce his ear with an awl, and he will serve him forever" (Exodus 21:5-6).

The male debt-slave is left with two options: first, he can exercise his right to release in the seventh year and go on his way; however, he would do so alone. His second option would be to remain with his wife and children, continuing to serve as a slave in the master's home. Because his wife and children are the property of the master, not subject to release after a set term of service, remaining with his family is contingent upon him dedicating himself to lifetime service to the master.[12] If the male debt-slave decides to remain with his master, wife, and children, he swears an oath of life-long servitude and is marked as a chattel slave.

The Female Slave (Exodus 21:7-11)

Having dealt with the rules for the male debt-slave, the text turns to the female slave.

> "And if a man sells his daughter as a female slave, she will not go out like the male slaves. If she is displeasing in the eyes of her master, who has designated her for himself,

then he must let her be redeemed. He may not sell her to a foreign people, as he dealt treacherously with her. And if he designates her for his son, he must treat her according to the custom of daughters. If he takes another wife for himself, her food, her clothing, and her marital rights he cannot diminish. And if these three things he does not do for her, then she will go out free without payment of money" (Exodus 21:7-11).

Here, the passage speaks of a man selling *his daughter* as a slave in order to satisfy a debt. In this case, she is entering into a sexual relationship with either her master or his son and, based on this relationship and its social and financial consequences to her value, she is to receive certain rights from her master. Her status must be changed – either to a wife or a concubine – as her sexual and reproductive capacities are now in use. This also means that, unlike the male debt-slave who was also used in a reproductive capacity but without the social and financial consequences, she is not to be released after six years. Essentially, the sexual activity of the female debt-slave irrevocably alters her status, while sexual activity of the male debt-slave is irrelevant to his social position.[13]

This legally-mandated change of status to wife or concubine affords her protection (as odd as that may sound), as her master must provide for her. Even if she falls out of favor with him, he cannot reduce her to the status of a simple slave and sell her to foreigners. He must continue to provide for her or allow her to be redeemed. Propp elaborates:

"A Hebrew maidservant is not released after six years . . . even if she is married to a Hebrew slave (21:4) . . . While at first glance this non-liberation of the maidservant may seem oppressive, the statute is designed to *protect* her. Instead of liberating a menial to shift for herself, the law encourages the owner to elevate her to the status of wife or at least concubine".[14]

Before we leave this section of Exodus, we should briefly consider the question of the daughter's consent in this situation: does she agree to be sold as a female slave? The text clearly is not concerned with her opinion on the matter. Propp agrees:

"In 21:7, the subject is the girl's father not her purchaser. In contract, the paraphrase in Deut 15:12, 'When your Hebrew brother or sister sells him/herself,' empathizes more with the slave, and in fact contains more liberal provisions. *Exodus stresses rather the woman's passivity,* subject to the authority first of her father and then of her purchaser" (emphasis mine).[15]

Mitigating Slave Abuse (Exodus 21:20-21; 26-27)

Perhaps no other passage is more frequently discussed in slavery debates than Exodus 21:20-21: "And if a man beats his male or female slave with a wooden rod so that they die immediately, he will surely be punished. However, if he survives a day or two, he will not be punished, because he is his property". It is unsurprising that these two verses carry so much significance in the discussion. The text describes a scenario in which either a male or female slave is beaten with a wooden rod, which sounds justifiably horrific to us. One might expect that this was the purpose of the law – don't beat your male or female slave with a wooden rod! Of course, we know that this was not the law's intent. The question is, how should we understand the purpose of this regulation?

While it might seem as though the law is giving a slaveholder a type of "manual" on how to legally beat their slave within an inch of their lives, this interpretation does not correctly understand the passage in its context. It is absolutely assumed that masters will beat their slaves; this passage indicates that, if a master beats their slave and they survive a day or two, then there is no punishment that will come to the master, as the slave is their property. However, this law is intended to provide the slave with some level of protection from physical abuse and murder.

We see in the Proverbs that physical punishment was an expected necessity:[16]

> *"By words alone a slave cannot be corrected, since he will understand, but not respond.* Do you see a man who is hasty with his words? There is more hope for a fool than for him. *A man who pampers his slave from youth, in the end he will be insolent"* (Proverbs 29:19-21, emphasis mine).

What we see in Exodus 21:20-21 is an example of this expected corporal punishment or correction inflicted upon a slave. The use of the rod in this context is unsurprising, given its common use as a tool of discipline for fools and children. For example, Proverbs 13:24 reads, *"He who withholds his rod hates his son,* but he who loves him diligently disciplines him". Similarly, Proverbs 26:3 explains, "A whip for the horse, a bridle for the donkey, *and a wooden rod for the back of fools*". Propp summarizes:

> "More likely, however, as with guiding a sheep or chastising a child, the rod was ordinarily used to direct and admonish slaves, notwithstanding the potential for abuse (Rashbam). The staff appears as a legitimate instrument of guidance also in Isa 9:3; Prov 10:13; 13:23; 19:25; 22:15; 23:13-14; 26:3. Moreover, in Prov 29:19, 'a slave is not chastised with words,' seems implicitly to advocate beating one's servants".[17]

What we see in Exodus 20:20-21, therefore, is a law regulating the beating of one's slave. The rationale of the law is likely focused on the intent of the master in the situation. If the master beat the slave so severely that the slave died immediately (v. 20), then there would be severe punishment (likely death). However, if the slave did *not* die immediately but survived for a day or two, then – according to this logic – the intent of the master was likely not murderous, and the death would be seen as accidental. Fox concludes:

> "None of the biblical law codes place restrictions on beating one's slaves (male or female). If, however, the owner kills a slave, vengeance of an unspecified sort is exacted (Exod 21:20). If the slave survives the beating, no compensation is required, for the slave 'is his (master's) money' (Exod 21:21)".[18]

Finally, in verses 26 and 27 we read:

> "And if a man hits the eye of his male slave or the eye of
> his female slave and destroys it, he must send him out free
> in place of his eye. And if a tooth of his male slave or a tooth
> of his female slave he knocks out, he must send him out in
> place of his tooth" (Exodus 21:26-27).

While it is clear that these laws are in place to benefit and protect the slave, they are often misunderstood in their context. In the preceding verses, the text is elaborating on the principle of talion, generally designated *lex talionis* or "the law of retaliation". In verses 23-25 we see, "And if there is serious injury, then you will give life for life, eye for eye, tooth for tooth, hand for hand, foot for foot, burn for burn, wound for wound, bruise for bruise".

In this context, we would expect that, if a slave were on equal footing with the master before the law, we would read something akin to, "An owner who hits his male or female slave in the eye and destroys it *will have his own eye destroyed*". This, of course, is not the case. The principle of retaliation – that the slave would have the right to the eye of the master – is not in play here because of their differing status. This is the same principle seen, for example, in the *Laws of Hammurabi*:

> "If an *awīlu* [free person] should blind the eye of another
> *awīlu*, they shall blind his eye. If he should break the bone
> of another *awīlu*, they shall break his bone . . . If an *awīlu*
> should knock out the tooth of another *awīlu* of his own
> rank, they shall knock out his tooth" (LH 196-197, 200).[19]

Notice, however, that the punishment is different when a free man performs these same actions against a "commoner": "If he [a free man] should blind the eye or break the bone of a commoner, he shall weigh and deliver 60 shekels of silver" (LH 198). In other words, while the price to be paid is still quite significant, it is not equal retribution, as the commoner does not have the right to the eye or bone of the free man. The same is true if a tooth is knocked out: "If he [a free man] should knock out the tooth of a commoner, he shall weigh and deliver 20 shekels of silver" (LH 201). What if the victim is a slave and the assailant is a free man? "If he [a free man] should blind the eye of an *awīlu*'s slave or break the bone of an *awīlu*'s slave, he shall weigh and deliver one-half of his value (in silver)" (LH 199).

Both the *Laws of Hammurabi* and the Hebrew Bible make it clear that only social equals have the right of "talionic retribution".[20] Houtman concurs: "Talio (21:23-25) only applies to the free citizen, not to a slave".[21] Thus, the slave is protected by the law — at least in theory — from abuse or excessive beatings. If they are killed as a direct result of a beating, it is considered murder, and the master is likely to be killed; if the master destroys or puts out an eye or tooth, the slave is forgiven their debt and set free.

The Goring Ox (Exodus 21:32)

Before we move on to Deuteronomy 15, we will briefly cover the laws concerning the goring ox found in Exodus 21:28-32.

> "And if an ox gores a man or a woman so that they die, the ox will surely be stoned to death and its meat will not be eaten, but the owner of the ox will be blameless. And if a

bull has been known to gore, and his owner has been warned, but he has not watched over it, and it kills a man or a woman, the bull will be stoned to death, and its owner will also be killed. If a ransom is imposed on him, then he may give the ransom for his life in accordance with what was imposed on him. Whether it gores a son or a daughter, according to this law it will be done to him. If the ox gores a male or female slave, he [the owner] will give 30 shekels of silver to his master, and the bull will be stoned to death" (Exodus 21:28-32).

Again, this passage is laid out in a fairly logical and straightforward manner. If a bull gores a man or a woman to death, the bull is killed, its meat is not to be eaten, but the owner is not held responsible. However, if the bull had done this kind of thing before, and the owner failed to take the necessary precautions to ensure the bull stayed penned up, then the owner is killed. In other words, the living victims of the crime have the right to the life of the bull's owner. The law allows, however, for the owner to compensate the family of the victim *if* they agree, and the owner must pay whatever they demand. This also holds true if the victim is a son or daughter of a free person.

But what about a slave? Does the law consider the life of the slave to be equal to that of a free person in this context? No. Instead, the slave is treated under property law, and the owner of the bull is to pay the master of the slave 30 shekels of silver as compensation. Gurtner writes, "The goring of a slave (v. 32) – male or female – is treated in terms of property loss".[22] Likewise, Haas concludes "If one's ox gores a slave to death, one is required to pay the slave's master an amount of money, likely the value of the slave (Ex. 21:32). In contrast, if one's ox gores a free Hebrew to death, the penalty is death (Ex. 21:28-31)".[23]

Deuteronomy 15:12-18 – Developments in Slavery

"If your brother – a male Hebrew or a female Hebrew – is sold to you, then he will serve you six years, but in the seventh year you must send him out from you free. And when you send him out from you free, you must not send him out with nothing. You will supply him liberally from your flock and from your threshing floor and from your wine vat. That which Yahweh has blessed you with, you must give to him. Now you must remember that you were a slave in the land of Egypt, and Yahweh your God redeemed you. Therefore, I myself am giving you this command today. And if it happens that he says to you, 'I will not go out from you, because I love you and your house, because it is good for me with you', then you will take the awl and put it into his ear and into the door, and he will be your permanent slave. And also for your female slave you will do this. It will not be considered difficult in your eyes when you send him away from you free, because double the service of a hired worker he has served you in six years, and Yahweh your God will bless you in everything that you do" (Deuteronomy 15:12-18).

As you can see, there are many similarities between what we saw in Exodus 21 and what appears here in Deuteronomy 15. The text speaks of Hebrew slaves who serve for six years and are released in the seventh.

The slave is also able to voluntarily serve for life, and a similar ritual is performed on that occasion. There are, however, differences between these passages. Notice that the laws here in Deuteronomy pertain not only to the Hebrew man, but also to the Hebrew woman (v. 12). In this passage, the woman is also to be released, or is allowed to remain a slave for life (vv. 12 and 17). More significant is the command for the master to provide a substantial amount of goods to the newly freed slave (vv. 13-14). The overall tone of the passage is one of encouraging the master not to hold back from his slave; as God has supernaturally blessed and provided for his people, he will continue to do so if they keep his covenant (Deut. 7:12-13; 15:4, 6, 10, 14, 18). In like manner, the master should also give generously to the slave. This concept of supernatural provision for obedience is seen prominently in Deuteronomy 28 and will be a central theme in the next chapter that we will analyze: Leviticus 25.

Leviticus 25 – Contrasting Israelite and Foreign Slaves

Leviticus 25 is likely familiar to most atheists and apologists who debate the issue of slavery, though probably to a very limited degree. Specifically, verses 44-46 are often cited to show the harsh reality of slavery in the Old Testament:

> "And as for your male slaves and female slaves that you may have: from the foreign nations that are around you, *from them* you may purchase male and female slaves. And even from the tenant foreigners that are living with you, *from them* you may purchase, even from their families who are with you, whom they have born in your land, and they will be your inherited property. And you may bequeath

them to your sons after you to receive as inherited property; you can make them serve permanently. But as for your brothers, the children of Israel, you must not rule over one another with violence". (Leviticus 25:44-46, emphasis mine)

Obviously, these verses are incredibly significant to the slavery discussion; however, before we investigate what they mean, it is important to establish the context in which they exist. Let's begin with Leviticus 25 as a whole. The beginning of the chapter (vv. 1-7) contains God's command to let the land of Israel have a year-long rest from farming every seventh year. In other words, they were allowed to till the ground and produce food for six years, but in the seventh year, they were commanded to let the land lie fallow.

The next section (vv. 8-17) commands the people to also hold a year of rest every fiftieth year; they were have to seven "sabbath years" (totaling 49 years), followed by a "Jubilee" in the fiftieth year. During this year of the Jubilee, people were to be returned to their land and debts were to be cancelled. However, this applied only to the Israelites.

Leviticus 25:18-22 returns to the seventh year sabbath, as God anticipates the very natural concerns that would come from the people. Verse 20 reads, "And if you say, 'What will we eat in the seventh year if we do not sow and do not reap our produce?'" God's response?

> "Then I will command my blessing for you in the sixth year, and it will produce yield for three years. And you will sow in the eighth year, but you will eat from the old produce

until the ninth year; until its produce comes in, you will eat the old produce" (Leviticus 25:21-22).

As we saw in Deuteronomy, God's supernatural provision would overcome any concern for finances or produce; if they would simply obey God's commands, he would provide.

This brings us to the critical section of the chapter for our purposes: laws concerning Israelites that become poor (vv. 25-55). There are three scenarios that are discussed in these verses with respect to an Israelite. In the first (vv. 25-34) we see, "If your brother becomes poor *and sells some of his inherited property...*" (v. 25). Israelites owned property in the land of Israel, and if they fell into poverty, selling (a portion of) their land was a viable option. The law required, however, that the land would eventually return to its original owner, either by a near relative redeeming it for them or during the year of Jubilee.

In the second scenario (vv. 35-38) we see:

> "And if your brother becomes poor and his hand falters with you, then you will take him as a resident alien, and he will live with you. Do not take interest from him, but fear your god, so that your brother can live with you. Your silver you must not give him at interest, nor sell him your food at a profit. I am Yahweh your God, who brought you out from the land of Egypt to give to you the land of Canaan and to be your God" (Leviticus 25: 35-38).

It appears that, in this case, the Israelite has already sold his property and still cannot make ends meet. Should this occur, the poor Israelite was to be cared for by their fellow Israelites, who were to loan them what they needed at no interest. They were to fear and obey God by supporting their poor brother, with the result that God would provide for them because of their obedience.

In the third scenario (vv. 39-43 and 47-55), the Israelite actually reaches the stage where he must sell himself into debt-slavery. The response of his fellow Israelites, however, is to differ substantially from what we see in both Exodus 21 and Deuteronomy 15:

> "And if your brother with you becomes poor and sells himself to you, *you must not make him serve with the work of a slave. As a hired worker or as a tenant foreigner he will be with you*, until the year of Jubilee he will serve with you. Then he will go out from you, he and his children with him, and he will return to his family, and to the inherited property of his fathers he will return. For they are my servants, whom I brought out from the land of Egypt, *they must not be sold in a slave sale. You must not rule over him with violence*, but fear your God" (Leviticus 25:39-43, emphasis mine).

It is easy to see the distinguishing feature of the treatment of Israelites in this section: *they are not to be treated as slaves*. In contrast to Exodus 21 and Deuteronomy 15 – where it was perfectly legitimate to keep an Israelite as a slave – this is no longer allowed in Leviticus 25; instead, they are to be treated as hired laborers.[24] As God has already brought the Israelites out of slavery, they cannot be returned to that status again (Leviticus 25:42).[25]

If Israelites can no longer purchase fellow Israelites as slaves, a natural question arises in this context: where should they get slaves? We get our answer in the verses that follow:

> "And as for your male slaves and female slaves that you may have: from the foreign nations that are around you, *from them* you may purchase male and female slaves. And even from the tenant foreigners that are living with you, *from them* you may purchase, even from their families who are with you, whom they have born in your land, and they will be your inherited property. And you may bequeath them to your sons after you to receive as inherited property; you can make them serve permanently. But as for your brothers, the children of Israel, you must not rule over one another with violence" (Leviticus 25:44-46).

If an Israelite becomes so poor that he has to sell himself to another Israelite, *he cannot be treated as a slave.* If you want slaves, *you have to get them from the foreigners.*[26] This contrast between the Israelite and the foreigner is quite pronounced; Jackson writes, "The distinction between temporary debt-slaves and permanent foreign slaves (who may be bequeathed 'to your sons after you, to inherit as a possession for ever') is made explicit in a later biblical source, *Lev.* 25:39-46 (*which rejects even the use of the term eved for the Hebrew debt-slave*)" (emphasis mine).[27]

Amongst other things, we learn from these verses that:

1) chattel slaves can be purchased from the foreigners living in the nations around Israel and from tenant foreigners living in Israel;

2) these slaves become their property;

3) that property can be passed on as inheritance to their children; and

4) they can be made to serve as slaves for life.

Dandamayev sums this up well:

> "The next source of slavery was obtaining slaves through purchase from neighboring nations. *This source was in every possible way encouraged by biblical instructions* (Lev 25:44-46, etc.; cf. also Eccl. 2:7). *Such slaves were legally considered the absolute property of their owners, and their status was permanent*" (emphasis mine).[28]

In the final section of Leviticus 25 (vv. 47-55), we see another possible scenario in which the Israelite could find himself: sold as a slave to a foreigner that is living in Israel. In this case, the foreign tenant farmer has done well, financially speaking, and is so wealthy that he can afford to purchase an Israelite slave. Should this happen, the text states that the Israelite debt-slave maintains the right to redeem himself or to be released in the year of Jubilee. In either case, as stated earlier in the text, they are not to be treated as slaves, but rather as hired workers.

In short, the Israelites were given special treatment as Yahweh's slaves; because they already had a master – Yahweh himself – they could not be treated as slaves by another master. Instead, they were to be treated as hired workers, whether under the control of an Israelite or foreign master. In contrast to this, foreign slaves were able to be purchased, kept as property, passed on as inheritance, and made to serve for life.

Slavery in the Old Testament and the Antebellum South

How many times have you been in a discussion or debate about slavery in the Old Testament and heard your opponent begin with, "Now, we know that 'slavery' in the Old Testament was *nothing like* the slavery that we saw in the antebellum South"? While such comparisons ultimately have little relevance to establishing the reality of slavery as portrayed in the Hebrew Bible, they are made often enough by apologists that they are worth investigating.

Before I continue – as I very often do – I want to draw to your attention that the history of the antebellum South is absolutely not my field of expertise. I will, nevertheless, do my best to provide a well-researched presentation on this matter.

Often, this particular argument does not use comparable datasets – we're not comparing apples to apples, so to speak. In other words, when an apologist argues that we should distinguish between slavery in the Hebrew Bible and in the antebellum South, they often focus on the *laws* that appear in the Old Testament and the *practice* that we saw in the antebellum South. Instead, we should be comparing **either** the laws **or** the practices from both periods.

Ironically, I often hear Christian apologists critiquing atheists for condemning the Bible by citing passages that *describe the actions of people in the stories.* For example, in Jeremiah 34, we see the people in Jerusalem keeping their slaves past the time allowed in the law, not freeing them in the seventh year (Jeremiah 34:14). They eventually did release them, but after a short period of time, the slaveholders decided to take back their slaves (Jeremiah 34:15-16). If an atheist were to point out such atrocious behavior, their opponent would normally push back, arguing, "That is just what sinful people *did*! It is not what God commanded in the law. You have to look at what the law prescribed, *not how people disobeyed it*".

Interestingly enough, this is not the approach that apologists generally take – in my experience – with respect to slavery in the antebellum South. They often compare the *laws* in the Old Testament to the *practices* of slaveowners in the South. Here, we will consider details on southern slavery laws, as well as the legal discussions that surrounded their development, particularly by the presiding judges. It is not, therefore, a comparison between what the *laws* in the Old Testament called for and *what people actually did* in the antebellum South; rather, we will seek to compare the laws governing slave-ownership in Old Testament to the laws that governed slave-ownership in the southern United States during the antebellum period.

We will examine the development of slavery laws from the Colonial period until the decades before the Civil War, and readers looking for more information should see Thomas Morris's book, *Southern Slavery and the Law, 1619-1860.*[29]

Slave Laws in the Colonial Period

One of the key tensions that appears to connect the slave laws in the Old Testament to those in the South was *the right of a master to beat their slave in order to ensure proper behavior* balanced against *keeping the master from abusing their slave*. As we saw, Exodus 21:20-21 is intended to mitigate abuse, but to do so in such a way that it allows for the expected (and encouraged) practice of corporal punishment on the slave.

Colonial lawmakers wrestled with this same tension. Concerning the Virginia law of 1669, Morris writes, "The lawmakers began with an obvious problem. Slaves could not be punished by the extension of their time in servitude so that their 'obstinacy' could only be suppressed by violence".[30] In other words, a slave was clearly a chattel in this scenario, as it was understood that the term of their service was indefinite. Thus, threats of extending such a term of service were unavailable to the slaveowner. Instead, it was reasoned, the only means to ensure good behavior and service from a slave was physical punishment.

In a 1723 law in Virginia, this reasoning resulted in the freedom of a master to beat their slave without retribution, *as long as it was done for correction*. Morris writes, "The law provided that there would be no punishment or prosecution if a slave died 'by reason of any stroke or blow given, during his or her correction'".[31] In South Carolina, in 1740, we see that Christianity played a role in the discussion, providing some motivation to avoid abusing one's slave: "Cruelty is not only highly unbecoming those who profess themselves christians, but is odious in the eyes of all men who have any sense of virtue or humanity".[32] Unfortunately, the penalty for murdering a slave under this South Carolina law was not death, but a fine of 700 pounds, and the guilty party was not allowed to hold public office.[33]

Of course, establishing that a "death by beating" rose to the level of murder was a difficult case to prove in such circumstances; the laws appear to have inadvertently allowed great loopholes for the slaveowners to exploit. Morris summarizes:

"These were the colonial statutory schemes . . . No free person could be executed for killing a slave in South Carolina no matter how grotesque or unjustified the killing might have been. Virginia, on the other hand, left open the possibility – however remote – that anyone, even a slave owner, could be executed for the homicide of a slave".[34]

Slave Laws following the Revolutionary War

There was a significant development – relatively speaking – in the legal system after the Revolutionary War.

"After the Revolution a growing 'humanitarian sensibility' led to changes in parts of the law of homicide when applied to slaves . . . State after state, whether through constitutions, judicial decisions, or statutes, extended greater legal security to slaves".[35]

For example, in Georgia's constitution in 1798, we read:

"Any person who shall maliciously dismember or deprive a slave of life *shall suffer such punishment as would be inflicted in case the like offence had been committed on a free white person*, and on the like proof, except in case of insurrection by such slave, and unless such death should happen by accident in giving such slave *moderate correction*" (emphasis mine).[36]

Thus, if it was determined that a slave master had abused their slave to the point of dismemberment or death, the penalty would be equal to the penalty for murdering a free white person.

Nevertheless, let's not forget the end of the law: "unless such death should happen by accident in giving such slave moderate correction". The tension remained in the eyes of the lawmakers. Masters *must* be allowed to beat their slaves for the purposes of correction. However far the law was progressing in an attempt to protect slaves from abuse, it seemed to always run up against the problem of corporal punishment for correction.

A similar law was adopted in North Carolina in 1791, outlawing the deliberate homicide of a slave, "unless the slave was killed in resisting or he died under a moderate correction", and dictating that "The homicide was to be punished the same as if the victim were white".[37] Concerning this period, Morris concludes that, regardless of variations in specific states, the killing of a slave was legally equivalent to the murder of a white person, unless the slave "resisted or died under moderate correction for some misconduct".[38]

Let's turn to some of the legal decisions that were made during the early 19th century in order to see what some of the judges considered when ruling on these matters. In North Carolina's 1801 case *State v. Boon*, Morris summarizes Judge Johnston's determination:

> "Johnston argued that the murder of a slave was the same as the murder of a white person under the right circumstances. It was, in fact, more despicable. It was a 'crime of the most atrocious and barbarous nature . . . It is an evidence of a most depraved and cruel disposition, to murder one, so much in your power, that he is incapable of making resistance, even in his own defense'".[39]

Murdering a slave was considered even more vile than the murder of a free white person, as it took advantage of one who was weak and powerless in the situation.

In North Carolina's 1823 *State v. Reed*, Morris notes Judge Henderson's argument: "The notion that the life of the slave was at the disposal of the master was 'abhorrent to the hearts of all those who have felt the influence of the mild precepts of Christianity'".[40] Henderson considered it horrific to allow the master to have complete and utter control over the life of the slave, a notion which he attributes (at least in part) to the influence of Christianity. Judge Peck came to a similar conclusion in Tennessee's 1829 *Fields v. State*: "That law which says thou shalt not kill, protects the slave; and he is within its very letter. Law, reason, Christianity and common humanity, all point out one way".[41]

In short, in the antebellum South where slavery flourished, laws were set in place in an apparent attempt to curb the abuse of slaves. Slaves were not to be at the absolute mercy of their masters, and should a master murder their slave, the punishment was the same as murdering a free white person. Whether these laws were in fact enforced is a separate matter (we know that they were generally not); the laws themselves strove for what they considered to be fair and humanitarian treatment of slaves, allowing only for moderate physical correction.

As we have seen in the legal sections of the Old Testament, the laws that governed the treatment of slaves in Exodus 21 were in many ways similar. Although the Exodus 21 laws pertained (most likely) to debt-slaves – and thus their release was set after six years of service – the rationale for the laws in Exodus 21:20-21 and 26-27 is quite similar.

Slaves were not to be at the mercy of their masters when it came to life and limb. Slaveowners must be allowed to apply moderate physical correction to their slaves; however, they should take care when doing so, as abuse which leads to death or loss of limb results in punishment. Indeed, sharp lines of distinction should not be drawn between Old Testament and antebellum laws, and we would do well to remember that *a very similar legal rationale in both periods resulted in the atrocities that we saw prior to the Civil War.*

Did God Put Up with Slavery? Analyzing a Theological Interpretation

While theological interpretations are not the focus of my investigation into the Hebrew Bible (and outside of my field of expertise), addressing certain theological arguments can open up the dialogue between skeptics and apologists in a meaningful way. In light of this, it is helpful to address an interpretation that – while certainly not new – has resurfaced with some frequency. This apologetic argument admits that the Old Testament endorsed slavery, but argues that this was God's way of slowly developing the morality of humanity, beginning with his chosen people. In other words, God allowed slavery in the Hebrew Bible, but was all the while slowly working to reveal to humanity that it was immoral.

There are a few pieces of evidence that are cited in this regard. First – and certainly foremost – is Matthew 19:3-8, where Jesus is tested on the subject of divorce:

> "And Pharisees came to him, testing him, and saying, 'Is it permitted for a man to divorce his wife for any reason?' And

he answered and said, 'Have you not read that the creator made them male and female from the beginning?' And he said, 'Because of this, a man will leave father and mother and will be joined to his wife, and the two will become one flesh, so that they are no longer two, but one flesh. Therefore, that which God has joined together, let not man separate'. They said to him, 'Then why did Moses command to give a certificate of divorce and to divorce her?' He said to them, 'Moses, because of your hard-heartedness, permitted you to divorce your wives, but from the beginning it was not so'" (Matthew 19:3-8).

We need not go into great detail in this passage, as the basic principle that is used to support the argument is relatively clear. [42] Jesus is confronted with a portion of the Mosaic law (Deuteronomy 24:1-4), which seems to contradict what Jesus had just taught. Jesus responded that Moses had (legally) "permitted" men to divorce their wives because of their "hard-heartedness" (Matthew 19:8). *This was not God's original intent, however.* In other words, in the beginning, God created man and woman to be united for all time; he later allowed for divorce because of the sinfulness of mankind.

This passage is then abstracted and applied to slavery, another situation – it is argued – that Jesus and the other New Testament authors were attempting to bring humanity out of. While slavery is not mentioned in the text, the principle of "returning to creation" can be similarly applied. Immediately following creation – before the fall – people were not enslaved to one another, but rather lived in equality. It was only later – when mankind became sinful and wicked – that God had to regulate their behavior in an attempt to bring them back to the pristine state of creation. France comments on Deuteronomy 24:1-4 and Matthew 19:8 in this way:

> "The Deuteronomic legislation is a response to human failure, an attempt to bring order to an already unideal situation caused by human 'hardness of heart' . . . It was the fact that divorce was taking place in defiance of God's stated intention for marriage that made it necessary for Moses to make appropriate provision. But it should never have been so. The existence of divorce legislation is a pointer not to divine approval of divorce but to human sinfulness".[43]

However, in order to effectively demonstrate that Jesus intended to bring about the abolishment of slavery – or even to draw attention to its immoral character – it would seem likely that two things would need to be present in the text or in history. First, Jesus and other New Testament authors would have condemned the practice in some overt way, and second, the early church would have recognized such condemnation. Is this what we see?

Jesus and the NT Authors Condemning Slavery?

In order to demonstrate that Jesus and the writers of the New Testament spoke out against or condemned slavery, there are several common passages that are cited by apologists. Setting aside general statements about loving one another (e.g., Matthew 7:12), Paul's letter to Philemon often appears early in the conversation. Here, it is argued, the apostle implores Philemon to free his slave Onesimus upon his return. Although the meaning of the book is debated,[44] assuming the interpretation most in favor of an anti-slavery position by the apostle, Onesimus would indeed have been a slave of Philemon, whom Paul was seeking to have freed. Lohse writes that, according to this type of interpretation, "The purpose of Phlm, it was assumed, was to illustrate in a novelistic fashion how the Christian communities in the post-Pauline period handled the question of slavery".[45]

Another text that is frequently cited comes from the so-called "Pastoral Epistles". In 1 Timothy 1:9-10, the writer is speaking on the purpose of the law, listing those for whom it was made:

> "Knowing this, that the law is not made for a righteous man, but for the lawless and rebellious, the ungodly and sinful, the unholy and worldly, for those who murder their fathers and mothers, murderers, the sexually immoral, homosexuals, *slave traders*, liars, perjurers, and whatever else opposes good instruction" (1 Timothy 1:9-10, emphasis mine).

In verse 10, the inclusion of "slave traders" in a list of immoral practices is used to support the New Testament's anti-slavery position.

The next verse that is cited in this regard is Galatians 3:28, where Paul writes, "There is neither Jew nor Greek, there is neither slave nor free, there is neither male nor female; for all of you are one in Christ Jesus". Betz summarizes the two ways in which this verse can be understood with respect to slavery:

"Taken alone the statement can be understood in two ways: (a) as a declaration of the abolishment of the social institution of slavery, or (b) as a declaration of the irrelevancy of that institution, which would include the possibility of its retainment".[46]

If the former position is taken, then one could argue that Jesus came to do away with the social institution of slavery.

One final set of passages comes up less frequently, but should also be included in this discussion: the parable of the talents found in Matthew 25:14-30 and Luke 19:11-27. The parable speaks of three slaves who are entrusted with different amounts of money to invest for their master, who then leaves on a journey. The first two slaves invested wisely, earning substantial returns on their investments. However, the third did nothing with the money, but instead hid it away safely until the master's return. While it might seem odd to include this parable in a discussion on the New Testament's condemnation on slavery, it could be argued that providing "slaves" with such substantial amounts of money, along with the freedom to invest it, suggests a very different slave-master relationship. Calling it "slavery", therefore, would simply be inaccurate and inflammatory.

Let's deal with each of these arguments in reverse order, beginning with the parable of the talents. While it may seem odd or out of place for a master to entrust sums of money to his slaves, this was common practice during this period. Luz writes:

"Jesus' hearers would hardly have been thinking of the practice, common in the Middle East, of doing business with borrowed capital, since that was possible only for free persons; here we are dealing explicitly with slaves. Instead, the parable assumes that among other things clever slaves were to do business with their master's money with the clear understanding that both the money and the profit earned belonged to the slave owner. Roman law designated the money given to slaves for this purpose as *peculium*".[47]

Concerning slavery in the ancient Near East, Westbrook writes, "A slave could act as agent for his master. In this capacity, he could make contracts with free persons and litigate. He could also manage property on his own behalf, in the form of a *peculium* given him by his master".[48] In other words, two things are clear in the passage. First, *these were slaves*, and second, the money they were given *was not their own*; all of the money and any interest or profit it brought belonged to the master.

Turning to Galatians 3:28, we remember that there are two ways of interpreting the phrase "neither slave nor free":

1) abolishing the institution of slavery; or

2) showing it to be irrelevant.

Betz notes, "The overwhelming evidence in early and later Christianity seems to recommend *only the second option viable*, a view taken by most commentators" (emphasis mine).[49] That the passage is not intended to do away with the social institution of slavery is clear for several reasons. First, the other two statements in the verse – "neither Jew nor Gentile" and (especially) "neither male nor female" – can hardly be understood as doing away with such distinctions. Whatever one would argue concerning the attitude of the New Testament writers on the role and status of women (another topic entirely), it would be difficult to maintain that passages like 1 Corinthians 14:34-35 would allow the social distinction between men and women to be ignored.

The point of Galatians 3:28, it would seem, is to express the unity that members of the "Body of Christ" share by being "in Christ". MacKnight writes, "To be 'in Christ' is to be in spiritual fellowship with him through God's Spirit. This is one way of defining what a Christian is: one who is 'in Christ'".[50] Although believers are now all untied and equal in the eyes of God – having been baptized into Christ – this does not negate the reality of social and role distinctions between members of the referenced social groups, *including slaves*. Avalos concludes:

> "Gal. 3.28 was clearly meant solely to establish the reckoning of believers as Abraham's seed regardless of their gender, ethnicity, or slave status. Other New Testament authors certainly did not see this passage as incompatible with having Christian slaves or ordering Christian slaves to serve their slavemasters (Eph. 5.24 or 6.5)".[51]

When we consider 1 Timothy 1:10, where "slave traders" are included in a list of vices, it may seem straightforward that this shows that the writer condemned slavery. This, however, is simply not the case. The Greek word *andrapodistes* is translated "slave-trader" and "kidnapper" in one of the standard New Testament Greek lexicons,[52] but only appears one time in the New Testament (here in our passage). Harrill describes slave dealers in this way:

"Slave dealers displayed vice at every stage of the slave-trading operation, from the illegitimate acquisition and the deceptive selling of merchandise to the polluting result such sale had on places and people. In acquiring merchandise when legitimate sources such as war captives did not offer enough supply, they were not above kidnapping free citizens, a criminal act against the law of nations".[53]

In fact, this word for slave trader appears in other so-called "vice lists" outside of the New Testament, clearly demonstrating that the act of stealing or illegally procuring another individual was not only considered immoral in the New (and Old) Testaments, *but also among the other nations*.[54] Avalos notes, "The fact that slave societies of Greece and Rome condemned an *andrapodistēs* indicates that pure slave trading cannot be meant".[55] Harrill concurs:

"Rather than revealing some alleged early Christian condemnation of slavery or the slave trade, the language of 1 Timothy articulates attitudes commonplace among masters in the Roman Empire. The term *andrapodistai* was derogatory only in the sense of the slave traders' exploitation (economic and sexual) of free citizens, and of their proverbial abuse of the law. The ancient world believed in the moral goodness of slavery yet condemned the immorality of slave traders".[56]

Finally, let's examine the book of Philemon. As we discussed above, apologists often turn to Philemon as a (perhaps subtle) statement on the position of Christianity on slavery. However one understands the situation being described in the book, we would be hard pressed to see it as presenting an over-arching declaration on the institution of slavery. Lohse writes concerning this view, "For good reasons this view has found no acceptance and today is no longer held by anyone. The letter to Philemon is neither the disguise of a general idea nor the promulgation of a generally valid rule about the question of slavery".[57]

Assuming that a slave-master relationship existed between Philemon and Onesimus, it seems clear that Paul leaves the decision to free Onesimus up to Philemon. In verses 8-9a, for example, Paul writes, "Therefore, although I have in Christ the confidence to order you to do the right thing, for the sake of love I implore you". Lohse comments, "It is the intercession of the Apostle in a concrete situation in which 'love' (ἀγάπη) must be promoted by decision and deed".[58] That the passage lacks of direct command – assuming the immoral character of the act of enslavement – is indeed problematic in the context. In other words, if we were to see a passage like 1 Timothy 1:10 as a direct indictment against the practice of slavery, *it is incredibly difficult to imagine a scenario in which Paul would say, "I'm leaving this up to you; I don't want to force you to set him free".*

Avalos says it this way:

> "Nowhere in the letter do we see Paul saying 'slavery is a sin, and you must free Onesimus'. Nowhere in the letter do we have anything even akin to the strong directive issued by Paul on such things as drunkenness and adultery (1 Cor.

6.8-9), incest (1 Cor. 5), or just not working hard enough (2 Thess. 2.10)".[59]

At best, it would seem, the book of Philemon is evidence of Paul encouraging Philemon to forgive and free his runaway slave in order that Onesimus might return to Paul to help him in the ministry. In no way is this a broad directive against owning other human beings as slaves.

Now that we've addressed the passages that are cited in support of this argument, let's turn to a few others that seem to show that slavery was not only accepted as a social norm, but was assumed to be the norm *for Jesus and his followers*. We will begin with Luke 17:7-10 and Jesus's statements about unprofitable servants:

> "But which of you, having a slave who plows or tends the sheep, who, coming in from the field, would say to him, 'Come here now and sit down'. Rather, would you not say to him, 'Prepare something that I may eat, and get dressed and serve me until I have eaten and drunk, and after these things *you* may eat and drink'? Would he thank the slave because he did what he was commanded? So also you, when you have done all the things you have been commanded, say, 'We are worthless slaves; that which we were supposed to do, we have done'" (Luke 17:7-10).

While Jesus's story is concerned with the actions and attitudes of his disciples, it also provides us with insight into current attitudes towards slavery. Green writes:

"Jesus is not so much inviting an allegorical reading of master-servant roles as drawing on a well-known reality of village life to teach something about faithfulness. Envisioned is a small landholder/farmer whose one slave performs the various outdoor and household duties that would be divided between slaves in a larger estate. The household, master/slave analogy has become a regular fixture of the Lukan narrative, providing a basis for important instruction on kinship, faithfulness, and status-seeking (e.g., 12:35-48; 16:1-9; cf. 22:24-27)".[60]

The message is that, just as a slave who performs his required duties is due no special thanks or treatment (and thus earns nothing by it), so also followers of Jesus, who perform their required duties, are due no special reward thereby. Fitzmyer writes, "In the present Lucan setting Jesus' words stress that the Christian disciple who is a 'servant' or 'slave,' and has well carried out his task, can only regard himself as an unprofitable servant".[61] What is assumed by this story, therefore, is:

1) the reality of slavery during Jesus's time;

2) the appropriateness of drawing the analogy based on the details of that reality; and

3) the complete lack of condemnation for the practice as described in the analogy.

Throughout the book of Luke, in fact, the parables and stories of Jesus show a reliance on the normalcy and acceptance of the practice of slavery. Charles calls attention to the stories of the slaves in Luke 12, who remain alert while awaiting their master's return in vv. 35-46, contrasted with those who received beatings for improper behavior (vv. 47-48), along with depictions seen in chapters 14-16. [62] Far from condemning the practice of slavery, Charles explains that Jesus (as he does throughout the gospels) "relied on a normative portrayal of the slave in antiquity to illustrate his teachings".[63] This pattern can also be seen Deutero-Pauline writings, as Glancy notes that the Pauline letters speak directly to Christian slaveholders and slaves, indicating "the presence within the local Christian community of both slaves and slaveholders".[64] She continues to say that *"The New Testament epistles consider slaveholding compatible with membership in the Christian body"* (emphasis mine).[65]

In the end, one would be hard pressed to argue that the New Testament – Jesus included – clearly and overtly condemns the practice of owning another human being as property. In fact, we see time and again that Jesus utilizes the well-known practice of slavery to teach principles of appropriate behavior and loyalty within the context of discipleship. Passages that are cited to support open or implied condemnation of the practice – including Galatians 3:28, 1 Timothy 1:10, the book of Philemon, or even the parable of the talents – are in fact not setting forth any such condemnation.

Slavery in the Early Church

If we see no overt condemnation of slavery in the words of Jesus or the other New Testament writers, it is likely that the early church took a similar stance. This is indeed what we see. Glancy writes:

"Every generation of Christians in antiquity included slaveholders. The persistence of slaveholding as a practice among geographically scattered Christians over a period of centuries testifies to the enduring power of the institution of slavery in antiquity. With rare and limited exceptions, Christian authors expressed no opprobrium towards Christian slaveholders. *Slaveholding was not considered a sin*" (emphasis mine).[66]

While it is not our intent to provide a detailed analysis and numerous examples of slavery in early Christianity, a few examples to support Glancy's argument will suffice. More information can be found in Glancy 2006 and 2011.

Hector Avalos summarizes his section on slavery in late antiquity with these words: "The first millennium of Christianity saw an overwhelming acceptance of slavery by significant theologians, higher clerics, Church councils, and the Pope himself". [67] The fact that slaves needed permission from their Christian owners to join various Christian bodies (including their access to religious training in the 3rd and 4th centuries C.E. and joining a monastery according to the Council of Chalcedon in 451) speaks to this institutional acceptance.[68]

The early church fathers also held slaves and saw no problem in doing so. When they spoke against the practice, it was often for reasons that we might not think. For example, Glancy writes, "Patristic authors objected to ownership of excessive numbers of slaves, *not out of concern for the slaves but out of concern for the owners. Owning slaves was associated with gluttony and dissipation*" (emphasis mine).[69] A similar position was held by John Chrysostom, who spoke against excessive self-indulgence.[70]

Furthermore, it was expected that slaves would receive corporal punishment. While abuse of slaves was condemned – as it was in the Hebrew Bible (cf. Exodus 21:20-21) – this did not mean that slaves were not to be beaten. Glancy writes,

> "Early Christian slaveholders punished slaves physically, sometimes brutally. In the early third century, Tertullian wrote casually, and seemingly without condemnation, 'You have subjected your slave's skin to stripes and shackles and branding' (*The Resurrection of the Flesh* 57)".[71]

Clement of Alexandria came to a similar position, condemning torture and abuse, *but emphasizing the use of the rod for discipline.*[72]

While we could multiply the examples that we have provided above, it is not necessary to make our point. What we see, in short, is that the New Testament authors – including the words of Jesus himself – not only fail to condemn slavery, but speak of the practice as a normal and expected way of life. This attitude was continued in the early church, as they owned slaves and disciplined them using corporal punishment.

Conclusion

With slavery and its effects still fresh in our minds – and present in our world – it is sometimes hard to imagine that a book that is considered divinely inspired would endorse such a practice. As we have seen, however, the legal sections of the Old Testament clearly do endorse the practice of both debt- and chattel-slavery, and the New Testament (at a minimum) assumes its common reality and in no way condemns it.

My goal in this chapter has been to examine what the Bible says about slavery (primarily in the Old Testament). We began by providing a brief overview and analysis of the three places in the legal passages of the Old Testament that deal with the practice of slavery. In Exodus 21, we saw that Hebrew debt-slaves could be kept and made to serve for six years and were to be released in the seventh. If they were provided with a wife by their master, the wife and any children were the property of the master and were to remain with him.

We saw that a father could sell his daughter as a female slave, who would take on the status of concubine or wife. Her status was changed as a form of protection and certain rules then applied to her treatment. Exodus 21 also attempts to curb abuse inflicted upon slaves; if a master murdered a slave by beating him to an immediate death, he received severe punishment (likely death). However, it was expected that a master would beat his slave (male or female) with a wooden rod, as this was considered a necessary form of moderate correction. If the master destroyed the eye or put out a tooth of the debt-slave, the slave was to be released. Although they were not due *lex talionis*, their debt was forgiven and they were set free. Finally, we saw that the penalty for the negligent death of a slave was not the same as that of a free person or their children.

We saw in Deuteronomy 15 similar laws to those in Exodus 21, though they differed in important ways. First, the laws concerning the Hebrew female debt-slave may have been intentionally developed, as the text calls for their release in the same way as the male debt-slave. More importantly, however, is the command to provide substantial provisions to the Hebrew debt-slave upon their release in the seventh year. The master was not to hold back, but was to trust in God, who would provide for them if they would obey his commands.

Finally, in Leviticus 25, we saw that the well-known passage on chattel slaves (vv. 44-46) is situated within a broader section dealing with the care of destitute Israelites. The sharp contrast between the treatment of an Israelite and a foreigner is pronounced, as the Israelites were no longer allowed to be treated as slaves. If the Israelites wanted to purchase slaves, they could now only do so from the nations around them or from foreign tenant farmers living in the land of Israel. These could be kept for life and passed on as inherited property.

We then briefly examined the claim that slavery as described in the legal sections of the Old Testament was nothing like slavery in the antebellum South. This is only true if one compares the *laws* in the Old Testament with the actual *practices* in the South. When we looked at the *laws* in the South prior to the Civil War, we saw many areas of similarity, most importantly as it related to the rationale for the proper and necessary treatment of slaves.

Finally, at the end of the chapter, we addressed a common apologetic argument that God allowed slavery in the Old Testament because of the wickedness of mankind. Slavery is compared to divorce in Matthew 19, where Jesus explains that Moses allowed the people in the Old Testament to divorce their wives, but only because of their "hard-heartedness". It is argued that, when we come to the New Testament,

God – perhaps subtly – condemns the practice of slavery. We saw, however, that this is not the case; neither Jesus nor the New Testament writers condemned the practice. Rather, they assumed it to be commonplace and drew many analogies based on its prevalence. Finally when we examined the practice of slavery in early Christianity, it appears that they saw no condemnation of slavery in the Old or New Testaments.

The topic of slavery is one that makes us uncomfortable, and yet it comes up time and again in discussions about morality and the God of the Bible. We would do well – whether as a believer or atheist – to understand what the Bible actually says about the practice of slavery, rather than building our conclusions and positions on faulty arguments or apologetics. Slavery was indeed endorsed in the Old Testament and the New Testament did not condemn its practice. The Old Testament laws concerning slavery were not so different from those in the antebellum South, which should give us pause; we must remember the atrocities that transpired prior to the Civil War, and *vigilantly guard against repeating the past* by understanding the nature of slavery, not only in the South, but in the laws of the Old Testament.

---

[1] United Nations 1948.
[2] Haas 2003: 778.
[3] Dandamayev 1992: 58.
[4] Westbrook 2003: 40.
[5] Bowen 2020a.
[6] Dozeman 2009: 76.
[7] Lemche 1992: 8.
[8] Bowen 2020a: 67-75.
[9] Hamilton 1990: 472.
[10] Kitchen 1962: 1195.
[11] Durham 2015: 321.
[12] Jackson 2006: 85.

[13] Jackson 2006: 89.

[14] Propp 2006: 196-197.

[15] Propp 2006: 196.

[16] Dandamayev 1992: 67.

[17] Propp 2006: 218.

[18] Fox 2009: 843.

[19] Translation Roth 1997: 121.

[20] Propp 2006: 231.

[21] Houtman 2000: 172. I disagree with Dozeman (2009: 536) who writes, "Exodus 21:26-27 extends the *lex talionis* to male and female slaves. If a master destroys an eye or knocks out the tooth of a slave, the compensation is freedom".

[22] Gurtner 2013: 392.

[23] Haas 2003: 780.

[24] Wells 2011: 140.

[25] Harrison 1980: 228.

[26] Bowen 2020a: 138-141

[27] Jackson 2006: 82.

[28] Dandamayev 1992: 66.

[29] Morris 1996.

[30] Morris 1996: 163.

[31] Morris 1996: 164.

[32] Morris 1996: 165.

[33] Morris 1996: 165.

[34] Morris 1996: 165.

[35] Morris 1996: 171-172.

[36] Cited in Morris 1996: 172.

[37] Morris 1996: 172.

[38] Morris 1996: 173.

[39] Morris 1996: 174.

[40] Morris 1996: 175.

[41] Morris 1996: 176.

[42] For analysis of the passage in greater detail, see Luz 2001: 488-496.

[43] France 2007: 648-649 electronic version.

[44] For a relatively recent and detailed discussion on the various interpretive positions, see Harrill 2006: 6-16.

[45] Lohse 1971: 188.

[46] Betz 1989: 192-193. See also MacKnight 1995: 201.

[47] Luz 2005: 251.

[48] Westbrook 2003: 42.

[49] Betz 1989: 193.

[50] MacKnight 1995: 199.

[51] Avalos 2013: 111.

[52] Danker 2000: s.v. ἀνδραποδιστής.

[53] Harrill 1999: 102.

[54] See Harrill 1999 for several examples.

[55] Avalos 2013: 126.

[56] Harrill 2006: 141.

[57] Lohse 1971: 188.

[58] Lohse 1971: 188.

[59] Avalos 2013: 130.

[60] Green 1997: 614.

[61] Fitzmyer 1985: 1145. It is interesting to note that, while the disciples are to recognize their association with the unprofitable servant(s), they are also to view the story through the eyes of the slave master. Jennifer Glancy observes, "In the only extant version of this parable, Jesus asks the hearer explicitly to identify with the slaveholder who benefits from the labor of the slave" (Glancy 2006: 128).

[62] Charles 2020: 107.

[63] Charles 2020: 107.

[64] Glancy 2011: 463.

[65] Glancy 2011: 463.

[66] Glancy 2011: 461-462.

[67] Avalos 2013: 171. The date range for Late Antiquity in this section runs from 150-1000 CE.

[68] Glancy 2011: 463.

[69] Glancy 2011: 464.

[70] Glancy 2011: 464, citing *Homiliae in epistulam i ad Corinthios* 40.6.

[71] Glancy 2011: 465.

[72] Glancy 2011: 465, citing *Paed.* 3.12.93.

CHAPTER SEVEN
Tired of Hearing about Tyre?
The Failed Prophecy of Ezekiel 26

Introduction

Atheist: "How do you know that the Bible is the 'Word of God?'"

Christian: "Because of the fulfilled prophecies that come from the
   Old Testament!"

Atheist: "What about the failed prophecy against Tyre in Ezekiel
   26?"

While Ezekiel's prophecy against the island city of Tyre is not the most frequently discussed topic among atheists and apologists, it is still familiar to both groups. Analyzing how several different Christian groups sought to defend this prophecy, atheist activist Aron Ra writes, "Biblical literalists are forbidden to admit that the Bible could ever be wrong about anything, which is why so many apologists are employed full time making up excuses trying to conceal the many errors of scripture".[1] And it is not a mystery why this prophecy comes up time and again: *because of its apparent failure to come true.* The prophet Ezekiel, speaking under divine inspiration, prophesied in some detail about the complete destruction and annihilation that was to come upon the island city. This judgment would be meted out by Nebuchadnezzar, the king of Babylon, acting as the agent of God. In the end, however, *Tyre was not destroyed.*

This apparent failure of Ezekiel's prophecy creates a problem for many Christians. Daniel Block puts it this way:

> "This oracle presents a *major hermeneutical dilemma.* Whereas chs. 26-28 had consistently envisaged a total and permanent destruction of Tyre at the hands of Nebuchadrezzar, delivered some fifteen years later, this prophecy seems to admit the failure of that campaign . . . how is this apparent failure of Ezekiel's prophecy to be explained?" (emphasis mine).[2]

Passages like Deuteronomy 18:21-22 are sometimes quoted in connection with this failed prophecy:

> "And you might say in your heart, 'How will we know the word that Yahweh has not spoken?' When a prophet speaks in the name of Yahweh and that word does not come to pass or come true, that is a word that Yahweh has not spoken; the prophet spoke over-confidently. You shall not fear him".

If Ezekiel prophesied that Tyre would fall to Nebuchadnezzar, and that prophecy failed to materialize, it is then assumed that Ezekiel was not a legitimate prophet of God.

Further complicating the issue is the fact that Ezekiel, writing some 15 years later, seems to openly admit that his earlier prophecy had not been fulfilled as he predicted. Nebuchadnezzar had indeed worked hard in besieging the island city of Tyre but was unable to breach its walls and receive "payment" for his efforts on God's behalf. In Ezekiel 29:17-20 we read:

"And in the twenty-seventh year, in the first month, on the first day of the month, the word of Yahweh came to me, saying: 'Human! Nebuchadnezzar king of Babylon worked his army in hard labor against Tyre – every head was made bald and every shoulder was rubbed bare – but he received no wages for his army from Tyre on account of the work that he performed against it. Therefore, thus says the Lord Yahweh: I am about to give to Nebuchadnezzar king of Babylon the land of Egypt, and he will take up its riches and plunder booty and pillage her spoils, then he will have wages for his army. For the work he performed against it, I have given him the land of Egypt, as they did it for me, says the Lord Yahweh'".

Kris Udd rightly asks, "Ezekiel has been acknowledged throughout the history of the church as a true prophet. What are we to make of the fact that, by his own admission, one of his prophecies did not come about?"[3]

This chapter will address Ezekiel's prophecy against the city of Tyre and its apparent failure to come to pass. We will begin by providing a historical overview of Tyre, particularly during the second half of the Neo-Assyrian period, in the centuries leading up to Ezekiel's prophecy. We will examine the significance of Tyre for these Neo-Assyrian kings, and why the submission of the city was important to their overall military strategies. We will then reconstruct the events surrounding Nebuchadnezzar's siege of Tyre, examining our available sources, noting what they can tell us about the events leading up to the siege, the siege itself, and its aftermath. Finally, we will skip forward to Alexander the

Great and briefly discuss his successful campaign against the island city of Tyre.

With this clear historical backdrop in place, we will then turn to the book of Ezekiel itself, noting its overall literary structure and where the prophecies against Tyre appear within that structure. We will look at the oracles against Tyre and how they are presented in chapters 26-28, looking specifically at the way that Ezekiel lays out the all-important prophecy in chapter 26. We will then turn to the specific details of that prophecy, asking questions like: "What does the prophecy entail? What are to be the results of the siege? Who is to act on God's behalf to carry out Tyre's destruction?" After careful analysis of the significant portions of this chapter, we will turn to the later prophecy in Ezekiel 29:17-20, in which Ezekiel seems to admit the failure of his initial prophecy.

Although it is not the primary purpose of this chapter, in order to demonstrate that this prophecy is clearly an interpretive problem, we will present some of the theological solutions that scholars have proposed to reconcile these passages. How have Christians sought to reconcile this failed prophecy with what they know about God's nature and the consequences for false prophets? This will also be useful to the reader should they desire to engage in a deeper investigation in any of these theological solutions.

Finally, we will address some of the other common objections and apologetics that are raised with respect to this prophecy. As many Christians do not accept some of the conclusions of consensus scholarship, it is necessary to examine their objections and address them from the text itself. Three of the most common objections are:

1) the use of the phrase "many nations" in Ezekiel 26:3 shows that Nebuchadnezzar was not the only king described in the prophecy who was to come against Tyre;

2) the shift in person from "he" to "they" in Ezekiel 26:12 confirms that Nebuchadnezzar was not the only one spoken of in the prophecy (see point 1); and

3) the distinction between the island city of Tyre and the mainland city of "Old Tyre" or Ushu indicates (at least to some) that the prophecy was actually about the mainland city of Tyre, not the island, at least as it concerned Nebuchadnezzar.

The problem of Ezekiel's prophecy against Tyre is not one that Christian apologists can easily sweep aside. The vast majority of scholars in the field – both evangelical and "liberal" alike – acknowledge that Nebuchadnezzar was the lone agent who was prophesied to destroy Tyre... and that he failed to do so. In spite of this consensus position, many apologists continue to argue that the prophecy did *not* fail, asserting that scholars have simply misinterpreted the data.

Historical Background

While a great deal has been written on the island city of Tyre, we will provide only a brief overview of its history as it pertains to Ezekiel's prophecies against it. Tyre was an island that was – prior to Alexander the Great's siege of the city – located somewhere between 600 and 750 meters off the coast (see figure 5).[4] In use since (at least) the mid-3rd millennium B.C.E., the island was originally two separate rocks, which were later connected – according to the (legendary) description of Josephus – during the reign of Hiram I (around the middle of the 10th c. B.C.E.).[5] Following the siege of Alexander, the island was "linked to the mainland by a dike, which has so broadened over the centuries through alluvial deposits that present-day Tyre is built upon a peninsula".[6] In

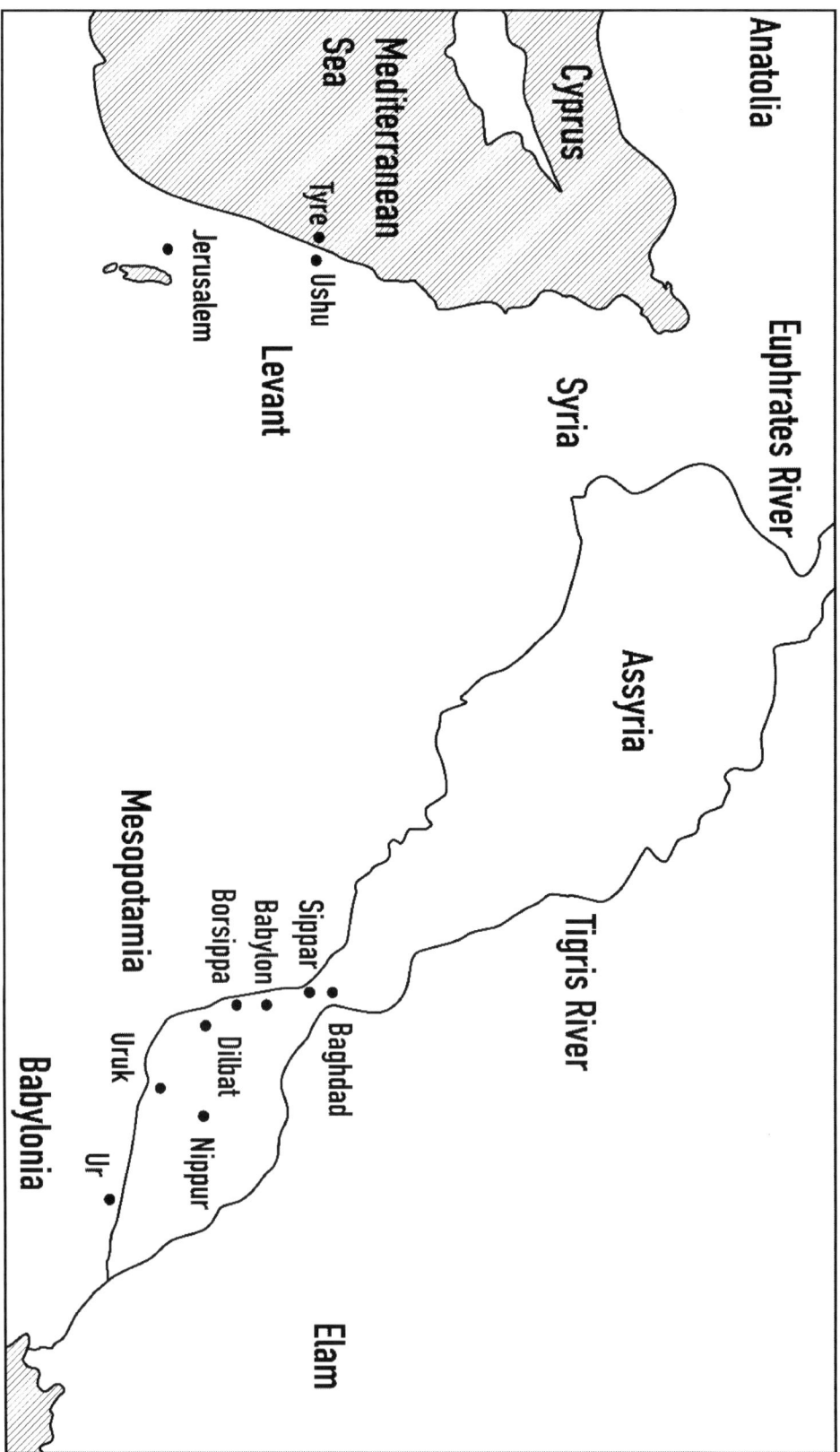

Figure 5. Map of the Ancient Near East showing Mesopotamia and the Levant.

other words, if you look at the island of Tyre on a Google map, the thick land bridge that connects it to the mainland was not always there. Following Alexander's conquest, the causeway that was built out to the island began to gather alluvial deposits and eventually formed what we see today.

In addition to the island city of Tyre, there were mainland cities that were often closely associated with it; most notable of these was Ushu, located somewhere opposite the island close to the shore. We read about Ushu in several ancient sources. For example, during the 14th c. B.C.E. (the Amarna period), the king of Tyre, Abi-Milku, wrote to the Egyptian pharaoh, asking for his assistance against one Zimredda, who had taken control of Ushu:

> "The king knows whether you installed me as commissioner in Tyre. (Still), Zimredda seized Usu from <his> servant. I abandoned it, and so we have neither water nor wood. Nor is there a place where we can put the dead. So may the king, my lord, give thought to his servant".[7]

Notice that the mainland city of Ushu is a source for things like freshwater and wood for the city of Tyre. This makes sense when one considers how difficult it was to procure these things on an island founded on a rock. Later sources refer to the mainland city of Ushu as Palaetyrus (Greek for "Old Tyre"), noting its particular importance as a source of freshwater for the island; Ushu was located near freshwater springs, and water was ferried from the mainland to the island city in boats.[8]

I emphasize the supporting role that Ushu played for the island because of its importance in understanding how kings, both Assyrian and Babylonian, went about attacking the island city of Tyre. As we will see below, because of the difficulties associated with besieging the island city directly – given the amount of water separating the army from the island – kings were often content with simply cutting off its supply lines, making it incredibly difficult to obtain necessities like freshwater.

Previous Attacks on Tyre

Why attack Tyre? Given its relatively small size and position "in the midst of the sea", what was the rationale for expending time and energy attacking it? Two factors stand out in this regard. First, as far as the Neo-Assyrian Empire was concerned – particularly during the late 8th and early 7th centuries – the city of Tyre and its environs represented a part of the path that had to be taken in order to engage in battle with the Egyptians. With respect to Esarhaddon's attacks on Egypt, Elayi writes:

> "Knowing his [Esarhaddon's] earlier policy, he obviously would not have launched his Egypt expedition without taking adequate rearguard precautions. This was all the more necessary if he used Tyrian territory as a logistical base for his campaign to Egypt, unless he set out from Ashkelon on this occasion".[9]

The path to Egypt took the Assyrians and Babylonians through the Levant, leaving their armies exposed to potential attack from cities like Tyre.

Another important feature of the city was its tremendous wealth, given its highly advantageous position on a variety of trade routes. Katzenstein notes concerning Ezekiel's depiction of Tyre, "The profits from the concentration of trade in the hands of Tyre must have been tremendous. The wealth of that city became a legend based upon fact".[10] Even during the Amarna period (14th c. B.C.E.), rival kings spoke of Tyre's great wealth: "Look, there is no mayor's residence like that of the residence in Tyre. It is like the residence in Ugarit. Exceedingly great is the wealth in it".[11] Tyre was ideally situated to maximize its trade and expand its great wealth. It was therefore not only a strategic point to bring under military control during a campaign to Egypt, but it was also a significant source of income through the exacting of tribute.

In this section, we will begin with the late 8th c. attack on Tyre by the Neo-Assyrian king, Sargon II. The king of Assyria brought many of the Phoenician cities under subjection, establishing vassal treaties and exacting tribute. However, King Luli of Tyre refused to submit to Sargon II. While we cannot be sure of the specific historical details, it appears that Sargon II borrowed a number of ships from his vassal Phoenician cities in order to attack Tyre. However, he was unsuccessful in defeating Luli and his fleet. Sargon then set up a blockade along the shore in order to cut off water and other supplies from the island.

According to Josephus:

> "[W]hen the Tyrians had come upon them in twelve ships, and the enemy's ships were dispersed, they took five hundred men prisoners, and the reputation of all the citizens of Tyre was thereby increased; but the king of

Assyria returned, and placed guards at their rivers and aqueducts, who should hinder the Tyrians from drawing water. This continued for five years; and still the Tyrians bore the siege, and drank of the water they had out of the wells they dug".[12]

Elayi writes:

"As we cannot vouch for the reality of the figures, we can merely note that Sargon II did not succeed in beating Luli's fleet or in capturing the island town of Tyre. He therefore organized his blockade to cut off the water supply".[13]

The blockade was apparently lifted upon the untimely death of Sargon II.

Only a few years later – in 701 B.C.E. – Sennacherib returned to lay siege to the island of Tyre. Sennacherib boasted of his military successes in the region:

"On my third campaign, I marched to the land of Ḫatti. Fear of my lordly brilliance overwhelmed Lulî, the king of the city Sidon, and he fled afar into the midst of the sea. The awesome terror of the weapon of the god Aššur, my lord, overwhelmed the cities Great Sidon, Lesser Sidon, Bīt-Zitti, Ṣarepta, Maḫalliba, Ušû, Akzibu, (and) Acco, his fortified cities (and) fortresses, an area of pasture(s) and water-place(s), resources upon which he relied, and they bowed down at my feet".[14]

Luli, having years earlier endured the siege by Sargon II, apparently knew that life was about to get difficult again on the island of Tyre; instead of holding out in the island fortress, he fled to Cyprus, where he was able to manage his kingdom from a distance. However, this move by Luli was not without consequence; Tyre was greatly diminished following Sennacherib's siege. Elayi writes, "Deprived of its mainland territory opposite the island, it [Tyre] held on to a few territories to the south of Mount Carmel and retained its colonies, but these possessions were a long way away".[15] The mainland cities, including Ushu, were critical for the success of Tyre; being deprived of them was a great blow to the city.

Following the reign of Sennacherib, attention was again turned toward Tyre by his successor, Esarhaddon. In spite of an initial treaty between Esarhaddon and King Baal I of Tyre, as often happened in the region, the king of Tyre shifted alliances. In 674, Baal I appears to have formed an alliance with Taharqa in Egypt, and when Esarhaddon sent orders for Baal I to provide materials for his new palace in 673, the Tyrian king refused. This resulted in a siege of Tyre:

> "In the course of my campaign, I set up fortifications against Ba'alu, the king of Tyre, who trusted in his friend Taharqa, the king of Kush, threw off the yoke of the god Aššur, my lord, and kept answering (me) with insolence. I cut off the supply of food and water that sustained their lives".[16]

Katzenstein observes:

> "A repetition of events, certainly a siege against the island
> of Tyre, which had to start with the occupation of Ushu, is
> quite normal, for a march against Philistia and Egypt had
> to pass this strip of country situated along the highways.
> As long as the Phoenician coastal towns were on friendly
> terms with the Assyrian king, no hostile action against
> them was necessary. But in alliance with Egypt each town
> might endanger the long lines of communications".[17]

Baal I quickly surrendered to Esarhaddon, yet the island of Tyre was
not breached.

Esarhaddon's son, Ashurbanipal, had his own problems with the city of
Tyre. In 662, Baal I revolted again, bringing about another siege against
the mainland and a blockade against Tyre.

> "On my third campaign, I marched against Ba'alu, the king
> of the land Tyre who resides in the middle of the sea.
> Because he did not honor my royal command(s and) did not
> obey the pronouncement(s) of my lip(s), I set up outposts
> against him. To prevent his people from leaving, I
> reinforced (its) garrison. By sea and dry land, I took control
> of (all of) his routes (and thus) cut off (all) access to him. I
> made water (and) food for the preservation of their lives
> scarce for their mouths. I confined them in a harsh
> imprisonment from which there was no escape. I
> constricted (and) cut short their lives. I made them (the
> people of Tyre) bow down to my yoke".[18]

Elayi explains in some detail:

> "The Assyrian king described his siege operations of Tyre:
> 'I encircled it with siege walls, and I blocked its sea and
> land routes.' These siege walls were constructed on Tyre's
> mainland territory in order to block the land access routes.
> To block the sea routes, Ashurbanipal organized the
> blockade of the whole island, or only its access to the coast.
> The overpopulated island of Tyre was totally dependent on
> the mainland territory for its water supply, agricultural
> products, and wood. Baal I knew this from experience,
> already having lived through Esarhaddon's blockade".[19]

The upshot was a quick surrender by Baal I, a substantial payment of tribute to the Assyrian king, and some of the mainland sections of Tyre's territory being turned into an Assyrian province.

Nearly two decades later, the mainland towns of Ushu and Akko rebelled against Ashurbanipal. Katzenstein writes:

> "Some time later, approximately in 644/43 B.C.E.
> Ashurbanipal was campaigning against some northern
> Arabian tribes for a second time. On his return from that
> expedition he had to suppress the rebellion of the towns of
> Ushu and Akko".[20]

Ashurbanipal's inscription reads:

> "On my return march, I conquered the city Ušû
> (Palaetyrus), whose location is situated on the shore of the
> sea. I slew the people of the city Ušû who had not been

obedient to their governors by not giving payment, their annual giving. I rendered judgment on (those) insubmissive people: I carried off their gods (and) their people to Assyria".[21]

It is worth noting the ease with which the mainland cities were apparently taken by the Neo-Assyrian kings; while the island fortress of Tyre remained unbreached, cities like Ushu were taken with little effort.

The Siege of Nebuchadnezzar II

Anyone who has studied the history of the Old Testament – or even read through the book of Daniel – probably recognizes the name Nebuchadnezzar. Following the fall of the Neo-Assyrian Empire at the end of the 7th c. B.C.E., the Neo-Babylonian Empire became the dominant power in the region. The first king, Nabopolassar, was succeeded by Nebuchadnezzar II, who made several campaigns to the west into the Levant. After dealing with several rebellions in Judah, he finally laid siege to Jerusalem, and in 586 B.C.E. the city fell.

We have two primary sources from which we reconstruct the events that followed at the city of Tyre: Josephus and Ezekiel. Josephus records:

> "I will now add the records of the Phoenicians; for it will not be superfluous to give the reader demonstrations more than enough on this occasion. In them we have this enumeration of the times of their several kings: 'Nebuchadnezzar besieged Tyre for thirteen years in the days of Ithobal, their king; after him reigned Baal, ten years; . . . [list of rulers that followed] . . . So that the whole

interval is fifty-four years besides three months; for in the seventh year of the reign of Nebuchadnezzar he began to besiege Tyre".[22]

Ezekiel reports on the siege in two primary sections: chapters 26 and 29. Predicting what the siege would look like, he writes in Ezekiel 26:8b-12:

"'[H]e will set against you a siege mound, and heap up against you an assault ramp, and raise up against you a large shield. And the blow of his battering ram he will set against your walls, and your towers he will tear down with axes. Because of the multitude of his horses, he will cover you with their dust; because of the sound of the cavalry and wagons and chariots, your walls will shake when he comes into your gates as one enters a breached city. With the hooves of his horses he will trample all your streets; your people with the sword he will kill, and your strong pillars will come down to the ground. And they will plunder your wealth and plunder your merchandise and tear down your walls, even your nice houses they will tear down, and your stones and timbers and dust they will throw into the sea'".[23]

Three chapters (and some 15 years) later, we read:

"And in the twenty-seventh year, in the first month, on the first day of the month, the word of Yahweh came to me, saying: 'Human! Nebuchadnezzar king of Babylon worked his army in hard labor against Tyre – every head was made bald and every shoulder was rubbed bare – but he received no wages for his army from Tyre on account of the work that he performed against it'" (Ezekiel 29:17-18).

While we cannot simply take these texts – either Josephus or Ezekiel – at face value, we can reconstruct the primary aspects of these events with reasonable certainty. It would seem that both sources agree that Nebuchadnezzar, having taken Jerusalem, proceeded to lay siege to Tyre. Josephus's statement that the siege lasted thirteen years seems to accord well with Ezekiel's two prophecies, which appear to be separated by fifteen years.[24] Greenberg notes:

> "This brief passage – the latest-dated in the book, aside from the enigmatic 1:1 – amends the unfulfilled oracles on Tyre and Egypt. By the twenty-seventh year of the exile (571) the thirteen-year siege of Tyre by Nebuchadnezzar had ended with the city subjected but intact – contrary to Ezekiel's predictions. Moreover, when seventeen years earlier, around the time of Jerusalem's agony, Ezekiel had proclaimed Egypt's fall and devastation, he had expected it to occur imminently".[25]

When we view the overall process described in Ezekiel 26 – taking the mainland cities and then moving on to the island of Tyre – the pattern should come as no surprise to us, given what we know about prior attempts to besiege Tyre, particularly by the Neo-Assyrian kings. Sargon II attempted to send ships to take the island, but having failed, set up a blockade to cut off supplies from Tyre. Sennacherib besieged Tyre in a similar fashion. Esarhaddon followed suit, taking the mainland cities and cutting off the island, as did Ashurbanipal after him. When only the mainland cities rebelled, Ashurbanipal was able to take them by force with relative ease.

In light of the actions of Nebuchadnezzar II and Ezekiel's prediction that he would slaughter the mainland cities and ultimately destroy the city of Tyre, what appears to have transpired fits quite well with historical precedent. Elayi summarizes:

> "All the mainland territory of Tyre, including its fortified towns, such as Ushu and Akko, was conquered by the Babylonians; it was plundered and devastated, its populations deported. Just as the Assyrian kings had done previously, Nebuchadnezzar II must have blocked the supplies of drinking water, food, and other resources from reaching the island of Tyre from its mainland territory, without succeeding completely because Tyre's fleet was too powerful".[26]

The upshot was the apparent submission of King Ithobaal III of Tyre, who was replaced by Baal II, a ruler placed on the throne by Nebuchadnezzar II himself. However, the island fortress was not breached and would remain that way until the siege of Alexander the Great more than 200 years later.

Alexander the Great

Although the siege and conquering of Tyre by Alexander the Great is mostly outside of the scope of this investigation, it is very frequently cited as the event being prophesied about in Ezekiel 26; therefore, this section will briefly summarize the events as they transpired. Alexander approached the city of Tyre in 333, meeting a delegation from Tyre in the city of Ushu. When Alexander was denied entrance into Tyre, he laid siege to the city. Elayi notes that Alexander "had the ingenious idea of having a causeway built that would link the island to the mainland, choosing the narrowest and shallowest part of the straight".[27] Although Alexander met significant opposition – both on the causeway and on the sea – in 332, he was able to successfully breach the walls, enter the city, and kill or enslave many of its inhabitants. The city was not destroyed, however, and Alexander appears to have even left Ozmilk on the throne. [28] This is an important point, as those who argue that Alexander's siege of Tyre is prophesied in Ezekiel 26 must contend with the fact that the island – even in Alexander's siege – was not completely destroyed.

The Structure of Ezekiel's Tyre Prophecy

Now that we have overviewed the historical background to the events being predicted in Ezekiel 26 (and referred to in Ezekiel 29), let's turn to the prophecy itself. As with most books in the Hebrew Bible, it can be difficult to understand a particular passage without having at least a general idea of its immediate and broader context. Ezekiel's prophecy against Tyre is no different. We will look at the overall structure of the book, then at the section in which the Tyre prophecy is contained, eventually narrowing our focus to the literary structure of the prophecy in Ezekiel 26 itself.

Generally speaking, the book of Ezekiel is laid out in three major sections: an initial call and a series of prophecies of destruction against Judah and Jerusalem (chapters 1-24); a series of oracles against the surrounding nations (25-32); and prophecies of restoration (33-48).[29] The book initially prophesies destruction to come upon God's chosen people, followed by prophecies against the surrounding nations. Finally, Ezekiel speaks words of encouragement to the people, prophesying their eventual restoration.

The prophecy against Tyre, naturally, falls within the second section of the book: the oracles against the surrounding nations (chapters 25-32). These types of oracles are not unique to Ezekiel; examples of similar groupings of prophecies against foreign nations can be seen in passages like Amos 1-2, Isaiah 13-19, and Jeremiah 46-51. Oracles against foreign nations were incredibly common among the Israelite prophets, and Collins notes that we can see the social context of these pronouncements in the story of Micaiah ben Imlah in 1 Kings 22, in which "the prophets conduct a virtual pep rally before the start of a military campaign".[30]

In Ezekiel 25-32, the structure of the oracles against the nations appears in this way:

1) Chapter 25: oracles against Ammon, Moab, Edom, and the Philistines.

2) Chapters 26-28: oracles against Tyre.

3) Chapters 29-32: oracles against Egypt.

While not the longest section among the oracles, the prophecies against Tyre take up a great deal of space when compared to all of the combined oracles against Ammon, Moab, Edom, and the Philistines.

This section on the literary structure of Ezekiel is based on the work of Daniel Block, whom the reader should see for a more exhaustive analysis of the book of Ezekiel.[31]

When we focus in on the oracles against Tyre, we see the following substructure:

1) Chapter 26: Judgment on Tyre.

2) Chapter 27: Lament over Tyre.

3) Chapter 28:1-10: Judgment on the King.

4) Chapter 28:11-19: Lament over the King.

Notice the pattern that is present: *judgment / lament / judgment / lament* (A/B/A/B). We will see as we move through this section that there is a very clear literary structure in these chapters; this also applies to Ezekiel 26. Block writes, "Several additional indications of intentional structuring are evident in the Tyrian oracles as a whole".[32] This will become important when we attempt to derive the intended meaning of the prophet, particularly with respect to the agent who will be responsible for bringing judgment against the island city. In other words, the structure will point to the person or nation that was supposed to have destroyed Tyre, whether Nebuchadnezzar himself or someone that was to come after him.

Structure of Ezekiel 26

When we move into the specific structure of chapter 26, we notice a definite pattern that appears in the text. In fact, as we will see, the pattern not only appears in this chapter, but in other places in the book of Ezekiel, functioning in a similar way. The literary pattern is important for our discussion, as it shows the reader not only which sections of the text are connected to others, but allows later texts to interpret or explain those that come before. If that sounds confusing, don't worry; it will become clear as we move through the passage.

The prophecy against Tyre in Ezekiel 26 breaks generally into four paragraphs, based on their content and the repetition of particular phrases. In the text below, you can see the pattern quite clearly.

> ¹**"And in the eleventh year, in the first of the month**, the word of Yahweh came to me saying, ²**Human!**...'"

> ³"'Therefore, **thus says the Lord Yahweh**...'"

> ⁷"'*For* **thus says the Lord Yahweh**...'"

> ¹⁵"'**Thus says the Lord Yahweh** to Tyre...'"

> ¹⁹"'*For* **thus says the Lord Yahweh**...'"

The chapter opens with Ezekiel giving the date of the prophecy, followed by the call from God to the prophet in verse 2: "Human!" The rest of the verse explains why God is about to bring judgment upon the city of Tyre. Subsequent phrases are introduced with either the phrase "'Thus says the Lord Yahweh...'", or "'For thus says the Lord Yahweh...'" In verse 3, we see the phrase "'Therefore <u>thus says the Lord Yahweh</u>'", a phrase that also appears in verses 7, 15, and 19. However, in verses 7 and 19, the phrase adds the Hebrew word *ki* "for", connecting what comes before to what comes after. Thus, the pattern is as follows:

1) Date of prophecy and "Human!"

2) "'Thus says the Lord Yahweh'" (v. 3).

3) "'For thus says the Lord Yahweh'" (v. 7).

4) "'Thus says the Lord Yahweh'" (v. 15).

5) "'For thus says the Lord Yahweh'" (v. 19).

The word "for" (*ki*) that appears in verses 7 and 19 acts as a type of connection between the paragraph beginning in verse 3 and the paragraph beginning in verse 7. The same is true with the "for" (*ki*) in verse 19; it connects the paragraph beginning in verse 15 with the one beginning in verse 19. Let's label the four sections that begin with this phrase Sections A, B, C, and D. The resulting structure and content of the passage can be laid out in this way:[33]

A. Judgment with Yahweh as the Agent (vv. 3-6).

B. Judgment of Yahweh with Nebuchadnezzar as the Agent (vv. 7-14).

C. International Response to Yahweh's Judgment against Tyre (vv. 15-18).

D. Waving Goodbye to Tyre (Her Descent into Sheol) (vv. 19-21).

But why is that significant? When we examine the content of Sections A and B, we notice that *Section A contains a more general set of statements or predictions* about what is to come; these statements are *further developed in greater detail in Section B*.[34] Allen explains it this way:

"The second oracle of vv 7-14, introduced by כי 'for' and a messenger formula, gives careful interpretation of the message of judgment in the first oracle".[35]

In other words, it would be like me saying to my kids: "We are going to have so much fun this weekend! We are going to go out, get some dinner, and see some friends". This would be a general statement about what we are going to do. However, if one of my kids was thinking of doing something else, I might try to persuade her by being more specific. "On Friday night, we are going to go out to Red Robin, get some burgers and shakes, and some donuts for desert. Then we are going to go to the Smith's house, and we will play some games and watch a movie, and afterwards you will spend the night". The first two sentences (Section A) give a general description of what we are going to do over the weekend, while the second two sentences (Section B) describe the same events, but in much greater detail. This is what we see happening in Ezekiel.

Comparing Sections A and B

Section A (Ezekiel 26:3-6) reads:

> "'Therefore, thus says the Lord Yahweh: I am now against you, Tyre! And I will bring up against you many nations, like the sea brings up its waves! And they will destroy the walls of Tyre and demolish her towers, and I will sweep away her dust, and I will turn her into a bare rock. A drying place for nets will she become in the midst of the sea, for I myself have spoken, declares the Lord Yahweh! And it will be for plunder for the nations. And her daughters, which

are in the field, will be killed by the sword, and they will know that I am Yahweh!'" (Ezekiel 26:3-6).

Before we compare the content found in these verses with that which is seen in verses 7-14, let's take a quick look at what these verses are saying. God is speaking in the first person ("I"), and declares that he will do things like "bring up against you many nations" (against Tyre) and "sweep away her dust" and "turn her into a bare rock". In other words, this first section focuses on Yahweh as the one who will bring judgment upon the city of Tyre, describing it in a fairly general way.

But what will Yahweh do to judge the city?

1) Bring many nations against Tyre (v. 3).

2) Destroy the walls of Tyre (v. 4).

3) Pull down the towers of Tyre (v. 4).

4) Sweep away the dust to make Tyre a bare rock (v. 4).

5) Make Tyre a place out in the sea for spreading fishnets (v. 5).

6) Cause Tyre to become plunder for the nations (v. 5).

7) Cause the mainland settlements to be ravaged by the sword (v. 6).

When we continue reading into Section B, we quickly see that *these same judgments are spoken of,* often using the *exact same words and phrases,* yet describing them in greater detail. Let's take a look at verses 7-14:

"'For thus says the Lord Yahweh: I am about to bring to Tyre Nebuchadnezzar king of Babylon from the north – the king of kings – with horses and with chariots and with horsemen and an assembly and many people. Your daughters in the field with the sword he will kill, and he will set against you a siege mound, and heap up against you an assault ramp, and raise up against you a large shield. And the blow of his battering ram he will set against your walls, and your towers he will tear down with his axes. Because of the multitude of his horses, he will cover you with their dust; because of the sound of the cavalry and wagons and chariots your walls will shake, when he comes into your gates as men entering a breached city. With the hooves of his horses he will trample all your streets; your people with the sword he will kill, and your strong pillars will come down to the ground. And they will plunder your wealth and plunder your merchandise, and tear down your walls, even your nice houses they will tear down, and your stones and timbers and dust they will throw into the sea. And I will bring the sound of your songs and the sound of your lyres will not be heard any longer. And I will turn you into a bare rock; it will be a drying yard for nets; you will not be built any longer, for I Yahweh have spoken, declares the Lord Yahweh'" (Ezekiel 26:7-14).

One can immediately see the connections – even on a surface level – between Sections A and B. Furthermore, it is apparent that the description in Section B is far longer and more detailed than that which is seen in Section A. The connections between these two sections becomes even clearer when one examines them more closely (see table 3 below).

Block identifies many of these connections in his analysis, where he explains that the elaborative purpose of Section B (Ezekiel 26:7-14) is clear from the substantial links between it and Section A (Ezekiel 26:3-6).[36]

As you can see, the parallels between Sections A and B are clear and numerous; *these two paragraphs are intimately connected with one another*. Section B is, essentially, a longer and more descriptive version of Section A. For example, in 26:4a the text reads, "'And they will destroy the walls of Tyre and demolish her towers'". The parallel description in 26:8-9 explains in more detail how this will be accomplished: "'and he will set against you a siege mound, and heap up against you an assault ramp, and raise up against you a large shield. And the blow of his battering ram he will set against your walls, and your towers he will tear down with his axes'".

Another example can be seen in 26:4b: "'and I will sweep away her dust'", which is developed in 26:12b, "'and your stones and timbers and dust they will throw into the sea'".

So, why does any of this matter? Why is it important to know that *the second section is essentially restating the predictions of the first section in more detail*? Looking at Ezekiel 26:3 and 26:7 provides us with a helpful example:

Verse	Section A	Verse	Section B
6	"And her daughters, which are in the field, will be killed by the sword"	8	"Your daughters in the field with the sword he will kill"
4	"And they will destroy the walls of Tyre and demolish her towers"	9	"And the blow of his battering ram he will set against your walls, and your towers he will tear down with his axes"
5	"And it will be for plunder for the nations"	12	"And they will plunder your wealth and plunder your merchandise"
4	"And I will sweep away her dust"	12	"And your stones and timbers and dust they will throw into the sea"
4b-5	"And I will turn her into a bare rock. A drying place for nets will she become in the midst of the sea"	14	"And I will turn you into a bare rock; it will be a drying yard for nets"

Table 3. Table showing the connections between Section A and Section B.

> "'And I will bring up against you many nations, like the sea brings up its waves!'" (Ezekiel 26:3).

> "'I am about to bring to Tyre Nebuchadnezzar king of Babylon from the north – the king of kings – with horses and with chariots and with horsemen and an assembly of many people'" (Ezekiel 26:7).

These two verses (one from Section A, and one from Section B) – *both identify who God is going to use to bring his judgment on Tyre: Nebuchadnezzar.* The shorter "many nations" is identified and developed with the longer description of Nebuchadnezzar and his armed forces.[37]

The reason that this elaborative structure is important to be aware of is that many apologists will argue that the "many nations" of verse 3 is not speaking only of Nebuchadnezzar and his armies. However, if we are familiar with the literary structure of the narrative, then we can clearly see that the structure of the passage argues strongly against this interpretation.

A similar literary technique (Sections A and B) is used several chapters later in Ezekiel 32; in verses 3 and 11 we see the familiar "'thus says the Lord Yahweh'" and "'for thus says the Lord Yahweh'", just as we saw in Ezekiel 26. Comparing verses 3 (Section A) and 11 (Section B) directly is again helpful:

> "'And I will spread over you my net *with an assembly of many peoples*, and they will lift you up in my net'" (Ezekiel 32:3).

"'The sword of the king of Babylon will come upon you. With the swords of the mighty men I will cause your multitude to fall'" (Ezekiel 32:11).

The "assembly of many peoples" referenced in verse 3 *is specifically identified in verses 11b and 12a* as the king of Babylon. Not only is the plural "many peoples" specifically identified with the king of Babylon, but – as in chapter 26 – the general description "many peoples" in Section A is specifically identified as "the king of Babylon" in Section B. Hummel explains:

> "The figurative language of the preceding verses is dropped and the message is summarized in literal terms: the imminent Babylonian devastation of Egypt . . . In the wider context, it is not even the king of Babylon's sword, as such, which is in mind, but Yahweh's, and he merely uses the king as his agent".[38]

Having examined the literary structure of the book of Ezekiel as a whole – and more specifically at the oracles against the nations, those against Tyre, and the specific prophecy against Tyre in chapter 26 – we can see that there is a clear and consistent literary structure in chapter 26, which breaks the narrative into four primary sections. Focusing in on Sections A and B demonstrated that they are intimately connected with one another, not only based on their content, but also on their specific words and phrases.

Examining Sections A and B more closely, we saw that Section A speaks in more general terms, while Section B describes the same people and events, but in a much more specific and concrete way (for example, "many nations" is specifically identified as "'Nebuchadnezzar, king of Babylon, from the north – king of kings – with horses and chariots and horsemen, and an assembly and many people'"). This style of writing appears in other places in Ezekiel, including chapter 32, where it functions in a very similar way.

Let's get into the details of the content of the chapter and see what the prophecy is actually describing, and what fate is supposed to befall the island fortress.

Content of the Ezekiel 26 Prophecy

So what is this prophecy actually describing? What is supposed to happen to the city of Tyre, according to Ezekiel? While this portion of the chapter is not a thorough commentary on any part of Ezekiel 26, its goal is to provide you with enough information to understand what this prophecy predicted would occur.

Following the opening "date formula" in verse 1, Yahweh speaks to Ezekiel and explains why he is about to bring judgment: "'because Tyre has said concerning Jerusalem, "Aha! The gateway of the peoples is broken; it has turned to me! I will be filled! She is desolate!"'" (v. 2). As you recall from our earlier discussion, Nebuchadnezzar had recently besieged the city of Jerusalem and destroyed it. The city of Tyre had taken some pleasure in their destruction; their rejoicing was now going to bring God's wrath against them.

"'Therefore, thus says the Lord Yahweh: I am now against you, Tyre! And I will bring up against you many nations, like the sea brings up its waves!'" (v. 3). God's judgment was immanent and would take the form of "many nations" coming against Tyre. This type of "wave" imagery is not unique to Ezekiel; in Jeremiah 51:42, the destruction of Babylon itself is described in a similar way: "The sea has gone up over Babylon; by its roaring waves it has been covered". Thompson writes of the passage in Jeremiah, "Babylon's foes would surge over her like the chaotic waters of the primeval ocean with their roaring waves, a vivid symbol indeed".[39]

The prophecy continues in Ezekiel 26:4-5a: "'And they will destroy the walls of Tyre and demolish her towers, and I will sweep away her dust, and I will turn her into a bare rock. A drying place for nets will she become in the midst of the sea'". The enemy hordes will leave nothing standing. The walls and defensive towers are to be torn down, and even the debris left behind following the destruction will be completely removed. This will leave Tyre as a "bare rock", a fitting word play, as the name "Tyre" (Hebrew *tsor*) comes from a word for "rock" or "flint".[40] In essence, Tyre will be scraped clean, returned to its original state – a bare rock – having value only as a place to spread out fishnets to dry them (v. 5a).

Finally, verses 5b and 6a read, "'And it will be for plunder for the nations. And her daughters, which are in the field, will be killed by the sword, and they will know that I am Yahweh!'" A full reversal of the fortunes of Tyre – following their return to a "bare rock" – would result in the wealthy trade center being reduced to nothing, with their wealth becoming plunder for the nations. The nations that had engaged in commerce with her, who had made her so wealthy, would take from Tyre all that she possessed.[41]

Not only will the island city of Tyre be destroyed, but its cities on the mainland will also feel God's wrath. As we saw above, when kings would besiege the city of Tyre, they would inevitably begin by taking control of the mainland cities, particularly Ushu, cutting off the island from its supply source. Eichrodt writes, "To strike a blow against these satellite cities of Tyre was a very effectual method of weakening the dominion of Tyre, which no attacker failed to strike".[42]

As we move into Section B (verses 7-14), we see the earlier, more general predictions described in greater detail. "'I am about to bring to Tyre Nebuchadnezzar king of Babylon from the north – the king of kings – with horses and with chariots and with horsemen and an assembly and many people'" (v. 7). We will discuss this below in more detail, but Nebuchadnezzar's army is often described as composed of a great and diverse multitude. Allen notes, "The title 'king of kings' is striking: politically it echoes Assyrian royal usage, while in terms of the first oracle it expresses his role as ruler of its '(many) nations' (vv. 3, 5)".[43]

Additionally, Nebuchadnezzar is described as coming "from the north", which is fitting from Tyre's perspective. The Levant represents the corridor through which armies would travel between Egypt and Anatolia, Syria, and Mesopotamia (see figure 5 above). From that point of view, Nebuchadnezzar would come west out of Mesopotamia and "from the north" down into the Levant.

Verse 8a parallels verse 6: "'Your daughters in the field with the sword he will kill'". After taking the mainland cities – where a siege of Tyre would naturally begin – verses 8b-9 continue:

"'[A]nd he will set against you a siege mound, and heap up against you an assault ramp, and raise up against you a large shield. And the blow of his battering ram he will set against your walls, and your towers he will tear down with his axes'" (Ezekiel 26:8-9).

Many commentators have noted that Ezekiel's description of the coming siege does not seem to fit with the idea of besieging an island city. We see, however, that Ezekiel has a certain set of words and phrases that he uses to describe attacks on cities. Hummel notes, "It appears, at least, as if Ezekiel had a sort of stock, stereotyped repertory of idioms to describe the fall of cities".[44] Allen suggests that there may not have been specific vocabulary to describe a naval attack.[45] There are several descriptions of siege tactics found in the book of Ezekiel, including 4:2; 17:17b; and 21:22 (Hebrew text 21:27). These three passages speak of the siege of Jerusalem, and each uses language that is – at least in part – quite similar to what we see in 26:8-9. In other words, Ezekiel had a particular way of describing a siege, and he used that stock language in chapter 26; it was not custom-tailored to the coming siege of Tyre.

Nebuchadnezzar is to lay siege to the island fortress and ultimately breach its walls. "'Because of the multitude of his horses, he will cover you with their dust; because of the sound of the cavalry and wagons and chariots your walls will shake, *when he comes into your gates as one enters a breached city*'" (v. 10, emphasis mine). Block ties these verses together nicely: "The last line of v. 10 is the key: the enemy will take the sea fortress by storm as if it were an ordinary walled city on the mainland".[46] This is another possible explanation for the use of stock siege imagery here in the passage.

Finally, Nebuchadnezzar's forces enter the city:

> "'With the hooves of his horses he will trample all your streets; your people with the sword he will kill, and your strong pillars will come down to the ground. And they will plunder your wealth and plunder your merchandise, and tear down your walls, even your nice houses they will tear down, and your stones and timbers and dust they will throw into the sea'" (vv. 11-12).

Nebuchadnezzar's forces will begin by killing the people of Tyre, allowing these soldiers to plunder the great wealth found therein. They will then tear down the walls, destroy the houses, and throw all the debris into the sea, leaving Tyre a bare rock. Notice that it is the debris from the *island city* that is thrown into the sea, not the debris from the mainland. This is important, as many will argue that this verse describes the actions of Alexander as he threw the mainland debris into the water to form a causeway out to the island.

Following a brief statement about bringing an end to their music (v. 13), the prophecy continues: "'And I will turn you into a bare rock; it will be a drying yard for nets. You will not be built any longer, for I Yahweh have spoken, declares the Lord Yahweh'" (v. 14). As we saw in Section A, God's judgment is supposed to leave Tyre a bare rock, a place for fishermen to dry their nets. In fact, according to the text, the city of Tyre is never again to be rebuilt. Nancy Bowen's summation is fitting:

> "Nebuchadnezzar will grind Tyre to dust, systematically dismantling the city and tossing it into the sea . . . Tyre is reduced to bare rock, useful only for spreading nets . . .

Tyre's silence is similar to Nebuchadnezzar's silencing of Jerusalem's singing (Ps 137:1-4; Lam 5:14-15). Unlike Jerusalem, which will sing once again (Isa 42:10; 51:3, 11; 52:9; 54:1), *Tyre's silence is permanent* (v. 14)" (emphasis mine).[47]

The majority of the specific judgments to fall upon Tyre are described in Sections A and B of Ezekiel 26. Section C (vv. 15-18) speaks of the reaction that those who witness Tyre's downfall will have, lamenting the once wealthy and powerful city. Section D (vv. 19-21) reiterates the permanent nature of Tyre's judgment, as Yahweh will make Tyre "a desolate city, like the cities that are not inhabited" (v. 19). He will also "make the deep go up over" Tyre (v. 20), and ultimately states, "I will set up terrors on you, and you will not be sought, and you will not be found again forever!'" (v. 21). As Allen notes:

"The 'never again' of v 21b echoes and intensifies the close of the first half of the overall unit (v 14). *This sealing of Tyre's fate in irrevocable finality* . . . is meant to assuage the passionate feelings of Ezekiel's fellow exiles" (emphasis mine).[48]

Let's quickly review what Ezekiel said would happen. The following list represents what the prophecy in chapter 26 predicts will befall Tyre:

1) "many nations" will come against it;

2) destroy the walls and towers;

3) scrape the city clean, turning it into a bare rock;

4) be plundered by the nations;

5) people in the city as well as on the mainland will be killed;

6) bring an end to their music; and

7) never to be rebuilt or inhabited.

Now we come to the crux of the matter: this prophecy did not come to pass. It is necessary to note at this point that I'm not just stating my own interpretation of the data; the vast majority of biblical scholars come to the exact same conclusion. A small selection of quotes will illustrate the point:

> "All of Ezekiel's anti-Tyre prophecies declare a disastrous defeat and destruction of the fortress city. Yet this did not happen; instead, Tyre held out in the siege, no doubt greatly assisted by the possibility of receiving supplies by sea. Although humiliated, the city was not defeated and ransacked".[49]

> "In the oracles against Tyre, the fall and devastation of Tyre and, quite explicitly in 26:7, her surrender to the great king from the north were expressed. The end of the siege of Tyre appeared quite differently. Whatever the details of the end may have been, Tyre was in any case not destroyed and plundered".[50]

> "The prediction of the siege of Tyre ending in its complete destruction provides an interesting case of the disconfirmation of prophecy, for by the time of the last anti-

Egyptian saying, dated sixteen years later (29:17-20), it was well known that the attempt of Nebuchadnezzar to reduce the city had failed".[51]

Clearly, Ezekiel prophesied complete destruction... but it never came to pass. How did the prophet respond to the failure of his prophecy?

The Later Prophecy of Ezekiel 29

Shortly after the fall of Jerusalem in 587/586, Ezekiel prophesied that Nebuchadnezzar would completely destroy the city of Tyre. Modern biblical scholars aren't the only ones who noted the failure of the prophecy... the prophet had noticed himself. Some 15 years later, lo and behold, a clarifying message from God came to Ezekiel:

> "And in the twenty-seventh year, in the first month, on the first day of the month, the word of Yahweh came to me, saying: 'Human! Nebuchadnezzar king of Babylon worked his army in hard labor against Tyre – every head was made bald and every shoulder was rubbed bare – but he received no wages for his army from Tyre on account of the work that he performed against it. Therefore, thus says the Lord Yahweh: I am about to give to Nebuchadnezzar king of Babylon the land of Egypt, and he will take up its riches and plunder booty and pillage her spoils, then he will have wages for his army. For the work he performed against it, I have given him the land of Egypt, as they did it for me, says the Lord Yahweh'" (Ezekiel 29:17-20).

As discussed above, it is likely that the king of Tyre ultimately submitted to Nebuchadnezzar, paying him tribute; however, it seems clear that the prophesied result of the siege did not come to pass. Block concurs:

> "But the present prophecy [29:17-21] seems to look on these developments as a failure. To be sure, Nebuchadrezzar would have made off with tribute payments of Tyre jingling in his pockets, *but this is a far cry from having conquered the city and confiscated all the precious loot that the merchant state had gathered into its treasure-houses*" (emphasis mine).[52]

In short, Ezekiel prophesied Tyre's complete destruction, but some 15 years later, it appeared that the prophet's word had gone unfulfilled. This follow-up prophecy in Ezekiel 29 helped to make sense of the historical developments. God was apparently in control, and was still working through Ezekiel, declaring that Nebuchadnezzar and his soldiers would not receive their compensation from Tyre, but instead from Egypt (another prediction that failed to come to pass).

Proposed Solutions

If Ezekiel were a true prophet, why does this later prophecy apparently concede the failure of Nebuchadnezzar's siege against Tyre?[53] As you might imagine, there have been several proposed solutions to this dilemma over the years. We will discuss a few of the more popular explanations, but for a more complete discussion the reader should refer to the work of Daniel Block and (more recently) Kris Udd.[54]

There are two older views that have been generally disregarded, given what we now know about the history of the period. The first argues that the prophecy *was actually fulfilled*; this position sees Nebuchadnezzar as God's agent of destruction in chapter 26 and argues that he actually was able to breach the walls of the island city of Tyre and take the city. As we have shown, however, the evidence simply does not support this conclusion.

A second interpretation that is similar to the first is that the prophecy was indeed fulfilled, but the wealth of the Tyrians was no longer on the island when Nebuchadnezzar breached it. This would account for Ezekiel's statements in chapter 29 concerning Nebuchadnezzar's failure to be "paid" for his efforts. One version of this interpretation argues that Nebuchadnezzar successfully took Tyre, but before he could get in, the people were able to ship all their treasures off of the island utilizing their fleet. Another interpretation involves seeing an absolutely precise fulfillment of Ezekiel 26:19-21, where the waters of the sea engulfed Tyre, washing away all its wealth. Unfortunately for Nebuchadnezzar, although he had just breached and destroyed the city, he was unable to plunder it, as the sea beat him to it.

Arguing for the latter position, the 19th century Rabbi Malbim concludes:

> "[N]either Nebuchadnezzar nor his army received any reward because after he had worked hard to conquer the city, it was destroyed not by him but by the ocean that inundated it. All the plunder was lost, and all the inhabitants were drowned. Hence, the army did not receive

any plunder, and Nebuchadnezzar gained neither subjects over whom to reign nor the fear due to one who destroys a country".[55]

However, as we have seen, there is sufficient historical evidence to conclude that neither this, nor the former "wealth-being-shipped-off-the-island" position, are historically likely.

A more recent and popular proposal attempts to reconcile the problem of the failed prophecy by examining the purpose of prophecy itself. Prophecies were intended to *do* something and often resulted in the recipients of these pronounced judgments turning from their wicked ways. A common example is Jonah and the city of Nineveh. Although Jonah prophesied that the city would be destroyed in 40 days, because the Ninevites turned from their evil ways, God decided not to carry out his plan.

If those threatened with a prophetic judgment were to repent, therefore, God was perfectly free to do likewise. If a condemned city changed its behavior, then God could change his judgement.[56] Thus, prophecy was inherently *contingent*. Block writes:

> "[T]hough preserved literary forms of oracles may contain no hint of conditionality, the outcomes announced were often contingent. Prophetic pronouncements did not possess inherent power so that the mere utterance of the word set in motion the events that they predicted, thus leading to an inevitable and mechanical fulfillment. The efficaciousness of the word lay not in the word itself but in

the power of the divine speaker to carry out what he had predicted".[57]

Kris Udd makes a similar argument:

"In answer to the initial question of what prophecy really is, there is good evidence to suggest that *it is the revelation of what God has planned or intends to do*, rather than simply a proclamation of future events based on passive foreknowledge . . . Ezekiel's God is one who plans and brings things to pass, but is *sometimes willing to flex with regard to his intentions*" (emphasis mine).[58]

These represent a few of the ways in which theologians have wrestled with the dilemma that is created by Nebuchadnezzar failing to take the island city of Tyre. However one makes sense of the events, it is important to recognize that Ezekiel indeed prophesied *the complete destruction of Tyre* and that *it failed to come to pass*, thus creating the theological problem to be solved.

Common Apologetic Objections

In this final section of the chapter, we will address some common objections or explanations that Christian apologists provide with respect to this prophecy. As you might imagine, there are many such arguments that are made in defense of Ezekiel 26; this failed prophecy ostensibly presents difficulties for many Christians who hold to a particular view of the inerrancy of the Bible. Because the prophet spoke for God, and God cannot lie or be in error, a failed prophecy – as we have seen – would show the prophet to be false, or God to have been either incorrect or incapable of bringing about his intended result. As noted above, many Christian apologists argue that, if you think the prophecy was not fulfilled as Ezekiel prophesied, then you have fundamentally misread and misunderstood the passage itself.

Perhaps the most common argument is that *Nebuchadnezzar was only the first agent of Yahweh*; he would do his part against Tyre but would be followed by Alexander the Great, who would finish the job against the island city. The arguments often go:

1) the prophecy in Ezekiel 26 speaks of "many nations", not simply Nebuchadnezzar; this is confirmed in the passage by the change from the pronoun "he" to "they" in Ezekiel 26:12. The "he" represented Nebuchadnezzar and his armies, while the "they" referred to Alexander the Great, who ultimately fulfilled the prophecy when he destroyed the island city centuries later.

2) Nebuchadnezzar did lay siege to Tyre, but it was "Old Tyre" (Ushu) on the mainland and not the island city of Tyre. After a thirteen-year siege, the Babylonian king *did* breach the walls of Ushu but found (much to his chagrin) that the inhabitants had been relocating with their possessions to the island city.

These arguments rest upon two premises: first, that the "many nations" and "they" refer to people or groups other than Nebuchadnezzar and his forces, and second, that the king besieged the mainland city of Ushu and not the island city of Tyre. This allows the prophecy to stand correct in its predictions. In the following section, we will argue that both of these premises are false; Nebuchadnezzar was the lone instrument of God in

Ezekiel's prophecy, and he besieged (and failed to breach) the island city of Tyre.

"Many Nations" and the "He/They" Distinction

As stated above, it is argued that Nebuchadnezzar was never prophesied to be the only agent to bring about Tyre's total destruction; many nations (Ezekiel 26:3) would come against Tyre, ultimately destroying the city and leaving it a bare rock. In Ezekiel 26:3 we read, "'Therefore, thus says the Lord Yahweh: I am now against you, Tyre! And I will bring up against you many nations, like the sea brings up its waves!'".

The reference to "many nations", at first glance, would seem to strongly indicate that the Neo-Babylonian Empire and its armies, headed by Nebuchadnezzar, would only be the first "wave" to come against the city of Tyre. If we only had this phrase to go by, this interpretation would likely be the natural reading of the text. However, several aspects of this passage, along with similar descriptions of Nebuchadnezzar's army in different contexts, argue against this conclusion.

Let's begin with Nebuchadnezzar and his army. The Babylonian king is the only agent of God spoken of in the text. The description of Nebuchadnezzar and his forces in verse 7 is meant to link with and develop the "many nations" of verse 3 (see the discussion above). We see in Ezekiel 26:7, "'For thus says the Lord Yahweh: I am about to bring to Tyre Nebuchadnezzar king of Babylon from the north – the king of kings – with horses and with chariots and with horsemen and an assembly and many people'".

There are several things to note in this verse. First, the Hebrew particle *ki* "for, because" appears at the beginning of verse 7, and directly connects the previous section to this concrete identification of Nebuchadnezzar and his army. Second, the use of the phrase "king of kings", along with the description of the various parts of the army (i.e., horses, chariots, horsemen), as well as an "assembly" and "many people", are almost certainly the "many nations" from v. 3. In fact, the adjective "many" in verse 3 is the same adjective used in verse 7 (Hebrew *rav*) to refer to the "many people". *This has led consensus scholarship to identify Nebuchadnezzar and his armies as the "many nations" in verse 3.* Block writes concerning this connection: "The *gôyim rabbîm* portrayed as waves beating on the rock in v. 3 are identified as Nebuchadrezzar (with his title of *melek melākîm*) and his hosts, referred to as *qāhāl we'am rāb*".[59]

Furthermore, Ezekiel's description of Nebuchadnezzar's forces is not unique. For example, in Jeremiah 34:1 we read:

> "The word that came to Jeremiah from Yahweh, when Nebuchadnezzar king of Babylon *and all his army and all the kingdoms of the earth – the dominion under his power – and all the peoples, were fighting against Jerusalem and against all its cities,* saying" (Jeremiah 34:1, emphasis mine).

Similarly, in the book of Ezekiel itself, we read another description of Nebuchadnezzar's army in 23:23 *"the Babylonians and all the Chaldeans, Pekod and Shoa and Koa, all the Assyrians with them,* all of the desirable ones, governors, and officials, and all of the adjutants and famous men, and riders of horses" (emphasis mine). Block writes concerning Ezekiel 23:23:

> "At their head are the 'magnates of Babylon,' the Chaldeans, followed by a triad of forces . . . The list concludes with a reference to 'all the magnates of Assyria,' *presumably the officials of western vassal states, formerly under Assyrian control but now in the hands of the Babylonians*" (emphasis mine).[60]

In other words, *the Babylonian army was made up of soldiers from a variety of vassal nations*; the descriptions seen in the above passages make it clear that the "many nations" of Ezekiel 26:3 refer to the multi-national makeup of Nebuchadnezzar's army.[61]

Furthermore, this apologetic interpretation concludes that the shift from the use of the singular pronoun "he" in Ezekiel 26:7-11 to the plural pronoun "they" in verse 12 *indicates a change in referent* from Nebuchadnezzar to the nation that would follow Nebuchadnezzar (ostensibly lead by Alexander the Great). [62] In other words, these apologists do not deny that Nebuchadnezzar was the agent prophesied about in verses 7-11; however, in verse 12, *the shift to the pronoun "they" indicates that the prophecy was then referring to Alexander the Great and what he would accomplish*, as he would be responsible for ultimately taking the island city of Tyre.

There are numerous problems with this interpretation, both with regard to parallel constructions that occur in other prophetic passages, as well as the internal logic of the prophecy in Ezekiel 26. First, there are other prophetic passages that are constructed with similar shifts in pronouns.

For example, in Jeremiah 20, we read about the priest Pashhur mistreating the prophet Jeremiah, who responds by pronouncing judgment upon him. In Jeremiah 20:4 we read:

> "For thus says Yahweh, 'I am about to set you as a horror to yourself and to all your friends, and they will fall by the sword of their *enemies* while your eyes see it, and all Judah I will give into the hand of *the king of Babylon, and he* will exile them to Babylon, and *he* will kill them with the sword" (Jeremiah 20:4, emphasis mine).

Notice that not only is the word "enemies" in the plural form, but the "king of Babylon" (singular) is the agent who will kill Pashhur's friends and bring the exiles to Babylon. However, in verse 5 the text reads:

> "'And I will give all the treasure of this city and all its possessions and all its valuables, even all the treasures of the kings of Judah I will give into the hand of their *enemies*, and *they* will plunder them and *they* will take them and *they* will bring them to Babylon'" (Jeremiah 20:5, emphasis mine).

We know, not only from this text, but also from external sources, that Nebuchadnezzar brought the kingdom of Judah into exile, and he was the lone agent of the prophecy here in Jeremiah 20. Yet, *there is a clear change in pronoun use from "he" to "they" in this passage.*[63] In other words, we would not postulate that some future nation would follow Nebuchadnezzar's attack as described in Jeremiah 20; instead, we recognize that the shift from "he" to "they" in the passage indicates something different.

If the switch from "he" to "they" in Ezekiel 26:12 does not refer to a future nation that would come up against Tyre, then to what is it referring? The internal logic of the passage makes it clear that Nebuchadnezzar's *soldiers* are the ones referred to as "they". In Ezekiel 26:7 – as we have seen – Nebuchadnezzar is described as coming with horses, chariots, cavalry, a host, and many people. He would kill the inhabitants on the mainland, set up a siege and battering rams, tear down the towers, etc. Of course, while Nebuchadnezzar would indeed be responsible for performing these actions – as the leader of the army – it is in no way intended by the prophet that Nebuchadnezzar *himself* would bring the towers down with a sword or set up a battering ram; this would be the work of his soldiers.

This idea is carried into verses 10 and 11, as the horses enter the city, raise a cloud of dust, shake the walls, trample the streets, and kill the inhabitants. In verse 12, the use of "they" *simply refers to the soldiers who have just breached the city and killed its inhabitants*: "'They will plunder your wealth and loot your merchandise; they will break down your walls and demolish your fine houses and throw your stones, timber and rubble into the sea'". Greenberg addresses this shift to the third person: "*They.* Nebuchadnezzar's soldiers; the shifts in subject portray the action from different viewpoints. In G [the Greek text] all the verbs of this verse are singular, continuing the person of the previous verb".[64] Here, Greenberg points to the Septuagint, the Greek translation of the text, which *maintains the third person singular pronoun "he" throughout*, demonstrating its understanding of the agent of destruction to be Nebuchadnezzar, as in the immediately preceding verses.[65]

To briefly summarize, the first pillar upon which this argument stands is the meaning of the phrase "many nations" in verse 3, which apologists often argue does not refer only to Nebuchadnezzar and his armies, but also to Alexander the Great. This is evidenced, according to this position, by the shift from the third person singular pronoun "he" in verses 7-11 to the third person plural "they" in verse 12. However, as we have seen, the "many nations" almost certainly simply refers to the "many people" that make up the armies of Nebuchadnezzar referred to in verse 7; this is in keeping with the other descriptions of the Babylonian army seen in Ezekiel 23 and Jeremiah 34.

Looking at the shift in pronouns, we saw that this is merely a change in perspective, as the "he" refers to Nebuchadnezzar as the representative of his armies, while the shift to "they" in verse 12 changes the perspective to the soldiers themselves. This conclusion is supported (amongst other things) by the reading of the Septuagint in verse 12, which maintains the third person singular pronoun "he" throughout. In short, there is no reason to suggest that anyone other than Nebuchadnezzar and his armies is referred to in the prophecy of Ezekiel 26.

Tyre vs. the "Daughters" on the Mainland

The second pillar of this argument is the identification of the besieged city of Ezekiel 26:7-11 as the mainland city of Ushu or "Old Tyre", rather than the island city of Tyre. It is sometimes argued that, for thirteen years, Nebuchadnezzar laid siege to the *mainland city of Ushu*, which was ultimately breached. However, when the king entered into the mainland city, instead of finding the people and their wealth, he discovered that, during the siege, the people of the city had secretly relocated to the island city of Tyre, taking their possessions with them. Thus, Ezekiel's prophecy was indeed accurate, for Nebuchadnezzar did breach the mainland city; however, he was unable to receive any plunder, because the people had taken it to the island city of Tyre.

Unfortunately, this interpretation is untenable for several reasons. First, the distinction between the city of Tyre (an island city) and the city of Ushu (a mainland city) is maintained in the ancient sources, and as far as we know, the word "Ushu" is never used by ancient sources to refer to the island city. Thus, the judgment prophesied against Tyre by Ezekiel was clearly against the island city, evidenced not only by this ancient distinction, but by the language of the passage in Ezekiel itself (for example, verse 5 speaks of Tyre "in the midst of the sea", contrasted with "her daughters, which are in the field [on the mainland]" in verse 6). Secondly, we know a fair amount about the mainland city of Ushu and the role that it played in the day-to-day life of Tyre. Although Ushu likely had fortifications of some sort to protect its natural springs, it had been captured and conquered with relatively minimal effort throughout history (even recent history from Ezekiel's perspective). Finally, as we saw earlier in this chapter, the siege of the island city of Tyre was predicated upon cutting off its supply lines, which came from the mainland, particularly Ushu. In other words, the siege of Tyre *began* with cutting off Ushu from the island city, and the defeat of Ushu did not constitute the defeat of Tyre. Let's examine these points in greater detail.

The island city of Tyre was distinct from its vulnerable mainland or "daughter" cities, including Ushu. Katzenstein writes, "Situated as it was, 'on an island in the midst of the sea,' Tyre's chief interest was her wide-spreading trade. While her mainland was vulnerable to attack, her splendid isolation was Tyre's trump card, which the king of Tyre knew how to play".[66] As we have seen, not long before Ezekiel's time, the Assyrian army had laid siege to Tyre under several Neo-Assyrian kings, including Sargon II, Sennacherib, Esarhaddon, and Ashurbanipal. These inscriptions reveal that Tyre was situated "in the middle of the sea", and that a crucial aspect of besieging the city was cutting off its supply lines, both from the land and the sea. Because Ushu represented a significant source of freshwater for Tyre, an invading king would begin a siege of Tyre by cutting off supply lines between the island and Ushu.[67]

We also saw from these inscriptions – particularly those of Ashurbanipal – that the mainland city of Ushu was comparatively easy prey for invading armies. This Neo-Assyrian king was able to conquer this rebellious daughter city on his return march home from his campaign. Ashurbanipal maintained the distinction between Tyre "in the middle of the sea" and Ushu, which was "situated on the shore of the sea" (see inscriptions above).

To briefly summarize this section so far, there was a clear distinction drawn between the island city of Tyre and the mainland city of Ushu, along with the other mainland cities along the coast. Ushu was a source of freshwater for the city of Tyre, and because of this, the initial stages of any siege included either directly controlling Ushu or cutting off the supply lines between Ushu and Tyre via blockade. Finally, we noted the relative ease with which armies were able to conquer the cities of the mainland.

The situation was no different in these respects for Nebuchadnezzar when he began his siege of Tyre around 585 B.C.E. Given the normal siege tactics that were historically used against Tyre, the first thing that we would expect the Babylonian king to do would be to defeat and secure the vulnerable mainland cities, cutting off supply lines (particularly of water) to the island of Tyre. This, of course, is what we see.

Block observes:

> "The description [in Ezekiel 26] begins appropriately with the fate of the mainland Tyrian settlements, which must be the first to experience Nebuchadrezzar's attack, followed by a more detailed account of the assault on the island city itself".[68]

Katzenstein agrees:

> "Nebuchadnezzar started a special Phoenician campaign, and apparently quickly conquered and subdued Sidon and Arvad. The mainland of Tyre, was occupied by the Babylonian forces too, but the island of Tyre did not open its gates to the Babylonian king. Thus in about 585 B.C.E., the seventh year of Ethbaal III, the siege of Tyre started . . . . We must assume that the siege of Tyre was actually a blockade of the island, from the mainland opposite. After the Tyrian mainland had been occupied . . . the siege of the island itself started. But the island was surrounded by strong and high walls, strengthened by high and mighty towers".[69]

These details about Ushu are quite significant for this apologetic argument. The contention is that Nebuchadnezzar did not besiege the island city of Tyre but the mainland city of Ushu. After a thirteen-year siege, he eventually did enter Ushu's gates, but found that, during the siege, all of the inhabitants had relocated to the island fortress. This interpretation not only flies directly in the face of what is recorded in the text of Ezekiel – which specifically differentiates between Tyre and its "daughters" or mainland cities – but contradicts the historical and logical progression of events that we know from previous historical sieges of Tyre.

Even if no other historical data were available to us concerning the siege of Nebuchadnezzar, it seems difficult to imagine that Ashurbanipal (for example), on a return from a separate campaign, could conquer the mainland coast and Ushu, but Nebuchadnezzar and his hosts could not breach the walls of this mainland city for thirteen years! It seems even more fantastic to suggest that Nebuchadnezzar would only besiege the mainland side of Ushu (under this suggested scenario), allowing the inhabitants of Ushu to essentially "sneak out the back door", relocating with their possessions to the island fortress. This seems all but ludicrous, particularly in light of the common practice of setting up a blockade to cut off Ushu and the mainland cities from providing supplies to the city of Tyre.

The prophecy of Ezekiel 26 is pronounced against Tyre, *the island city*, and not Ushu, the city on the mainland. Although Ushu was likely fortified to protect its freshwater springs, it was vulnerable to attack and was repeatedly conquered during the 1st millennium B.C.E., along with the other mainland cities. In fact, a siege of the island city of Tyre would begin with either conquering or isolating Ushu and the other cities on the mainland in order to cut off supply lines to Tyre. Thus, in addition to the historical evidence available to us, given that:

1) Ushu was weak and repeatedly conquered; and

2) blockades of Ushu were the norm when laying siege to the island;

it is difficult to imagine a scenario in which Nebuchadnezzar would lay siege to Ushu – and only from one side – allowing its inhabitants to sneak out of the city and flee to the island fortress during a thirteen-year siege.

What Can We Say?

According to some apologists, the prophecy found in Ezekiel 26 against Tyre did not fail, but rather referred to (at least) two separate agents of Yahweh's destruction: Nebuchadnezzar and Alexander the Great. This interpretation is primarily based on the phrase "many nations" in verse 3 and the shift in pronouns from "he" to "they" in verse 12. Furthermore, it is argued that Nebuchadnezzar did not besiege the island city of Tyre, but instead the mainland city of Ushu, later referred to as "Old Tyre".

As we have demonstrated, neither of these conclusions are justifiable. First, the agent referred to in chapter 26 is Nebuchadnezzar, and attempting to assign any portion of the prophecy to a later agent is extremely problematic. The "many nations" almost certainly refers to Nebuchadnezzar and the vast hosts that he was to bring against Tyre, and a similar shift in pronouns can be seen in other prophetic passages, where they refer to only one agent. In Ezekiel 26:12, it is clear that the "they" refers not to some future conquering nation, but rather to the soldiers of Nebuchadnezzar, shifting the perspective of the text, evidenced by the continued use of the singular "he" in the Septuagint.

Finally, we have demonstrated that the normal, historical process of besieging Tyre began with conquering or isolating the mainland cities, particularly Ushu, as it was a supply line for food and freshwater for the island. It seems highly unlikely, having been so easily and repeatedly conquered by previous kings, that Ushu would not only hold out during a siege by Nebuchadnezzar for thirteen years, but that its citizens would also be able to leave the city undetected to flee to the island fortress of Tyre.

Conclusion

This chapter has focused on one of the more intriguing prophecies in the Old Testament: the oracles against the island city of Tyre in Ezekiel 26. As we have seen, the prophet Ezekiel predicts the impending doom that is to befall this wealthy and secure city in the midst of the sea; God would bring "many nations" against her, "like the sea brings up its waves" (Ezekiel 26:3). King Nebuchadnezzar II of Babylon, along with his hordes, was to ravage the mainland and breach and destroy the island city, reducing it to a bare rock. This prophecy is a frequent topic of debate, particularly on social media, because of its apparent failure to come true.

We learned that the failure of Nebuchadnezzar II to take the city of Tyre is not only known from extra-biblical sources but was also reported by the prophet himself. In chapter 29, Ezekiel explains that, although Nebuchadnezzar and all his forces worked tirelessly to take Tyre, his efforts were unsuccessful. As a result, the king and his army would be given Egypt as plunder to repay them for their efforts. In short, although Ezekiel waved goodbye to the island fortress in chapter 26, the "waves" of judgment were unable to break down her walls, leaving the interpreter with a significant theological problem.

This chapter has sought to provide the reader with a more holistic approach to the prophecy, providing the historical background of the book of Ezekiel and its prophecies against Tyre. We examined the literary structure of the book as a whole, the group of "oracles against the nations" in which the Tyre prophecies are contained, and finally the specific prophecy in chapter 26.

Ezekiel 26 is relatively clear concerning what the prophecy entailed, particularly with respect to who was to bring about the destruction of Tyre. We examined the later prophecy of Ezekiel 29 and briefly discussed the admission of Ezekiel concerning Nebuchadnezzar II's failure, along with several solutions that have been proposed by theologians that attempt to make sense of this failed prophecy. Finally, we addressed a common set of apologetic responses often heard in defense of Ezekiel's prophecy.

How are we to understand Ezekiel's failed prophecy? How have theologians sought to reconcile the word spoken by an all-knowing deity's spokesperson and its failure to come to pass? Did the prophecy actually fail? What are we to make of all of this? The evidence leaves us with little doubt on the following points:

1) Ezekiel prophesied that the island city of Tyre would be completely destroyed by Nebuchadnezzar.

2) Nebuchadnezzar neither destroyed Tyre, nor was able to even breach the city walls.

3) Ezekiel's later prophecy acknowledges this failure.

Consensus scholarship agrees on these basic data, and it is within these bounds that theologians have sought to reconcile the failure of the prophecy with the validity of God's prophet and his message.

While the question of theological interpretation is an interesting one, it is beyond the scope of this work. Instead, my only goal – as with all of the topics in this book – is to ensure that we are all beginning at the same place, building on the data points that scholars agree upon. When it comes to the prophecy against Tyre, it is important that we recognize the problems in the text – whether we are arguing as an atheist or theist – and work to structure our arguments accordingly. The prophecy of Ezekiel against Tyre went unfulfilled; any solution – theological or historical – must accept and begin with that fact.

---

[1] Ra 2016: 42. Aron provides a lengthy discussion on the issue that is well worth reading on pages 42-50.
[2] Block 1998: 147.
[3] Udd 2005: 36-37.
[4] Katzenstein 1997: 9-10. The exact distance differs in various sources.
[5] See Aubet 2018: 709. "The legend, as reported by Flavius Josephus (*Contra Ap.* I, 113), tells us that Hiram joined the two islands or reefs together, forming a single island, on which he erected temples for Melqart, Astarte, and Ba'al Shamem". For a general overview of 3rd millennium occupation, see Edwards & Katzenstein 1992: 687.
[6] Katzenstein 1997: 9.
[7] Letter EA 149, lines 47-54 (BM 29811, rev. 10-17), translated in Moran 1992: 236. Letters EA 148 and 150 also mention Usu in similar contexts.
[8] Katzenstein 1997: 14.
[9] Elayi 2018: 171.
[10] Katzenstein 1997: 218.
[11] Translation of lines 48ff of EA 89 in Moran 1992: 162.

[12] *Antiquities* Book 9, chapter 14, 286-287, translated in Whiston and Maier 1999: 332.
[13] Elayi 2018: 161.
[14] Grayson & Novotny 2012: 63, Sennacherib 4, lines 32-34. Elayi notes, "His title 'king of Sidon' indicates that the dual kingdom had briefly been reestablished after the lifting of Sargon II's blockade of Tyre" (Elayi 2018: 162).
[15] Elayi 2018: 165.
[16] Leichty 2011: 87, Esarhaddon 34, lines 12'-14'.
[17] Katzenstein 1997: 279.
[18] Novotny & Jeffers 2018: 61, Ashurbanipal 3, lines ii 38-49.
[19] Elayi 2018: 176.
[20] Katzenstein 1997: 293.
[21] Novotny & Jeffers 2018: 260, Ashurbanipal 11, lines ix 115-121.
[22] *Against Apion*, Book 1, 21, 155-159a, translated in Whiston and Maier 1999: 946.
[23] Ezekiel 26:9-12.
[24] Elayi 2018: 199-200.
[25] Greenberg 1997: 616.
[26] Elayi 2018: 200.
[27] Elayi 2018: 281-282.
[28] Elayi 2018: 282.
[29] Block 1997: 23.
[30] Collins 2018: 316.
[31] See Block 1998: 28.
[32] Block 1998: 28.
[33] See Block 1998: 33-34 for a more detailed discussion.
[34] Block 1998: 33-34.
[35] Allen 1990: 73.
[36] Block 1998: 38-39.
[37] Eichrodt 1975: 371.
[38] Hummel 2007: 944.
[39] Thompson 1980: 764.
[40] Block 1998: 29.
[41] Greenberg 1997: 531.
[42] Eichrodt 1975: 370.
[43] Allen 1990: 76.
[44] Hummel 2007: 812-813.
[45] Allen 1990: 75-76.
[46] Block 1998: 41.
[47] Bowen 2010: 162.
[48] Allen 1990: 76.
[49] Clements 1996: 122.
[50] Zimmerli 1983: 119.
[51] Blenkinsopp 1990: 115-116.
[52] Block 1998: 149.

[53] Block 1998: 147.

[54] Block 1998: 147-149; Udd 2005.

[55] See Rosenberg 2000: 254, quoting Malbim (Rabbi Meir Leibush ben Yehiel Michal).

[56] Chisholm 2010: 571.

[57] Block 1998: 148.

[58] Udd 2005: 40-41.

[59] Block 1998: 39.

[60] Block 1997: 749-750. See also Greenberg 1997: 481.

[61] A similar reference to a multiplicity of people groups can be seen in Ezekiel 32:3, where the Babylonian army is referred to as "many peoples" (Hebrew *ammim rabbim*) compared to "many nations" (Hebrew *goyim rabbim*) in 26:3.

[62] This also leads to a problem of "many nations" having to refer to only two – Babylonia and Greece.

[63] This third person singular/plural shift can also be seen in Jeremiah 21:4-10, as the king of Babylon, Nebuchadnezzar, and his army, are referred to in both the singular and the plural, although the army of Babylonia is the single referent.

[64] Greenberg 1997: 534.

[65] As we discussed above, there is not only internal logic to connect verse 12 to the preceding section, but the literary structure of the chapter unifies the prophecy and its topics.

[66] Katzenstein 1997: 217.

[67] Katzenstein 1997: 14-15.

[68] Block 1998: 40.

[69] Katzenstein 1997: 330-331.

CHAPTER EIGHT
Conclusion

Perhaps the most important question to ask at the end of a book like this is, "What have we learned?" Another might be, "Have we accomplished what we set out to do in the introduction?" Let's answer the first question by taking a look back at the key points of the book.

In chapter one, we went on a journey through the first half of the "story" of the Old Testament. We weren't concerned with things like how Genesis chapter one squares with what we know of history, if Abraham was a real person, or if three million Israelites walked out of Egypt in the 15th c. B.C.E. Our sole purpose was to understand the narrative of the Hebrew Bible on its own terms. What did the writers set down as the canonical story of the Old Testament? We began with the primeval history – from creation to the Tower of Babel – followed by the story of the patriarchs: Abraham, Isaac, and Jacob. Each had their own stories, some of which appear quite similar.

As the book of Exodus opened, we saw the Israelites fall into slavery in Egypt, only to be miraculously delivered by Moses, who – by the power of God – brought the people out into the wilderness. They continually failed to trust God and were finally condemned to wander the wilderness until that generation died out. Through the book of Numbers, we saw the wilderness wanderings, and when we came to Deuteronomy, we heard Moses's farewell address, just outside of Canaan, before he died. The story will continue in volume II of this series, where Joshua will lead the Israelites into the land of Canaan.

Having covered the first half of the narrative of the Old Testament, we broadened our scope and surveyed the history of the wider ancient Near East. Although we could certainly not cover everything, the goal was to lay out the major time periods from the early 3rd millennium B.C.E. until the conquest of Alexander the Great. We saw the major powers in Mesopotamia and their interactions with Egypt, the Levant, Anatolia, and Elam to the east. In the end, the reader was left with a broad understanding of the history of the ancient Near East, allowing them to place individual events in history – be they in the Bible or elsewhere – into the broader framework of ancient history.

Chapter three focused on archaeology, beginning with how archaeology is actually done. Following this brief introduction to its practice, we moved on to "biblical archaeology" and saw how the field developed from a "handmaiden" of the Bible to an independent (and far more secular) field. No longer do biblical archaeologists dig "with a spade in one hand and a Bible in the other". Archaeologists have stopped basing their excavations on the biblical texts, and the discipline has greatly improved because of it. Finally, by way of example, we looked at two groups of people on whom the light of archaeological discovery has been effectively shed: the Canaanites and the Philistines. We learned that we know a great deal about the ancient Canaanites, and what we know – both archaeologically and historically – is a far cry from what we see in the descriptions of the Hebrew Bible. In a similar vein, we looked at the Philistines, including what archaeology can tell us about their origin and when they came into the area. While there is still debate concerning the specifics, we saw that the early portrayal of the Philistines that appears in Genesis is not in keeping with the archaeological data.

In chapter four, we began to examine individual issues that come up frequently in debates and discussions between atheists and Christian apologists. The first was the authorship of the Pentateuch... did Moses actually write it? Although tradition seemed to support that view, the evidence makes it clear that a single person could not have written the Torah. We saw that the rationale for this conclusion was not some anti-God bias, but dealing with the literary contradictions and inconsistencies that appear in the Pentateuch itself. We evaluated only a handful of such problematic passages, including the two creation accounts in Genesis 1 and 2, the contradictions in the flood story in Genesis 6-9, and the problems seen in the Joseph story in Genesis 37. We concluded by examining the contradictory accounts of the renaming of Bethel, the problems with identifying Moses's father-in-law, and inconsistencies in the laws concerning Hebrew slaves. In short, we saw that there are literary inconsistencies that have led scholars to abandon a single-authorship paradigm, including Mosaic authorship.

We then moved, in chapter five, to the dating of the book of Daniel. Conservative evangelical scholars will sometimes date the writing of the book to the late 6th c. B.C.E., when Daniel appears to have prophesied about coming events. However, the consensus view among biblical scholars is that Daniel was written during the 2nd c. B.C.E., at the time of Antiochus IV Epiphanes, although the Aramaic tales could have come from a century or so earlier. The chapter on the dating of Daniel was divided essentially into three sections, looking at linguistic evidence from the Aramaic language; the linguistic evidence from the Hebrew; and the historical problems that can be seen in Daniel, along with many of the common apologetic arguments in support of an early date. All the evidence examined supported (to a greater or lesser extent) a later dating of the book rather than earlier.

In chapter six, we provided an overview of slavery in the Hebrew Bible. Discussion was limited primarily to slavery in the Old Testament, along with consideration of selected apologetic arguments. Thus, after providing a general outline of the three major legal passages that discuss slavery, we examined arguments that are used from the New Testament to show that Jesus, the Gospels, and/or Paul implicitly (or even explicitly) condemn slavery. We showed that this simply is not the case, evidenced not only by the New Testament passages in question, but even by what we know from early Christianity. Finally, we briefly examined some of the points of comparison between what appears in the legal portions of the Old Testament and the laws on slavery in the antebellum South. We saw that, while there is not a one-to-one correspondence between the laws from these two periods, there is a significant amount of commonality in the apparent legal rationale used in deciding cases.

Finally, we looked at the failed prophecy that can be found in Ezekiel 26, where the prophet predicts the complete annihilation of the island city of Tyre. Because of the overt failure of this prophecy to come true as Ezekiel described, it has been a source of contention and discussion among theologians and apologists for quite some time. We examined the relevant sections of Ezekiel 26 in some detail, noting the literary structure of the passage, and how it reveals that Nebuchadnezzar was the lone agent who was to utterly destroy Tyre, the island city, and not Ushu, the mainland city. We examined historical evidence from the period, seeing how previous rulers had conquered or besieged Tyre and what Nebuchadnezzar did when he attempted to take the city. Finally, we looked at some of the theological attempts that have been made to circumvent this problematic prophecy.

Although we have covered a great deal of material in volume one, there is a lot left to cover. Volume II will continue the story of the Old Testament, covering the conquest of Canaan under Joshua, the period of the Judges, and the run of the united and divided monarchies. We will then show how Judah was taken into captivity by the Babylonians, only to be released approximately seventy years later by the Persians in order to rebuild their city and temple. We will also continue our examination of the ancient Near East, this time focusing on other aspects of their culture, including religion, laws, cosmology, and literature, as well as providing an overview of ancient Egyptian history.

We will examine the archaeological and historical data that we have concerning the actual formation of the nation of Israel during the latter part of the 2nd millennium B.C.E. and the different views that scholars hold on this reconstruction. This will lead us to examine the historical and archaeological evidence that we have for both the Exodus from Egypt and the Israelite conquest of Canaan. We will then turn to a detailed overview of prophecy in the Old Testament, including ancient apocalyptic concepts, messianism, and specific examination of passages like Psalm 22, Isaiah 7, and Isaiah 53. There will be a chapter on violence and genocide, women's rights (including rape, adultery, and abortion), as well as homosexuality in the ancient Near East and Hebrew Bible.

As we conclude this volume, let's answer our second question from above, "Have we accomplished what we set out to do in the introduction?" The primary goal was to provide the atheist and skeptic with a background to the Old Testament narrative, ancient Near Eastern history, and archaeological methods and data. Building on these introductions and general outlines, we could then examine in some detail several of the more contentious topics that atheists encounter in debates with Christians and apologists. Hopefully this book has accomplished that goal!

It is my hope that you feel not only grounded and confident in the general frameworks that we have introduced in this volume, but also well informed and equipped with scholarly sources to begin to form your own thoughts and opinions on how to best present this material to those with whom you come in contact. While this book has been predicated on the inherent struggle that exists between atheists and apologists, that struggle need not always find expression in antagonistic or hostile interactions. For example, there is an online group known as *The Atheist Round Table*, which hosts debates and discussions with atheists, Christians, and anyone else who wishes to have a civil discourse on difficult biblical issues. Although these interactions can become intense and animated, the intent (and quite often the result) is that the discussion will generate more light than heat.

This should be the aim of most of our interactions, in my opinion. Having been armed with the information in this book, it is my hope that you will engage in these discussions honestly and vigorously, but do so with the end result in mind: all of the participants gaining a greater understanding and appreciation of the details of the ancient past. By focusing on leading yourself and others to further clarity of the ancient world – including the Old Testament – we can seek to achieve a higher level of development, both in what we know and how we treat one another.

Index to Biblical Verses and Ancient Sources

Bibliography

Allen, Leslie.

    1990   *Ezekiel 20-48*. Word Biblical Commentary. Dallas, TX: Word Books.

Anderson, Steven.

    2014   *Darius the Mede: A Reappraisal*. CreateSpace Independent Publishing Platform.

Aubet, María.

    2018   Phoenicia During the Iron Age II Period. Pp. 706-716 in *The Oxford Handbook of the Archaeology of the Levant c. 8000-332 B.C.E.*, eds. M. Steiner and A. Killebrew. Oxford: Oxford University Press.

Avalos, Hector.

    2013   *Slavery, Abolitionism, and the Ethics of Biblical Scholarship*. Sheffield: Sheffield Press.

Baden, Joel.

    2012   *The Composition of the Pentateuch: Renewing the Documentary Hypothesis*. New Haven, CT: Yale University Press.

Bagg, Ariel.

    2011   *Die Assyrer und das Westland: Studien zur historischen Geographie un Herrschaftspraxis in der Levante im 1. Jt. V.u.Z.* Orientalia Lovaniensia Analecta 216. Leuven: Peeters.

Baker, D. and Alexander T.

    2003   *The Dictionary of the Old Testament: Pentateuch*, ed. D. Baker and T. Alexander. Downers Grove, IL: InterVarsity Press.

Bauer, Alexander.

    1998   Cities of the Sea: Maritime Trade and the Origin of Philistine Settlement in the Early Iron Age Southern Levant. *Oxford Journal of Archaeology* 17: 149-68.

Beaulieu, Paul-Alain.

    1989   *The Reign of Nabonidus King of Babylon 556-539 B.C.* New Haven, CT: Yale University Press.

    2009   The Babylonian Background of the Motif of the Fiery Furnace in Daniel 3. *Journal of Biblical Literature* 128: 273-290.

    2018   *A History of Babylon, 2200 BC – AD 75.* Hoboken, NJ: John Wiley & Sons.

Betz, Hans.

    1989   *Galatians.* Hermeneia. Minneapolis, MN: Fortress.

Black, J.A., Cunningham; G., Fluckiger-Hawker; E., Robson, E. and Zólyomi, G.

    1988-2006   The Electronic Text Corpus of Sumerian Literature (https://www.etcsl.orient.ox.ac.uk/). Oxford.

Blenkinsopp, Joseph.

    1988   *Ezra-Nehemiah.* Old Testament Library. Louisville, KY: John Knox Press.

    1990   *Ezekiel.* Interpretation. Louisville, KY: John Knox Press.

    1992   *The Pentateuch: An Introduction to the First Five Books of the Bible.* New Haven, CT: Yale University Press.

Block, Daniel.

    1997   *The Book of Ezekiel: Chapters 1-24.* The New International Commentary on the Old Testament. Grand Rapids, MI: Eerdmans.

    1998   *The Book of Ezekiel: Chapters 25-48.* The New International Commentary on the Old Testament. Grand Rapids, MI: Eerdmans.

2008 *Israel: Ancient Kingdom or Late Invention?*, ed. D. Block. Nashville, TN: B&H Publishing.

Bowen, Joshua.

2017 *A Preliminary Study of the Sumerian Curricular and Lamentational Texts from the Old Babylonian City of Kish*. Dissertation. Baltimore, MD: Johns Hopkins University.

2020a *Did the Old Testament Endorse Slavery?* Mechanicsville, MD: Digital Hammurabi Press.

2020b *Learning to Pray in a Dead Language: Education and Invocation in Ancient Sumerian*. Mechanicsville, MD: Digital Hammurabi Press.

Bowen, Nancy.

2010 *Ezekiel*. Abingdon Old Testament Commentaries. Nashville, TN: Abingdon Press.

Brinkman, John.

1984 *Prelude to Empire: Babylonian Society and Politics, 747-626 B.C.* Occasional Publications of the Babylonian Fund, 7. Philadelphia: University of Pennsylvania Museum of Archaeology and Anthropology.

Buck, Mary Ellen.

2019 *The Canaanites: Their History and Culture from Texts and Artifacts*. Eugene, OR: Cascade Books.

Bunimovitz, Schlomo.

1990 Problems in the "Ethnic" Identification of the Philistine Material Culture. *Tel Aviv* 17: 210-222.

Carr, David.

2020 *The Formation of Genesis 1-11: Biblical and Other Precursors*. New York, NY: Oxford University Press.

Charles, Ronald

2020   *The Silencing of Slaves in Early Jewish and Christian Texts*. Routledge Studies in the Early Christian World. New York, NY: Routledge.

Charlesworth, James.

1983   *The Old Testament Pseudepigrapha, Volume One: Apocalyptic Literature and Testaments*. Peabody, MA: Hendrickson.

Chisholm, Robert.

2010   When Prophecy Appears to Fail, Check Your Hermeneutic. *Journal of the Evangelical Theological Society* 53: 561-577.

Clements, Ronald.

1996   *Ezekiel*. Westminster Bible Companion. Louisville, KY: Westminster John Knox Press.

Cline, Eric.

2015   *1177 B.C.: The Year Civilization Collapsed*. Princeton, NJ: Princeton University Press.

Cogan, Mordechai and Tadmor, Hayim.

1988   *II Kings: A New Translation with Introduction and Commentary*. The Anchor Bible 11. New Haven, CT: Yale University Press.

Collins, John.

1993   *Daniel: A Commentary on the Book of Daniel*. Hermeneia. Minneapolis, MN: Fortress.

2015   *Apocalypse, Prophecy, and Pseudepigraphy: On Jewish Apocalyptic Literature*. Grand Rapids, MI: Eerdmans.

2016   *The Apocalyptic Imagination: An Introduction to Jewish Apocalyptic Literature, Third Edition*. Grand Rapids, MI: Eerdmans.

2018 *Introduction to the Hebrew Bible, 3rd Edition.* Minneapolis, MN: Fortress.

Connan, Jaques; Imbus, Kendra; Macko, Stephen; Nissenbaum, Arie and Zumberge, John.

2006 Asphalt in Iron Age Excavations from the Philistine Tel Miqne-Ekron City (Israel): Origin and Trade Routes. *Organic Geochemistry* 17: 1768-1786.

Cook, Stephen.

2003 *The Apocalyptic Literature.* Nashville, TN: Abingdon Press.

2018 *Ezekiel 38-48: A New Translation with Introduction and Commentary.* Anchor Yale Bible Commentaries. New Haven, CT: Yale University Press.

Cooper, Jerrold.

1986 *Sumerian and Akkadian Royal Inscriptions, I: Pre-Sargonic Inscriptions.* New Haven, CT: American Oriental Society.

Cooper, Jerrold and Heimpel, Wolfgang.

1983 The Sumerian Sargon Legend. *Journal of the American Oriental Society* 103: 67-82.

Culbertson, Laura.

2011a Slaves and Households in the Near East. Pp. 1-17 in *Slaves and Households in the Near East*, ed. L. Culbertson. Oriental Institute Seminars 7. Chicago, IL: University of Chicago.

2011b *Slaves and Households in the Near East*, ed. L. Culbertson. Oriental Institute Seminars 7. Chicago, IL: University of Chicago.

Dandamayev, Muhammad.

1992 Slavery. Pp. 58-65 in *The Anchor Bible Dictionary (Si-Z),* ed. D. Freedman. New York, NY: Doubleday.

Danker, Frederick.

>2000 *A Greek-English Lexicon of the New Testament and Other Early Christian Literature, 3rd Edition.* Chicago, IL: University of Chicago Press.

Davis, Thomas.

>2004 *Shifting Sands: The Rise and Fall of Biblical Archaeology.* New York, NY: Oxford University Press.

Demsky, Aaron; Maier, Aren; Wimmer, Stefan and Zukerman, Alexander.

>2008 A Late Iron Age I / Early Iron Age II Old Canaanite Inscription from Tell eṣ-Ṣâfī/Gath, Israel: Paleography, Dating, and Historical-Cultural Significance. *Bulletin for the American Schools of Oriental Research* 351: 39-71.

Dever, William.

>2020 *Has Archaeology Buried the Bible?* Grand Rapids, MI: Eerdmans.

Dewrell, Heath.

>2017 *Child Sacrifice in Ancient Israel.* Winona Lake, IN: Eisenbrauns.

Dothan, Trude.

>1990 Ekron of the Philistines. Part I: Where They Came from, How They Settled down and the Place They Worshipped in. *Biblical Archaeology Review* 16: 26-36.

>2002 Bronze and Iron Objects with Cultic Connotations from Philistine Temple Building 350 at Ekron. *Israel Exploration Journal* 52: 1-27.

Dothan, Trude and Dothan, Moshe.

>1992 *People of the Sea: The Search for the Philistines.* New York, NY: Macmillan.

Dothan, Trude and Zuckerman, Alexander.

2004   A Preliminary Study of the Mycenaean IIIC:1 Pottery Assemblages from Tel Miqne-Ekron and Ashdod. *Bulletin for the American Schools of Oriental Research* 333: 1-54.

Dothan, Trude; Gitin, Seymour; Gunneweg, Jan and Perlman, Isadore.

1986   On the Origin of Pottery from Tel Miqne-Ekron. *Bulletin for the American Schools of Oriental Research* 264: 3-16.

Douglas, J. D.

1962   *The New Bible Dictionary*, ed. J. D. Douglas. Grand Rapids, MI: Eerdmans.

Dozeman, Thomas.

2009   *Exodus*. Eerdmans Critical Commentary. Grand Rapids, MI: Eerdmans.

2017   *The Pentateuch: Introducing the Story of the Torah*. Minneapolis, MN: Fortress Press.

Durham, John.

2015   *Exodus*. Word Biblical Commentary. Grand Rapids, MI: Zondervan.

Edzard, Dietz Otto.

2009   *Geschichte Mesopotamiens: Von den Sumerern bis zu Alexander dem Großen*. München: C.H.Beck.

Edwards, Douglas and Katzenstein, H.J.

1992   Tyre. Pp. 686-692 in *The Anchor Bible Dictionary (Si-Z)*, ed. D. Freedman. New York, NY: Doubleday.

Eichrodt, Walther.

1975   *Ezekiel: A Commentary*. Old Testament Library. Philadelphia, PA: Westminster Press.

Elayi, Josette.

2018   *The History of Phoenicia*. Nottingham: Lockwood Press.

Fagan, Brian and Durrani, Nadia.

    2016   *Archaeology: A Brief Introduction, Twelfth Edition.* New York, NY: Routledge.

Finkelstein, Israel and Silberman, Neil Asher.

    2001   *The Bible Unearthed: Archaeology's New Vision of Ancient Israel and the Origin of Its Sacred Texts.* New York, NY: Simon and Schuster.

Fitzmyer, Joseph.

    1985   *The Gospel According to Luke X-XXIV: A New Translation with Introduction and Commentary.* Anchor Bible. Garden City, NY: Doubleday.

Foster, Benjamin.

    2005   *Before the Muses: An Anthology of Akkadian Literature, Third Edition.* Bethesda, MD: CDL Press.

Fox, Michael.

    2009   *Proverbs 10-31.* Anchor Yale Bible Commentaries. New Haven, CT: Yale University Press.

Frahm, Eckart.

    2017   The Neo-Assyrian Period (ca. 1000-609 BCE). Pp. 161-208 in *A Companion to Assyria*, ed. E. Frahm. Blackwell Companions to the Ancient World. Hoboken, NJ: John Wiley & Sons.

France, R.T.

    2007   *The Gospel of Matthew.* New International Commentary on the New Testament. Grand Rapids, MI: Eerdmans.

Frayne, Douglas.

    1993   *Sargonic and Gutian Periods (2334-2113 BC).* Royal Inscriptions of Mesopotamia: Early Periods, Volume 2. Toronto: University of Toronto Press.

Freedman, D.

    1992a *The Anchor Bible Dictionary, (H-J)*, ed. D. Freedman. New York, NY: Doubleday.

    1992b T*he Anchor Bible Dictionary, (Si-Z)*, ed. D. Freedman. New York, NY: Doubleday.

Fuchs, Andreas.

    2014 Die unglaubliche Geburt des neubabylonischen Reiches oder: Die Vernichtung einer Weltmacht durch den Sohn eines Niemand. Pp. 26-71 in *Babylonien und seine Nachbarn in neu- und spätbabylonischer Zeit*, eds. M. Krebernik and H. Neumann. Münster: Ugarit-Verlag.

Garr, W. R. and Fassberg, S.

    2016 *A Handbook of Biblical Hebrew, Volume 1: Periods, Corpora, and Reading Traditions*, eds. W.R. Garr and S. Fassberg. Winona Lake, IN: Eisenbrauns.

Gertzen, Thomas.

    2008 "Profiling" the Philistines: Some Further Remarks on the Egyptian Depictions of Philistine Warriors at Medinet Habu. *Ancient Near Eastern Studies* 45: 85-101.

Glancy, Jennifer.

    2006 *Slavery in Early Christianity*. Minneapolis, MN: Fortress Press.

    2011 Slavery and the Rise of Christianity. Pp. 456-481 in *The Cambridge World History of Slavery, Volume 1: The Ancient Mediterranean World*, eds. K. Bradley and P. Cartledge. Cambridge University Press.

Gitin, Seymour; Mazar, Amihai and Stern, E.

    1998 *Mediterranean Peoples in Transition: Thirteenth to Early Tenth Centuries B.C.E.* Jerusalem: Israel Exploration Society.

Glassner, Jean-Jacques.

>2004 *Mesopotamian Chronicles*. Atlanta, GA: Society of Biblical Literature.

Goldingay, John.

>2019 *Daniel*. Word Biblical Commentary. Grand Rapids, MI: Zondervan.

Goldstein, Jonathan.

>1993 Alexander and the Jews. *Proceedings of the American Academy for Jewish Research* 59: 59-101.

Grabbe, Lester.

>1987 Fundamentalism and Scholarship: The Case of Daniel. Pp. 133-152 in *Scripture: Meaning and Method. Essays Presented to Anthony Tyrrell Hanson for His Seventieth Birthday*, ed. B. Thompson. Yorkshire, England: Hull University Press.

>1988a Look at the Gestalt of "Darius the Mede". *The Catholic Biblical Quarterly* 50: 198-213.

>1988b The Belshazzar of Daniel and the Belshazzar of History. *Andrews University Seminary Studies* 26: 59-66.

Grant, Jim; Gorin, Sam and Fleming, Neil.

>2015 *The Archaeology Coursebook, Fourth Edition: An Introduction to Themes, Sites, Methods and Skills*. New York, NY: Routledge.

Grayson, Albert.

>1975 *Assyrian and Babylonian Chronicles*. Texts from Cuneiform Sources, Volume 5. Locust Valley, NY: J.J. Augustin.

Grayson, Albert and Novotny, Jamie.

>2012 *The Royal Inscriptions of Sennacherib, King of Assyria (704-681 BC), Part 1*. The Royal Inscriptions of the Neo-

Assyrian Period, Volume 3/1. Winona Lake, IN: Eisenbrauns.

Green, Joel.

1997   *The Gospel of Luke.* New International Commentary on the New Testament. Grand Rapids, MI: Eerdmans.

Green, Peter.

1990   *Alexander to Actium.* Berkeley, CA: University of California Press.

Greenberg, Moshe.

1997   *Ezekiel 21-37: A New Translation with Introduction and Commentary.* Anchor Bible. New York, NY: Doubleday.

Grossman, Jonathan.

2019   *Creation: The Story of Beginnings.* Jerusalem: Maggid.

Gurtner, Daniel.

2013   *Exodus: A Commentary on the Greek Text of Codex Vaticanus.* Leiden: Brill.

Haas, Gene.

2003   Slave, Slavery. Pp. 778-783 in *The Dictionary of the Old Testament: Pentateuch,* ed. D. Baker and T. Alexander. Downers Grove, IL: InterVarsity Press.

Hamilton, Victor.

1990   *The Book of Genesis 1-17.* New International Commentary on the Old Testament. Grand Rapids, MI: Eerdmans.

Harrill, James.

1999   The Vice of Slave Dealers in Greco-Roman Society: The Use of a Topos in 1 Timothy 1:10. *Journal of Biblical Literature* 118: 97-122.

2006   *Slaves in the New Testament: Literary, Social, and Moral Dimensions.* Minneapolis, MN: Fortress.

Harrison, R. K.

    1980   *Leviticus: An Introduction and Commentary*. Tyndale Old Testament Commentaries. Downers Grove, IL: InterVarsity Press.

Hartman, Louis and Di Lella, Alexander.

    1978   *The Book of Daniel: A New Translation with Notes and Commentary*. Anchor Bible. Garden City, NY: Doubleday.

Heimpel, Wolfgang.

    2003   *Letters to the King of Mari: A New Translation, with Historical Introduction, Notes, and Commentary*. Winona Lake, IN: Eisenbrauns.

Hodge, Bodie and Mortenseon, Terry.

    2011   Did Moses Write Genesis? Answers in Genesis 28 June 2011 (https://answersingenesis.org/bible-characters/moses/did-moses-write-genesis/) Accessed 14 February 2021.

Houtman, Cornelis.

    2000   *Exodus, Volume 3: Chapters 20-40*. Leuven, Belgium: Peeters.

Hummel, Horace.

    2007   *Ezekiel 21-48*. Concordia Commentary. St. Louis, MO: Concordia Publishing House.

Jackson, Bernard.

    2006   *Wisdom-Laws: A Study of the Mishpatim of Exodus 21:1-22:16*. Oxford: Oxford University Press.

Japhet, Sara.

    1993   *I and II Chronicles: A Commentary*. Old Testament Library. Louisville, KY: Westminster John Knox.

Karageorghis, Vassos.

    1984   Exploring Philistine Origins on the Island of Cyprus. *Biblical Archaeology Review* 10: 16-28.

Katzenstein, H. Jacob.

    1997   *The History of Tyre: From the Beginning of the Second Millennium B.C.E. Until the Fall of the Neo-Babylonian Empire in 539 B.C.E., Second Edition.* Beer Sheva: Ben-Gurion University of the Negev Press.

Killebrew, Ann.

    1998   Ceramic Typology and Technology of Late Bronze II and Iron I Assemblages from Tel Miqne-Ekron: The Transition from Canaanite to Philistine Culture. Pp. 379-405 in *Mediterranean Peoples in Transition: Thirteenth to Early Tenth Centuries B.C.E.*, eds. S. Gitin, A. Mazar, and E. Stern. Jerusalem: Israel Exploration Society.

    2013   Early Philistine Pottery Technology at Tel Miqne-Ekron: Implications for the Late Bronze-Early Iron Age Transition in the Eastern Mediterranean. Pp. 77-119 in *The Philistines and Other "Sea Peoples" in Text and Archaeology,* eds. A. Killebrew and G. Lehmann. Atlanta, GA: Society of Biblical Literature.

Killebrew, Ann and Lehmann, Gunnar.

    2013   *The Philistines and Other "Sea Peoples" in Text and Archaeology.* Atlanta, GA: Society of Biblical Literature.

Kitchen, Kenneth.

    1962   Slave, Slavery. Pp. 1195-1199 in *The New Bible Dictionary*, ed. J. D. Douglas. Grand Rapids, MI: Eerdmans.

Knapp, A. Bernard.

    1985   Review of L. Hellbing, "Alasia Problems", D.E. McCaslin, "Stone Anchors in Antiquity: Coastal Settlements and Maritime Trade Routes in the Eastern Mediterranean", and J. Strange, "Caphtor/Keftiu, A New Investigation". *Journal of Field Archaeology* 12: 231-250.

Kratz, Reinhard.

2016 The Analysis of the Pentateuch: An Attempt to Overcome Barriers of Thinking. *Zeitschrift für die alttestamentliche Wissenschaft* 128: 529-561.

Kuhrt, Amélie.

1997 *The Ancient Near East c.3000-330 BC, 2 Volumes.* New York, NY: Routledge.

2007 *The Persian Empire: A Corpus of Sources from the Achaemenid Period, Volume 1.* New York, NY: Routledge.

Lam, Joseph and Pardee, Dennis.

2016 Standard/Classical Biblical Hebrew. Pp. 1-18 in *A Handbook of Biblical Hebrew, Volume 1: Periods, Corpora, and Reading Traditions*, eds. W.R. Garr and S. Fassberg. Winona Lake, IN: Eisenbrauns.

Leichty, Erle.

2011 *The Royal Inscriptions of Esarhaddon, King of Assyria (680-669 BC).* Royal Inscriptions of the Neo-Assyrian Period 4. Winona Lake, IN: Eisenbrauns.

Lemche, Niels.

1992 Ḫabiru, Ḫapiru. Pp. 6-10 in *The Anchor Bible Dictionary (H-J)*, ed. D. Freedman. New York, NY: Doubleday.

Liverani, Mario.

2003 *Israel's History and the History of Israel.* Translated by Chiara Peri and Philip R. Davies. London: Equinox.

Lohse, Eduard.

1971 *Colossians and Philemon.* Hermeneia. Minneapolis, MN: Fortress.

Longman III, Tremper.

    1999   *Daniel*. NIV Application Commentary. Grand Rapids, MI: Zondervan.

Lucas, Ernest.

    2002   *Daniel*. Apollos Old Testament Commentary. Downers Grove, IL: InterVarsity Press.

Luz, Ulrich.

    2001   *Matthew 8-20: A Commentary*. Hermeneia. Minneapolis, MN: Fortress.

    2005   *Matthew 21-28: A Commentary*. Hermeneia. Minneapolis, MN: Fortress.

MacKnight, Scot.

    1995   *Galatians*. The NIV Application Commentary. Grand Rapids, MI: Zondervan.

Magdalene, Rachel F. and Wells, B.

    2009   *Law from the Tigris to the Tiber: The Writings of Raymond Westbrook*, eds. R. Magdalene and B. Wells. Winona Lake, IN: Eisenbrauns.

Mazar, Amihai.

    1985   The Emergence of the Philistine Material Culture. *Israel Exploration Journal* 35: 95-107.

    1992   *Archaeology of the Land of the Bible: 10,000 – 586 B.C.E.* New York, NY: Doubleday.

Milgrom, Jacob.

    1990   *The JPS Torah Commentary: Numbers*. Philadelphia, PA: Jewish Publication Society.

Millard, A. R.

    1977   Daniel 1-6 and History. *Evangelical Quarterly* 49: 67-73.

Melville, H.

    1851   *Moby Dick*. New York, NY, Harper and Brothers.

Moran, William.

    1992   *The Amarna Letters*. Baltimore, MD: The Johns Hopkins University Press.

Morgenstern, Matthew.

    2016   Late Biblical Hebrew. Pp. 43-54 in *A Handbook of Biblical Hebrew, Volume 1: Periods, Corpora, and Reading Traditions*, eds. W.R. Garr and S. Fassberg. Winona Lake, IN: Eisenbrauns.

Morris, Thomas.

    1996   *Southern Slavery and the Law, 1619-1860*. Chapel Hill, NC: University of North Carolina Press.

Newsom, Carol.

    2014   *Daniel: A Commentary*. Old Testament Library. Louisville, KY: Westminster John Knox.

Nickelsburg, George.

    2001   *1 Enoch 1*. Hermeneia. Minneapolis, MN: Fortress.

Novotny, Jamie and Jeffers, Joshua.

    2018   *The Royal Inscriptions of Ashurbanipal (668-631 BC), Aššur-etel-ilāni (630-627 BC), and Sîn-šarra-iškun (626-612 BC), Kings of Assyria, Part 1*. The Royal Inscriptions of the Neo-Assyrian Period, Volume 5/1. Winona Lake, IN: Eisenbrauns.

Peek, Celicia.

    1996   Alexander the Great Comes to Jerusalem: The Jewish Response to Hellenism. *Brigham Young University Studies* 36/3: 99-112.

Pomponio, Francesco.

> 1994   The Hexapolis of Šuruppak. Political and Economic Relationships between Šuruppak and the Other Towns of Central and Southern Mesopotamia. Pp. 10-24 in *Early Dynastic Administrative Tablets of Šuruppak*, eds. F. Pomponio and G. Visicato. Napoli.

Pomponio, F. and Visicato, G.

> 1994   *Early Dynastic Administrative Tablets of Šuruppak*, eds. F. Pomponio and G. Visicato. Napoli

Propp, William.

> 1999   *Exodus 1-18: A New Translation with Introduction and Commentary*. Anchor Bible Yale Commentaries. New Haven, CT: Yale University Press.

> 2006   *Exodus 19-40: A New Translation with Introduction and Commentary*. Anchor Bible Yale Commentaries. New Haven, CT: Yale University Press.

Ra, Aron.

> 2016   *Foundational Falsehoods of Creationism*. Durham, NC: Pitchstone Publishing.

Rahlfs, Alfred.

> 1979   *Septuaginta*. Stuttgart, Germany: Deutsche Bibelgesellschaft.

Rendsburg, Gary.

> 1987   Gen 10:13-14: An Authentic Hebrew Tradition Concerning the Origin of the Philistines. *Journal of Northwest Semitic Languages* 13: 89-96.

Rosenberg, A.J.

> 2000   *Ezekiel Volume II: A New English Translation*. New York, NY: Judaica Press.

Roth, Martha.

    1997   *Law Collections from Mesopotamia and Asia Minor.* Atlanta, GA: Scholars Press.

Sallaberger, Walther and Westenholz, Aage.

    1999   *Mesopotamien: Akkade Zeit und Ur III Zeit.* Göttingen: Vanderhoeck und Ruprecht.

Sarna, Nahum.

    1989   *The JPS Torah Commentary: Genesis.* Philadelphia, PA: Jewish Publication Society.

Schneider, A. W. and Adali, S.F.

    2014   "No Harvest Was Reaped": Demographic and Climatic Factors in the Decline of the Neo-Assyrian Empire. *Climatic Change*, 127: 435-446.

Seeman, Chris and Marshak, Adam.

    2012   Jewish History from Alexander to Hadrian. Pp. 30-69 in *Early Judaism: A Comprehensive Overview.* Grand Rapids, MI: Eerdmans.

Seow, Choon-Leong.

    2003   *Daniel.* Westminster Bible Companion. Louisville, KY: Westminster John Knox.

Shai, Itzhaq; Ilan, David and Kletter, Raz.

    2009   An Aegean Fire-Stand from Tel Nagila. *Palestine Exploration Quarterly* 141: 160-166.

Shea, William.

    2001   The Search for Darius the Mede (Concluded), or, The Time of the Answer to Daniel's Prayer and the Date of the Death of Darius the Mede. *Journal of the Adventist Theological Society* 12: 97-105.

Ska, Jean-Louis.

2006   *Introduction to Reading the Pentateuch*. Winona Lake, IN: Eisenbrauns.

Stavrakopoulou, Francesca.

2004   *King Manasseh and Child Sacrifice: Biblical Distortions and Historical Realities*. New York, NY: Walter de Gruyter.

Strange, John.

1980   *Caphtor/Keftiu: A New Investigation*. Leiden: Brill.

Thompson, B.

1987   *Scripture: Meaning and Method. Essays Presented to Anthony Tyrrell Hanson for His Seventieth Birthday*, ed. B. Thompson. Yorkshire, England: Hull University Press.

Thompson, J. A.

1980   *The Book of Jeremiah*. New International Commentary on the Old Testament. Grand Rapids, MI: Eerdmans.

Tigay, Jeffrey.

1996   *The JPS Torah Commentary: Deuteronomy*. Philadelphia, PA: Jewish Publication Society.

Udd, Kris.

2005   Prediction and Foreknowledge in Ezekiel's Prophecy against Tyre. *Tyndale Bulletin* 56: 25-41.

United Nations.

1948   *Universal Declaration of Human Rights*. (https://www.un.org/en /universal-declaration-human-rights/). Retrieved 20 February 2021.

Van De Mieroop, Marc.

2005   *King Hammurabi of Babylon: A Biography*. Malden, MA: Blackwell.

2007   *A History of the Ancient Near East ca. 3000-323 BC.*
       Malden, MA: Blackwell.

Vanderkam, James.

2020   *Jubilees: The Hermeneia Translation.* Minneapolis, MN:
       Fortress Press.

Veenhof, Klaas and Eidem, Jesper.

2008   *Mesopotamia: The Old Assyrian Period.* Göttingen:
       Vandenhoeck & Ruprecht.

Vermes, Geza.

2012   *The Complete Dead Sea Scrolls in English, Revised
       Edition.* London: Penguin Publishing.

Waltke, Bruce.

2001   *Genesis: A Commentary.* Grand Rapids, MI: Zondervan.

Wells, Bruce.

2011   The Quasi-Alien in Leviticus 25. Pp. 135-155 in *The
       Foreigner and the Law: Perspectives from the Hebrew
       Bible and the Ancient Near East*, eds. R. Achenbach, R.
       Albertz, and J. Wöhrle. Wiesbaden: Harrassowitz Verlag.

Wenham, Gordon.

1987   *Genesis 1-15.* Word Biblical Commentary. Grand Rapids,
       MI: Zondervan.

Westbrook, Raymond.

2003   *A History of Ancient Near Eastern Law*, ed. R. Westbrook.
       2 vols. Leiden: Brill.

2009a Cuneiform Law Codes and the Origins of Legislation. Pp.
       73-95 in *Law from the Tigris to the Tiber: The Writings of
       Raymond Westbrook*, eds. R. Magdalene and B. Wells.
       Winona Lake, IN: Eisenbrauns.

2009b Slave and Master in Ancient Near Eastern Law. Pp. 161-
       216 in *Law from the Tigris to the Tiber: The Writings of*

Raymond Westbrook, eds. R. Magdalene and B. Wells. Winona Lake, IN: Eisenbrauns.

Westbrook, Raymond and Wells, Bruce.

2009 *Everyday Law in Biblical Israel*. Louisville, KY: Westminster John Knox.

Whiston, William and Maier, Paul.

1999 *The New Complete Works of Josephus*. Grand Rapids, MI: Kregel.

Winter, Irene.

1985 After the Battle Is Over: The *Stele of the Vultures* and the Beginning of Historical Narrative in the Art of the Ancient Near East. Pp. 11-32 in *Pictorial Narrative in Antiquity and the Middle Ages*, eds. H. Kessler and M. Simpson. Washington, D.C., National Gallery.

Wiseman, D.J.

1965 Some Historical Problems in the Book of Daniel. Pp. 9-18 in *Notes on Some Problems in the Book of Daniel*, ed. D.J. Wiseman. London: Tyndale Press.

1995 *Nebuchadrezzar and Babylon: The Schweich Lectures*. Oxford: Oxford University Press.

Zimmerli, Walther.

1983 *Ezekiel 2: A Commentary on the Book of the Prophet Ezekiel Chapters 25-48*. Trans. J. Martin. Hermeneia. Philadelphia, PA: Fortress.

About the Author

Dr. Joshua Bowen is the author of *Did the Old Testament Endorse Slavery?* (spoiler: yes, it did!), the best-selling *Learn to Read Ancient Sumerian: An Introduction for Complete Beginners*, and *Learning to Pray in a Dead Language: Education and Invocation in Ancient Sumerian*, a book about schools and prayer in the ancient world. He is dedicated to opening up the world of academia to interested non-specialists and breaking down the walls of the ivory tower.

Joshua graduated from The Johns Hopkins University in 2017 with a Doctor of Philosophy in Near Eastern Studies, where he majored in Assyriology and minored in Hebrew Bible. His dissertation was entitled *A Preliminary Study of the Sumerian Curricular and Lamentational Texts from the Old Babylonian City of Kish*, and he specializes in the Sumerian language. Joshua was awarded the American Fulbright Scholarship, as well as the German Deutscher Akademischer Austauschdienst (D.A.A.D.) Scholarship for the 2014-2015 academic year, allowing him to spend the year in Tubingen, Germany, working with Dr. Konrad Volk on his dissertation project.

As well as his Doctor of Philosophy in Near Eastern Studies, Joshua holds a Bachelor of Science in Religion from Liberty University, a Master of Theology in the Old Testament from Capital Bible Seminary, and a Master of Arts in Near Eastern Studies from The Johns Hopkins University. Prior to entering academia, Joshua was a chaplain in the U.S. Air Force, where he also earned an Associate in Arts in Avionics.

Joshua is a periodic contributor to the Digital Hammurabi YouTube channel and podcast. He lives in Southern Maryland with his wife, and (very-soon-to-be) five children. In his free time – when he's not researching his latest publication – he is researching something else… or being climbed on by kids. Sometimes both at the same time.

Printed in Poland
by Amazon Fulfillment
Poland Sp. z o.o., Wrocław
21 September 2021

980b2a5d-9e15-49a4-b1bd-f3ddd9c00a01R01